PLAYS TWO

David Pownall

PLAYS TWO

BEEF
MY FATHER'S HOUSE
THE VIEWING
KING JOHN'S JEWEL
BLACK STAR

OBERON BOOKS
LONDON

First published in this collection in 2002 by Oberon Books Ltd.
Electronic edition published in 2013

Oberon Books Ltd
521 Caledonian Road, London N7 9RH
Tel: +44 (0) 20 7607 3637 / Fax: +44 (0) 20 7607 3629
e-mail: info@oberonbooks.com
www.oberonbooks.com

A catalogue record for this book is available from the British
Library.

PB ISBN: 978-1-84002-077-9
E ISBN: 978-1-78319-406-3

Cover design: Andrzej Klimowski

eBook conversion by Replika Press PVT Ltd, India.

Contents

BEEF

for Michael McKay

Characters

CON

CUSACK

MAEVE

CUCKOO

ALI

FERGUS

JANET

Set in Dublin, 1979

Beef was first performed on 5 February 1981 by Paines Plough at the Theatre Royal, Stratford East, with the following cast:

CON, Garret Keogh

CUSACK, Richard Leech

MAEVE, Fiona Victory

CUCKOO, Mannix Flynn

ALI, Sean Caffrey

FERGUS, James Donelly

JANET, Anne Hayden

Director, John Adams

ACT ONE

Sunday, 30 September 1979, 7:15 am, a sunny day.

The yard and open despatch room of the north-eastern abattoir, Dublin. A steel gantry and running rail with hooks goes from left to right. A large steel guts tray stands near the back wall and other trays are piled up nearby. On some of the hooks there are clothes hanging. The walls are tiled white. Lights fade up. Birdsong. Enter CON in smart, casual clothes with a white coat over his arm and a white hat on his head. He carries a Sunday newspaper which has a big spread of colour photographs.

CON: Cusack! Are you around? (*Takes a tray and puts it in the sun, then slips on the white coat.*) Cusack! If he's late again, he'll be in for it.
(*CUSACK sticks his head over the rim of the guts tray. He is bleary and dishevelled.*)
CUSACK: Good morning, Mr Sheehan.
CON: What? You frightened the life out of me! Have you been sleeping on the premises again? I'll take your key off you next time.
CUSACK: (*Climbing out of the tray.*) I missed the last bus home.
CON: (*Sitting down on the tray in the sun.*) Well, you see that container is thoroughly cleaned before it's used again, d'you hear? And no more using the abattoir as a doss-house or there'll be trouble.
CUSACK: Understood, Mr Sheehan. (*Takes a white coat and hat from a hook and puts them on.*) But getting in to work on a Sunday morning is murder for me from our side of town. There's no transport running.
CON: Buy a bike. (*Looks at his watch.*) Time's getting on. Where are the men?
CUSACK: Don't start getting het up now. Relax for a minute. Mr Sheehan, you know that we've been doing these Sunday overtime shifts on worn-out stock all this year and, nothing daunted, you called another for today of all days?
CON: The whole of Irish industry can't grind to a halt just because the Pope's here, you know.

CUSACK: Oh, agreed! But on Friday there were mutterings from the locker room when I put it to the lads that they might turn up this morning.

CON: I did anticipate some resistance from the genuinely devout churchgoers, i.e. none of them. They wouldn't turn down eight hours at double-time twelve weeks from Christmas, not those greedy beggars.

CUSACK: Mr Sheehan, as I was circulating in the city last night, traipsing round from house of religion to house of religion in search of peace, I bumped into the lads, many of them on their knees, and I got the impression that none of them had the slightest intention of reporting here for work this morning.

CON: Are you saying that we haven't got a shift?

CUSACK: The great mass that the Pope held in Phoenix Park was just too much for them, and the little masses that followed well into the night obliterated all sense of practical reality.

CON: Cusack, old son, this job is urgent. We're bound by a very tight contract. By tomorrow morning at ten this consignment has to be at the docks ready for loading. Now, it's my name that's at risk. I said, yes, we can deliver. Now you're letting me down.

CUSACK: Don't panic now, don't panic

CON: I'm not panicking. I left it to you, didn't I? There're penalty clauses in that contract. I could get hammered.

CUSACK: Don't worry. I fixed it, I fixed it.

CON: With no labour? Who's going to do the job? You and me? Listen, those two bulls we've got coming in are colossal creatures, old as the hills, tough as nails. It will take every man we've got to handle them.

CUSACK: Mr Sheehan, everything is under control. Last night I moved around in the twilight world I favour for a Saturday night out. I like a wander into the old haunts that haven't changed for centuries. The talk is good and the music unparalleled. You can get any job you like done down there. All you have to do is put the word out on the grapevine.

CON: Don't tell me you mean casuals?

CUSACK: Fine men, in general. Devils for work.

CON: Christ almighty, Cusack! You can't use casuals in highly specialised slaughtering! I need trained men!

CUSACK: And you'll have them. I put the word out that only experts need bother to turn up.

CON: What about the union? They'll go mad.

CUSACK: I squared it with the union. They're not bothered. They say that if our lads don't want the overtime and it's an urgent job, then we should use temporary labour.

CON: I'm very doubtful, Cusack, old son. It strikes me that you've made a mess of the arrangements.

CUSACK: I haven't. Everything will be all right.

CON: You know this contract is for our biggest customer?

CUSACK: The importance of the job has not escaped me. I wouldn't disappoint a British pet-food company for the world.

CON: If we let them down.

CUSACK: Unthinkable. Unthinkable. Would I heap more pain and frustration on the heads of people with licensing laws like they've got?
(*Pause. CON sighs and opens his newspaper. CUSACK looks nervous.*)
Your Sunday paper there looks thick and juicy.

CON: I like to keep up-to-date, as you know. No doubt your own choice of literature is more mind-improving.

CUSACK: (*Picking a black book up out of the guts tray.*) Not at all. Far inferior, I assure you. (*Riffles the pages.*) My bedtime reading for last night. Terrible stuff it is. (*Riffles the pages.*) Solid sex and violence. Not recommended for those of delicate sensibilities. (*Riffles the pages.*) To be kept away from those who cannot stand the sight of blood. (*Riffles the book again.*) Fantasies, lies for the enjoyment of idiots.

CON: (*From his newspaper.*) The Pope has become a national hero overnight, by the look of it. The man is a veritable star.

CUSACK: Did you go to the mass in Phoenix Park?

CON: No, I watched it at home on the box. Very moving. I admire this pope tremendously. You could feel the integrity and radiance coming out of him, and that being said by a man with no religion. I'll tell you, he has the power and charisma to change the situation. There's a great mood of optimism running through the country right now

CUSACK: It was there last night until closing-time.

CON: The gunmen will be listening and watching everything he does on television. It will affect them, you'll see.

CUSACK: The gunman? Whoever thought that they watch TV? Their behaviour would be ten times worse if they did. (*CUSACK riffles the book. Uproar off, at some distance. He looks up, smiles, then throws the black book into the guts tray. CON looks up from his paper, listening to the din. It fades, stops.*)

CON: Listen to that. People going off to early morning mass in that condition. Is it any wonder that some of us turn to science for comfort?

CUSACK: Atrocious behaviour.

CON: D'you know, they calculate that by the time the Pope leaves for America he will have been seen, in the flesh, by three-quarters of the people?

CUSACK: And here you have the consequences, roaming the street.

(*Uproar rises again.*)

CUCKOO: (*Off.*) Wham! Wham! Wham! Wham!

(*A crushed beer can lands in the yard.*
CON jumps to his feet, alarmed.)

CON: Look at that. Straight out of the boozer into the church.

CUSACK: Priests, war and alcohol, Mr Sheehan. Blood and religion. Vandalising and the Virgin Mary. It's the cocktail they call Michael Collins and the emotion we call Saint Patriotism.

(*Enter CUCKOO, FERGUS, ALI and MAEVE yelling 'Wham! Wham! Wham! Wham!' And battering empty beer cans against their foreheads. All four of them are garbed in greasy leathers, bones, beads, chains, earrings. They are wearing body-paint tattoos and layered hair-colouring in their long, wild unkempt locks. CUCKOO carries a long bundle wrapped in cowhide.*)

FERGUS: Look at this then! I've got it flat as a pancake. Totally destroyed.

CUCKOO: I could perform that feat with an iron-hooped barrel and not bring pain upon myself.

ALI: I could do it with a full one, but that was the last. (*He throws the crushed can into a tray.*)

CON: Hey! That'll be enough of that. (*Retrieves the can from the tray.*) Now, out of here you lot, and take your litter with you!

(*CON throws the crushed can back at ALI who catches it then throws it back at CON, who throws it back at ALI then the four of them throw their crushed cans into the tray with a defiant crash. Pause.*)

CUCKOO: Do you know who you're challenging?

CON: On your way, all of you. There's no thoroughfare.

ALI: Well, we're not looking for a fight or a short-cut.

CON: Look, I'm instructing you to get off this property! You're trespassing. Well, don't just stand there with your mouth open, Cusack! Do something!

CUSACK: What exactly?

CON: Get these piss-heads out of here!

CUSACK: All right, all right. It's only a bunch of lads having a laugh. Don't get excited now. Leave them to me.

CUCKOO: Wham! Wham! Wham! Wham!

CON: Don't you threaten me. Oh, yes, you're great when there's four of you.

CUCKOO/FERGUS: (*Together.*) Wham! Wham! Wham! Wham!

CUSACK: Now what would a collection of obvious vegetarians like yourselves be wanting in a place of this nature?

ALI: There's an important job that needs to be done. Are you the man?

CUSACK: No, that's the man, in there. Mr Sheehan. I think we have been found by the casuals.

CON: No, I'm not having that drunken rabble in here. Go on hop it!

CUSACK: You're all experienced animal mortality operatives?

ALI: We are indeed. Got it off to a T.

CUSACK: Cash in hand. No questions asked. I think these are good lads, Mr Sheehan. I like the look of them.

CON: Cusack, old son, I said no, definitely. They're filthy dirty.

CUSACK: A good scrub and some disinfectant will cure that. Once we have them in the white coats and white wellies with the rubber gloves on they'll be unrecognisable from ordinary clean and decent people.

CON: They stink. Those clothes are falling off them.

CUSACK: I'll keep their clothes under guard on the pavement outside, chained down while they do the job.

CON: Sorry, Cusack, old son. They won't do. Too unhygienic for me.

ALI: Is there a problem of some sort? Anything I can help with?

CUSACK: Come on now, Mr Sheehan. They're first-rate. How long have you been out of work, lads? Look at them. Insecure, unwanted, mocked in the streets. I bet people get up and move when they sit next to them in the alehouse. These lads can't afford soap, Mr Sheehan.

FERGUS: All we want to do is work.

CUCKOO: Wham! Wham! Wham! Wham!

ALI: We heard there was a job going. A big job.

CON: (*Edging out.*) Cusack, old son, I don't think it's a feasible proposition. Send them away. I expected…look, this is a clean place…it has to be…they can't work with hair like that…

(*FERGUS ties his hair up and sticks it down his collar.*)

CUSACK: See? Quick-thinking. And look at the arms on this one. Hey, show him your arm.

(*CUSACK taps MAEVE on the shoulder. She rolls up her sleeve. It reveals a white, smooth, woman's arm. She clenches her fist and flexes her bicep.*)

Look at that. Sprung steel. Let's get going. A shower for all of you, and that will include a shampoo. Will you supervise them directly, Mr Sheehan? Or shall I appoint a charge hand from within the group?

(*CON is looking intently at MAEVE's arm.*)

MAEVE: I'll be the chargehand.

CON: It's a woman!

ALI: Maeve will supervise.

MAEVE: Naturally.

CUSACK: Ireland's first slaughterperson, Mr Sheehan. It had to come sooner or later.

CON: Not in my abattoir!

CUSACK: My abattoir, is it? Since when?

CON: I'm not having a woman working here!

MAEVE: What have you got against women? Not your weapon, I'll be bound.

CON: That's it! Enough is enough.

CUSACK: I thought I was supposed to be sorting this out?

CON: I don't know what's got into you, Cusack old son.

CUCKOO: (*Chanting.*)
Heads hacked off, blood spouting,
battles roaring, men screaming,
heroes hovering like hawks!

CUSACK: Well, you're a sight for sore eyes, my friends. I'm glad you could make it.

MAEVE: We made the beginning, Cusack. It is only right that we should make the end.

CUCKOO: I heard the Pope give the Druid's snapping-mouth and the high hero's scream down in Drogheda yesterday.

FERGUS: He demanded a change in us all. Speaking in a voice of thunder which could be heard for miles, he shouted that the old times were over, then flew into the air, roaring and swaying in the wind.

ALI: You know how long we've waited for peace, Cusack. No one will believe it but the hero longs for nothing else, so he can rest and dream of the old days. He does not want his deeds repeated.
(*CON retreats.*)

CON: I'm leaving it to you, Cusack, old son, just as you said.

MAEVE: The bulls are on the move then?

CUSACK: At first light this morning they started out.

MAEVE: I can feel the land tensed up, waiting for the brunt of it.

CUSACK: It will be a blow of catastrophic proportions.

CUCKOO: (*Chanting.*) Cattle coming over old roads paved
    with slabs of dried blood, thick hooves treading on the
    broken shields of smashed armies, on twisted weapons
    and women red-eyed with grieving over this long track of
    killing.

CON: Cusack, old son, make a move, eh? Out, if you don't
    mind. Now. Immediately…

FERGUS: (*Chanting at CON.*)
    The field of slaughter bloomed red
    with body-flowers, white with bone-blossoms
    blue with staring eyes, green with bile,
    brown with bowel, all the colours
    were there to entertain the ravens
    kindle the kite's appetite.

CUCKOO: There will be such a shuddering! Such a shaking!
    Great feats of strength!

FERGUS: Do the leap over a poisoned stroke!
    (*CUCKOO leaps high in the air.*)

CUCKOO: Done!

FERGUS: The noble chariot-fighter's crouch!
    (*CUCKOO snarls, crouches, leans forward.*)

CUCKOO: Done! Look at this!

ALI: Cuckoo! I have a feat for you today.

CUCKOO: Name it!

CON: What a gang of cretins.

ALI: It is a hard one.

CUCKOO: The harder the better!

ALI: Stepping on a spear in flight then straightening erect on
    its point.
    (*Pause.*)

CUCKOO: Ah-um.

ALI: Bit rusty on that one?

CUCKOO: Well what about the apple-feat? Nine apples
    juggled with only one touching one hand at any one time?
    (*Pause.*) No apples. No apples. (*Slumps down.*) No apples.

MAEVE: Don't let him get the dooms. We're going to need
    him soon.

FERGUS: Cuckoo, come on, cheer up. (*Strokes his head.*)

CUCKOO: (*To CON.*) When did you last see the feat of the

Hero's Coil on the Spike of Spears?

CON: Lad, I'm sorry for you. You're wasting your breath.

CUCKOO: Climbing up a spear then performing a dance on its point without making the soles of the feet bleed. It's easy when you know how.

CON: Is it indeed? No doubt you're the only man in the world who can strike a match on wet soap. Push off, will you?

CUCKOO: We're not wanted, Maeve. All that journey for nothing. They don't want us. What do they care about the bulls.

MAEVE: (*Stroking CUCKOO'S head.*) Help him. Don't let him get into his doom-slide. Come now, Cuckoo. What do we care if we're wanted or not? Did we expect a great reception when it has all been spent on the Pope? We just have our task to perform.

CUCKOO: Who will watch us? Who cares?

MAEVE: History will care, and the future.

ALI: (*Stroking CUCKOO's head.*) Remember how hard it is to be a hero in your own time, never mind someone else's.

MAEVE: (*Catching a louse in CUCKOO's hair.*) Well, we something of our own with us. They last well, these lice. Your hair is teeming with them, Cuckoo.

CON: Oh no, lice! In here! We'll have to go though the whole place with a fumigator…do something, Cusack! They're crawling with vermin!

MAEVE: The big ones are helping the little ones over the gaps between the hairs. Why, here's a crowd camped just above your ear.

ALI: Ooooh, Cuckoo, I can see a hundred heroes in here arming themselves before dawn, strapping on harness, rubbing grease into their chariot-axles. Wha! Here's a gang of stone-slingers, whirling away in your head. Get ready to duck!

CON: Cusack!

CUSACK: Sssssh! You're taking a risk with yourself, Mr Sheehan.

CON: Bloody vermin! They'll be leaping all over the

premises. Look, Cusack, old son, these ruffians are a health-hazard. Get rid of them!

CUSACK: Not yet. I asked them round, you see. I thought they might be able to help with a problem which concerns you short-term hero, the Pope.

FERGUS: (*Searching CUCKOO's head for lice.*) In this gloomy forest here all I have eyes for are the naked women, running races, climbing up trees to see the armies coming, vaulting over streams. Ah, here's one with her belly full of children trying to outpace a golden chariot. (*Catches the louse.*) You lost that one, love of mine.

CUCKOO: We should go back, Maeve. It won't work.

MAEVE: It will, I promise you. (*Kisses his head.*) We will do it, together. Don't despair, Cuckoo. Your strength will still be needed. True courage is in short supply.

(*MAEVE takes CUCKOO, FERGUS and ALI in her arms and holds them, crooning gently.*

CON paces round them, vexed and frustrated.)

CON: Don't let the bastards fall asleep! We'll never get rid of them. They're not relatives of yours are they? Those nephews from Galway?

CUSACK: Oh, we all have a spot of their blood in our veins, Mr Sheehan. Aren't we all heroes on the sly, when no one is looking? But treat them carefully. They're not in a mood to be fooled with.

CON: Neither am I. As manager of this place –

CUSACK: Come off it, will you? All that's out in the open now. You stand exposed. Don't forget, I know… I know. There are more lice in your mind than there are in his head. D'you know what the staff call you?

CON: I don't. Nor do I care.

CUSACK: Can't you face a little truth like that?

CON: (*Pause.*) Cusack, old son, er I can see that I've upset you somehow. I must admit, I don't know why…

CUSACK: They call you Slackarse.

CON: Good of them. Cusack, old son, is it anything to do with that salary increase I put you up for but you didn't get? Now that wasn't my fault.

CUSACK: Don't worry. I remember your heroic battle on my

behalf. Mr Sheehan, your in-tray is a gaping void and your out-tray is a yawning chasm. In between is the desert of Eternity.

CUCKOO: Cusack, Cusack, I don't like this place. I don't like the smell. Couldn't we ambush the bulls on the road? Look at it...none of the old colour and encrustation of the old spots of sacrifice. It doesn't feel right. For Death, it's too clean, too clean.

MAEVE: As scrubbed as the neck of a virgin on her wedding night. But she falls, doesn't she? (*Kisses CUCKOO's neck and ears.*)

CUSACK: (*To CON.*) While the wise Queen Maeve has her tongue down the ears of Ireland's heroes I will make a confession to you. If you were a man of any religion I might stand a chance of being believed in the sin which I must reveal. But you, with your analytical mind, will merely become incredulous, not being trained to the lewd and impossible as is the ear of a priest. Amongst my sins there is one that is paramount. It towers above all the others. It is an unnatural sin. It is a sin that creates more sin, in envy. There is no worse sin in the world, and I have suffered for it. Without blessing, without permission, by a twist of Time and Nature,
I have lived over eight hundred years.

CON: Quite a night you must have had, Cusack, old son. You might have said you were still motherless.

CUSACK: Don't look my age, do I? Want to know my secret?

CON: Behave like a prick if you want to. I'm taking this as a temporary lapse. We'll both get over it.

FERGUS: Maeve, will we ever get back?

MAEVE: No, Fergus, my love. Once we've done the job and the air has been cleared, I think we will fade away.

FERGUS: Where to, Maeve?

MAEVE: Some bone-yard somewhere. Peaceful enough. The idea is for us to be forgotten about. Cusack has told you, Fergus, heroes like us are redundant. We have to get out of the way. Death is best for us four.

ALI: But the great Druid, the flying John Paul who stands on a spear and straightens erect on its point, surely that man is a hero? Look at his hands. Look at his head. Look how he circles the world checking his honour like a farmer checks his fence-posts.

MAEVE: Ah, he is a true hero of today, Cusack says. On his back he does not carry harness but ideas. In his hand he has no weapon, only the record of his talk. In his eyes are mirrors to reflect the questions. He does not prophecy, nor visit oracles. He shouts only the known words.

FERGUS: Could we try again, Maeve? (*Pause.*) Oh, I've made you sad.

CUSACK: (*To CON.*) *You* must forgive them if they slip and slide in your scientific brain, Mr Sheehan. Like new born infants, they're covered in mild, metaphorical jelly, incapable of standing still and making Anglo-Saxon sense. Pity them. The ground was never steady under their feet. All impulse you see. No plan, except for today, and I sketched that one out for them.

CON: So you are responsible?

CUSACK: Oh, you know how responsible I am, Mr Sheehan.

CON: You and me will have things to talk about once this is over. I'm not laughing, Cusack, old son, not laughing at all.

CUSACK: I should hope not. Me and my friends are very serious about what we're doing.

CON: Which is what, exactly?

CUSACK: In all your reading up there in the office while the killing was going on under your feet but out of your mind, did you ever get round to any yarns about the Irish heroes of old?

CON: I can't say I did.

CUSACK: Well, you might be equally indifferent to meeting them now – Queen Maeve and King Ali of Connaught, Fergus her lover, betrayer of Ulster, and Cuckoo – the hero of Ulster. Now, I'm eight hundred years old and I don't feel a day over forty, but they're knocking on two thousand – hence the smell.

CON: The smell I believe in.

CUSACK: They were the authors of their own deeds. What actions they took rattled in the air until it got hot and radiant? The reverberations never died away in Ireland,

not from the first century until the Normans came. People
kept them alive by word of mouth only. Now me, I was
unemployed at the end of the twelfth century – always
a traditionalist, you see – and my parents put me in
the monastery at Clonmacnois on the east bank of the
Shannon. Hired as a man of prayer, I found myself
frustrated as I had no faith in Anglo-Norman Christianity
and couldn't open my mouth to an alien god. One day the
Bishop of Leinster found me idling around and said – give
that lazy sod something to do. What? says the brother in
charge of me. The Bishop thought for a minute and then
said – conscious as he was of the great cultural changes
taking place and the danger of the people losing their
identity – let him collect and write down the full text of the
Cattle Raid of Cooley from the lips of the peasants. (*Pause.*)
So it was that I took charge of their lives, these heroes,
and we came to know each other intimately. I toured the
country gathering lies and fantasies from the memories of
whores, beggars, charlatans. I had to haunt every shebeen
in the four kingdoms. It had an everlasting effect upon my
liver.

CON: And your brain by the sound of it.

FERGUS: Watch your tongue! Are you doubting the word of
our friend and preserver?

CUSACK: Do you have the habit of denying the evidence
of your own eyes? Here are the heroes. (*Reaches into the
guts tray.*) And here is the book. (*Pause. They smile at CON.*)
I'm not saying that it was an easy rescue. The Church had
almost battered the stories from the peasant mind, but I
found people only too willing to give me the shreds, the
fragments. I was leapt on from behind walls, importuned
through the window of my cell, followed through the fields
by folk who wanted to sell me tales of these devils – filthy,
feuding, fornicating fiends. Irish heroes to the bone.
(*Pause. They smile at CON.*)

CON: Sure. For once we might agree.

CUSACK: But God would not accept that he'd created them.
The question arose as to who had? The Church could not
advise me. It would agree that God had created Lucifer,

who had fallen, but not this lot, which had never got off the ground. Now, Mr Sheehan, who can walk around in any chronology without a creator? Someone had to take on the responsibility.

CUCKOO: I had a house made from human heads. All my windows were made from the hip-bones of queens and my lintels from the thigh-bones of priests. That was what people said of me, and that was what was true.

CON: Who would waste time doubting it? (*Pause.*) Cusack, I don't think you're yourself today. I know you have a habit of picking up strange companions in your wanderings on a Saturday night, but bringing them to work is well past my sense of humour.

CUSACK: You interpret my old routines correctly. I am a lonely man. I do love a drink and a talk, and I do get enthusiastic about new friends. All this I admit. Ask my landlady. (*Pause.*) But these are the heroes.

(*CON turns away.*)

MAEVE: What time are the bulls due?

CUSACK: Eight o'clock.

MAEVE: And you're sure they're the ones?

CUSACK: The white bull of the south and the brown bull of Ulster.

MAEVE: Did you tell the drivers that if they get the bulls here on time they'd have the use of my friendly thighs as a bonus?

CUSACK: Maeve, what would stop them speeding and taking chances with their cargo if I told them that? They're simple men.

MAEVE: I want the scheme to work, Cusack. We didn't come here for nothing.

CUSACK: I've done everything I could. Do you think the Pope will understand a tribute like this? He's not one for sacrificing beasts on altars.

MAEVE: Ach, come off it. Everybody is.

CUSACK: The carcases are intended for the British dogmeat trade. You don't mind that?

MAEVE: Let the flesh look after itself. It's the thought behind the sword that counts. The lives of those two old horrors will go out like a pair of summer storms. They'll do the job, put the pressure in the right place.

CUSACK: But how will I persuade this man that we're telling the truth?

CON: You've been telling this riff-raff stories about me, haven't you?

CUSACK: If I have, they were full of compliments. How you keep your mind active...at home, with your experiments and inventions. How you use your time intelligently – sleep in the office, for which you get paid, work in your spare-time to make a fortune. D'you know this man here has come up with a substance extracted from animal fats which can dry-clean blotting paper? The world will recognise him one day.

CON: Christ, Cusack, old son – you hate me, don't you? All these years I've spent sticking up for you and this is the thanks I get.

CUCKOO: Fight him. Weapons. Blood. Hacking. Heads flying. Revenge. Watch the crows peck out his eyes. Put his head over your door to smile for ever. Hate will get you high up. High up. Yaaah! (*He leaps into the air.*
Enter JANET SOAMES. She is dressed in a smart white outfit with matching gloves, shoes and handbag.
CUCKOO lands in front of her and puts his hands out towards her breasts. A frozen pause.)
That is the country where I would rest my weapon. (*Smiles and claps his hands together, leaping in the air and tumbling.*)
The heroic salmon-leap, the feat of Cat and the feat of Body all in one. What d'you think of that?

JANET: I apologise for the intrusion, Mr Sheehan. I was passing so I thought I'd check that everything was all right with our order...everything is all right is it? No problems have arisen, I hope.

CUSACK: I'll get an armchair.

JANET: No thank you. I'm not stopping.

CON: Well, the beasts haven't arrived yet, I'm afraid.

JANET: Haven't they?

MAEVE: We're all waiting for them, impatiently. This man will tell you. He's lucky to have us.

CON: Nothing to do with me. Trouble-makers. You know, last night the whole of Dublin was on its ear…they just came in off the street. I'm sorry.

JANET: Well, I hope you manage to get rid of them soon. We are looking forward to our order being met in a satisfactory manner. Being importuned by vagrants will not be accepted as a reasonable excuse.

MAEVE: Vagrants? Do you think we haven't got a home to go to?

JANET: I hope everything works out, Mr Sheehan. I'll ring you in the morning when your premises have been washed out. Ten o'clock, number three.

(*MAEVE grabs JANET by the hips from behind.*)

MAEVE: Now would a child get through there, never mind an army?

JANET: Let go of me! Mr Sheehan!

CON: Hey, cut that out.

(*CON goes to pull MAEVE off JANET, FERGUS bounds into the air, his sword whirling and crashes it down, flatbladed, on CON's head, knocking him out.*)

FERGUS: (*Standing over CON – chanting.*)

Leap of the Cat
the blade beats
crow's winged
the queen-handler
sleeps, lucky
to live. No sword.

JANET: Don't hit him again. I get the picture. Now, I suppose that was to frighten me. An example. I understand. Is he breathing?

FERGUS: It was a kiss of great skill. A mere touch on the head.

JANET: I would think that you are an expert. Months of training. Complete dedication. Yes, I accept that. I know what I'm dealing with. Well, should we get down to business?

CUSACK: Business?

JANET: Of course.

CUSACK: What business?

JANET: Look, I've been expecting something like this to happen for a long time. The company has prepared me. We have had a pamphlet circulated.

(*CON groans and gets to his feet.*)

CUSACK: Miss Soames, you're misjudging these characters here. All they've come for is to do a slaughtering job.

CON: Keep your distance, Cusack! I won't forget this!

JANET: You have taken us hostage. That's obvious. What else could it be? (*Pause.*) It has all the signs. (*Pause.*) You have taken us hostage, haven't you?

MAEVE: I think the woman wants us to say yes.

CUSACK: A pamphlet is a powerful thing.

JANET: The first step is for me to ascertain what you want from us. In writing, if possible.

MAEVE: Well, Cusack does all the writing for us.

CUSACK: Miss Soames, you're a natural born extremist, you know that?

JANET: You are holding us here, aren't you?

CUSACK: Long enough to pass the time of day, that's all.

JANET: That's what they all say. You wouldn't tell us that you intend to keep us here for ever. Once you've made your demands...

CUSACK: Who to? All the police, army and world press are fluttering around following the Pope's helicopter over the countryside this morning. Dublin is empty.

JANET: (*Disappointed.*) Oh.

CON: You won't get anywhere with them while they're in this mood. They're enjoying themselves at our expense. What they're doing is buying time. Cusack brought them here, didn't you?

CUSACK: I did. To do a simple job that needs doing. A job they are desperate to do for Ireland's sake.

JANET: An old story, if you like.

CON: They want to work on the carcases for your consignment. That's all I can get out of them so far.

JANET: The bulls for this morning?

CON: That's right. They want nothing else out of life. See

what I mean?

JANET: And when the place is besieged and the streets fill up with sightseers and barricades, ambulances and fire engines, that's what they'll announce to the authorities and the media? They're keeping us here so they can kill bulls? Everyone will think they're mad.

CON: Useful in court later on. It's a cover so they can plead insanity.

JANET: I insist on knowing! Are you from the IRA? The UDA? The UDF? The UFF? The UUU?

MAEVE: Is that a spell she's chanting? Are you chanting a spell at me? Don't act the druid if you haven't got the powers.

JANET: Why be so secretive about it? It's not fair! We must know.

CON: Cusack, for Christ's sake, find out what they want. We're not going to resist. If they're going to hold us hostage that's fine…these things can be arranged…

JANET: He's with them. There's no point in asking him for help.

CON: Cusack? Never. (*Pause.*) In spite of appearances I think the man is still loyal to me. He's been indoctrinated. It's tragic.
(*CUCKOO and FERGUS are unwrapping their weapons out of the sacking. Each has a sharpening-stone, which they start to use. The sound is monotonous – but sinister. CUCKOO and FERGUS lick the blades and spears.*)

CUSACK: Don't get us wrong now. Mr Sheehan, I've reached the natural end of my employment here. There must be some other sucker in Dublin who could come along and run this place while you play the gentleman slaughterer, pretending the job isn't there. Failed his degree at Trinity, I'm afraid. He was to have been Ireland's Nobel Prize for Physics – the man who gave the Irish Government the atom bomb. You never got over the shock, did you, Mr Sheehan? It induced a strange paralysis of the nine-to-five nervous system. Butchery is below him.

JANET: Would you tell us what you want? Must we make a telephone call? Write a letter with your demands. Have

our photographs taken looking suitably terrified. Name it –
let's get down to business, please. (*Pause.*) Look, we do not
intend to resist! But tell us what you want.

CON: I think Cusack wants my nose rubbed in the dirt, don't
you?

CUSACK: Why d'you take the job on if you didn't mean to
do it?

CUCKOO: (*Chanting.*) Cutting death flowers
stretched in my strength
slitting the chariot cushion
my heroic hard hand
never at rest!

CUSACK: Mr Sheehan, a while ago you believed that an
ordinary mortal man could fly out of the sky and perform
a miracle in Ireland. (*Waves the newspaper at CON.*)
Remember? Well, we don't believe that he can do it alone.
So we're going to help him.

JANET: We intend to co-operate in every way possible.
Please, let us all keep calm. I have had instructions from
my company head office that I am to avoid heroics.

CUCKOO: Yaaaah! Scream! Sword-edge and sloped shield!
Thunder-feat!

JANET: Stop him yelling at me!

CUCKOO: I'll show you the spurt of speed, the stroke of
precision! With my massive stroke-dealing sword I'll hack
bits as big as babies' heads off those bulls. I'll strangle them
with their own dewlaps!

CUSACK: All right, Cuckoo, they'll be here soon. Don't get
impatient.

CUCKOO: Lumps like boulders I'll hack off!

JANET: He's a psychopath! Do something about him.

CUSACK: He's not interested in you. Did I tell you that
I was eight hundred years old?

JANET: No, but I'm not surprised. Look, will you stop beating
about the bush? Why do these friends of yours want to kill
our bulls so much?

MAEVE: Your bulls? What are you talking about? They've
belonged to us for two thousand years. We're making a gift
of them…they're all we've got left to sacrifice.

FERGUS: The Pope will soon be at Clonmacnois where
Cusack wrote us down and gave us eternal life – which
we don't want any more. We don't belong. The Pope's
going there to venerate the Christian saints and poets but
he hasn't been told that the great power created in that
monastery was always us, greater heroes than any of them.

CUSACK: Miss Soames, have you opened up your mind to
us? We are everything that we say we are.

MAEVE: She must have proof, Cusack. Why should she
believe that we're genuine? (*Pause.*) You've never seen
a blood-stained altar, have you? Never seen the red fog
rolling out of the bull's entrails into the clear air. We were
brought up on it as children.

ALI: You can do a lot with death which you can't with life.

MAEVE: And our druids were thoughtful men, men who
could take the initiative, like this pope. Ours would try
anything – anything – to get rid of a plague or a piece
of bad luck which was affecting the people. They'd turn
themselves inside-out, experiment, take chances with
their own lives. I've seen druids who've fallen asleep at
the altar, covered in blood, having sacrificed every sort of
living creature they could until they found the right one.
Sometimes it was as small as a mouse or a wren. They
never gave up. (*Pause.*) We get the idea from all the show
and shouting, that if this visit doesn't work, the Pope will
think there is nothing else to be done. No one has told him
about the bulls, you see. He doesn't know that they're still
roaming around. (*Pause.*) He hasn't made them a part of his
calculations.

CON: This isn't happening. Confirm that for me, Cusack, old
son.

CUCKOO: (*Sniffs the air.*) Aaaaah! Wham! Wham!

FERGUS: Have you got the scent, Cuckoo? Can you smell
them coming, those two enormous old devils!?

CUSACK: Mr Sheehan, you have more diplomas in meat
management than I have so it is reasonable to suppose
that you have, by far, the firmer grasp on reality. I don't
see that any one layer of the stuff has more relevance than

the other. But I'm very uneducated in this field, seeing so
many alternatives and states of being when I'm assured
by yourself that there's only one. But we haven't got the
tools for philosophy here, have we? We're left out of
the mainstream. Even psychology is left out of our lives
because of the shortage of snakes in Ireland. (*Pause.*) Have
you ever seen a snake here, Miss Soames?

JANET: No.

CUSACK: There you are then. (*Pause.*) How am I doing,
Maeve?

MAEVE: I still get the feeling that these two aren't with us
body and soul. They're not entirely convinced.

CUSACK: Then I will have to reveal all – down to the
last detail. Today we are going to create what Ireland
needs most. It's nothing very complicated. A child could
understand it quite easily. You could work it out yourselves.
(*Pause.*) Ireland needs a great natural disaster.

CUCKOO: Wham! Wham! Wham! Wham!

CUSACK: Irish disasters in the past have always been without
flair or drama, having at their middles either vegetables or
the seven virtues. But no natural cataclysms – nothing that
just came out of the earth or the sky. Well, we're going to
remedy that. I bet you can't guess, what it is?

CON: Lagging far behind you, Cusack, old son, far behind
you.

CUSACK: We're going to make an earthquake.

CON: Are you now?

CUSACK: Followed by a tidal wave of such huge proportions
that it will wash out the country from coast to coast. (*Pause.*)
Isn't it on the tip of your tongue to ask us how we're going
to do that? (*Pause.*) I thought it was. When the Pope jams
himself into the cramped little cell at Clonmacnois where I
made immortal the violence of an older Ireland, there will
obviously be a major disturbance. But that would not be
quite enough to split the earth. So we're going to project
the souls of those two terrible, ridiculous, discredited old
bulls into the same force-field at the precise moment of his
entry. With Ireland more sensitive to reverberations today

than any other for two thousand years, it cannot help but produce a convulsion of the beloved, suffering earth which will shake the Irish down to the back teeth, together. That's the thing. Together. (*Pause.*) I haven't got through to you, Miss Soames?

JANET: Yes, yes. The Irish must be shaken. I'm all for it, honestly.

MAEVE: Oooh, come on, come on, this waiting is itching my insides!

CUCKOO: It's the smell I can't stand, the smell of trees, pine trees, but no forest. Where's the forest?

CON: Look, I'll give them a full day's pay, double-time, to leave us alone. I want to close up now. Sorry, Miss Soames, the shipment won't be made tomorrow.

CUCKOO: (*Taking deeper and deeper breaths.*) I can smell the forest but there are no trees! I can smell the forest but there are no leaves! I can smell the forest but there are no rrrrrroots!

(*CUCKOO goes into an immense convulsion, foaming, yelling, striking out at the air, twisting and turning all his limbs. Suddenly he stops dead, frozen.*)

CON: Control the bastard, can't you?

JANET: He's getting ready to do it again. He's making himself do it, the animal! Oh, God, look at him!

(*CUCKOO breathes deeply and breaks into another furious convulsion.*

FERGUS and ALI circle him like sheep-dogs controlling his sphere of movement.

CUCKOO stops dead again, his eyes staring.)

MAEVE: The power is still in him. That was a good warp-spasm, Cuckoo.

CUSACK: What did you see then?

JANET: I presume it was some kind of fit or symptom.

CON: Ach, it's drying-out time. Sunday morning and the eight o'clock horrors.

CUSACK: You will have to stay until the bulls are slaughtered.

CON: Cusack, old son…

JANET: We undertake to leave here and not go to the police. Agreed, Mr Sheehan?

CON: Absolutely. You can trust us.

CUSACK: You hear them, Maeve? Cuckoo puts on his warp-spasm and it's a fit. Cuckoo puts on his warp-spasm and it's a symptom! Did I not tell you the truth when I said terror was dead?

MAEVE: In my own court I took the heads of any people who had deliberately blinded themselves. Self-mutilation is a sin. Now, didn't you see Cuckoo as we did?

CON: Yes, yes, of course.

ALI: Will you pardon me if I suggest that you might have overlooked the fact that he became a monstrous article vile, terrible and shapeless?

CON: Yes, yes, I did notice.

FERGUS: And did you notice how his shanks and his joints, every knuckle and knee-bone, every angle and artery and organ from top to bottom shook like a tree in the flood or a reed in the stream? Woman! You saw all that?

JANET: Yes. Of course.

MAEVE: Good. No doubt you were enthralled and entertained with the way his whole body made a tearing twist inside his skin so that all his flesh was loosened and wallowed around in him like a new-born pig in a bag. And did you see his feet, knees and shins switch round until they were facing the wrong way? The balled sinews of his calves flew round like big knots of a ship's rope. On his mighty head the veins of his temples writhed... didn't they?

JANET: If you say so.

MAEVE.: Oh, I do, I do. Just as I say that the sinews of his neck gathered into a knob the size of a month-old child's head and his face and features were thrust back until they became a deep, red bowl. You caught that?

JANET: Yes. Yes. If that's what you want, yes.

ALI: Did you see that special feature of his then? He sucked one eye so deep into his skull that a wild crane couldn't get at it with its long beak probing!

CON: Yes, we saw that too.

FERGUS: The other popped out of the socket and dangled there like a bell's clapper bumping against the cheek-bone. His mouth grew wider and wider in a terrible cave of distortion until all the skin was unrolled from the jaw and out heaved his liver and lungs from the gullet, flapping there like a great red flag while flakes of flaming blood flew all round his head. No doubt you captured these moments as well?

JANET: Yes, yes, yes.

MAEVE: This is truly a day of hope. Now I am sure that they must be capable of seeing the last and most terrible sign of the hero's warp-spasm, coming as it does as an afterthought.

CUSACK: What is that, Queen Maeve?

MAEVE: Oh, who should need reminding of the feature? Over Ireland, in the clear air, full, steady and straight, from the very dead centre of his skull, will rise a fountain of blood, a spout as high as a whale will throw the ocean, or a boy will throw a ball.

(Pause. They all look at CUCKOO who tenses himself, squeezing his eyes shut, clutching his balls. He starts to wail in anguish. FERGUS, ALI and MAEVE join him. It becomes a long, high, urgent song, sad and terrible. From the centre of his skull rises a stream of blood which showers over the white tiles, the white coats of CON and CUSACK, and JANET's white outfit. The song increases in pitch, then dies slightly as CUCKOO crumples to the ground, holding his head, moans. The keening rises again, now deeper, softer, darker. Red light fades in. CUSACK, CON and JANET hold out their arms as if crucified. They join in the Celtic grief.)

CUSACK: Ireland will change, as it was changed before; by pure belief.

(The heroes take the blood-stained clothes off CUSACK, CON and JANET and dress CUSACK as a monk, CON as a bishop and janet as a nun. CON and JANET turn their backs on the audience and stand in opposite corners. The keening changes to a Gregorian chant as the heroes stand the big guts tray on its end, centre. The black book

*slides out onto the floor. CUSACK picks it up and enters
the guts tray. He produces quills and vellum from the folds
of his habit. CUCKOO does his salmon-leap and knocks a
part of the gantry steelwork so that it snaps into a crucifix.
The heroes squat at the feet of CUSACK, searching each
other for lice.)*

Right, snippets of the heroes. If you peasants have rested
and cleaned up after your journeys here to Clonmacnois,
let us start.

FERGUS: Will we have the money first?

CUSACK: You will not. Money comes after the information.
Who's first?

FERGUS: That's me.

MAEVE: It is not! I got here long before you. Did you not see
me sitting here getting my thoughts together?

CUSACK: Well then, young woman. What do you know of
the story of the two bulls of Ireland?

MAEVE: I know a small portion.

CUSACK: What about?

MAEVE: Queen Maeve.

CUSACK: Let's hope you've got something good to say about
her. All I've got so far is the most unmitigated filth.

MAEVE: Mine is a very simple and straightforward story
illustrating the queen's essential humanity.

CUSACK: Well, that sounds very encouraging. Let's have it
then.

MAEVE: It is soon told. Queen Maeve's son-in-law, Ferdia,
was told to go out and fight the unbeatable Ulster hero,
Cuckoo. Ferdia got himself ready and drove over in
his chariot to say farewell. He did not think much of
his chances of survival. At Maeve's tent he found her
squatting in the darkness over something and saying, quite
affectionately, 'Are you still asleep?'

CUSACK: 'Are you still asleep?'

MAEVE: My grandmother, from whom I learnt the story,
thought that Maeve was pissing in the king's ear.

CUSACK: Why should she be doing that?

MAEVE: My grandmother said that it was the only way to
talk to some men.

CUSACK: And that is your contribution?

MAEVE: I've walked fifty miles to tell it to you.

CUSACK: Here. (*Gives her a coin.*) If you've got any more like that then leave them at home. Who's next?

(*FERGUS stands up.*)

FERGUS: That's me.

CUSACK: What story have you brought me?

FERGUS: The story of an encounter; a fight, if you like. (*CON and JANET turn round and step from their corners. CUSACK gets to his feet. The peasants scramble up to their knees.*)

CON: No, no, don't get up. Carry on. Pretend I'm not here. (*Pause. CUSACK sits down. He fixes FERGUS with a hard stare.*)

CUSACK: Go on. I hope it's an improvement on the last one.

FERGUS: Much better, brother monk, much better. It is soon told.

CUSACK: Get on with it then.

FERGUS: An Ulsterman called Ilech came against the army of the south at a place called Ath Feidli. His chariot was highly decrepit and falling to bits and it was pulled by two old jaundiced horses, spavined and knock-kneed to the degree where they could only shamble. Ilech had his old chariot full of stones and clods of earth and he threw these at the people who came to stare at him, for the old warrior was fighting stark naked and his worn-out weapon and bollocks hung down through a hole in the chariot floor, banging on the ground.

CUSACK: (*Covering his eyes.*) Oh God.

FERGUS: The army of the south jeered at Ilech and told him to get out of the way or they would trample on him. Ilech pulled his old worn-out weapon up and whirled it round his head, then cast it at the army of the south, catching a hundred warrior in a noose from which he hanged them from a tree while battering their brains out with his bollocks.

CUSACK: Have you finished?

FERGUS: That's the only bit I can remember.

CUSACK: Here. (*Gives FERGUS a coin and goes over to CON.*)
　　Your Grace, I apologise.

CON: Think nothing of it.

CUSACK: Your mistress', sorry, the holy sister's ears I
　　wouldn't want to pollute them further... Your Grace,
　　couldn't I be taken off this job and put on something else...
　　breaking rocks, digging ditches...anything, anything.

CON: Remember, my son, this is a pre-Christian poem we're
　　dealing with. We can't expect the same high standards of
　　decency as we observe ourselves.

CUSACK: But they only remember the filth! Why?

CON: Oh, to tease us. You know the Irish. They're probably
　　making it up as they go along.

CUSACK: (*To JANET.*) Please forgive them. They are lowly
　　people with no idea of what they're saying.

JANET: I think it is charming, charming.

CUSACK: That's enlightened of you, Sister. I fear there may
　　be worse to come.

JANET: Nothing can shock me, brother. Before I came over
　　from England I was trained in the ways of the Irish.

CUSACK: I could do with some of that myself. What
　　mysteries did they explain?

JANET: Their natural courtesy and hospitality. Their good
　　humour. Their particular sensitivities.

CUSACK: Aha! Could you enumerate for the sake of this
　　rabble? They might learn something about themselves.

JANET: The Irish, I was told, have a highly-developed sense
　　of wonder about human affairs. They are full of admiration
　　for the business of being alive but often regret the intensity
　　of the experience. They are prone to boiling over and
　　overstatement.

CUSACK: Let it never be said!

JANET: Tremendous respect for family ties and bonds. An
　　almost supernatural addiction to the ceremonies of death.

CUSACK: This is a course I must get on. Your Grace. Send
　　me to England for a refresher.

CON: Your great work must not be disturbed, my son.
　　England would only confuse you. As an Irishman born

and bred you might find much in the life of such a highly civilised people which struck you as worthless, over-practical and mercenary. Stick with it.

CUSACK: As an exercise in futility, your Grace, I think this must beat flagellation and all forms of mortification. (*Sits down.*) Next.

ALI: That's me, brother.

CUSACK: You have a story?

ALI: I do.

CUSACK: Is it in any way to do with bodily functions?

ALI: Mine is about healing.

CUSACK: Ah. (*Nods at CON and JANET.*) That sounds more like it. Gentleness, mercy, understanding.

ALI: It is soon told. An Ulsterman called Cethern arrived at Cuckoo's camp with his guts round his feet after a fight. 'Get me a doctor,' he said. There were no Ulster doctors so Cuckoo sent word to the enemy to send one of theirs, and he came. When he saw Cethern's guts round his feet he said: 'You won't survive this.' 'Neither will you,' Cethern cried and fisted the doctor until the healing-man's brains splashed over his feet. Then Cuckoo found fifty more doctors to come to Cethern and they were all killed in the same way

CUSACK: (*Interrupting.*) Fifty?

ALI: Fifty. I can see my great-grandfather saying it now, a cup at his knee. Fifty.

CUSACK: Cethern killed fifty doctors for saying he wouldn't survive. Go on, go on.

ALI: The fifty-first doctor only got a glancing blow and Cuckoo saved his life.

CUSACK: Decent of him.

ALI: So Cuckoo sent to Ulster for a doctor and one called Fingin came from the king's own court. He looked at Cethern's injuries and said: 'The blood is black here. You were speared at an angle, right through the heart. All your guts have been cut off from each other and lie in a heap like a ball of wool, rolling round your body. I can't promise to cure you...'

CUSACK: So he killed him as well, splashing his brains over his feet.

ALI: Not at all, at all. Just hold your horses, brother. Then the doctor Fintan went on to say: 'I'll tell you no lie, but your case is plain to me. A whole army has left is mark in your tripes and one way or another your life is nearly over.' Then Cethern fisted him and sent him across the chariot's two shafts and smashed the chariot to bits. But he didn't kill him, and the doctor picked himself up and said: 'Either your wounds will have to be treated for a year and you'll live, or I can do it in three days and three nights and give you enough strength for one last fight. Take your pick. (*Pause.*) Which choice did the Ulster warrior take, do you think?

CUSACK: You're telling the story.

ALI: What does the bishop say? Or the nun? What does anyone say who's here? Don't we know what the man's choice was? (*Pause.*) Give me the three days of strength. (*CON nods wisely.*
CUSACK sighs.)
The doctor bound the frame of Cethern's chariot around the spilled guts to hold them in and took wooden ribs to replace some that had been broken in the warrior's chest. Strapped up like this, Cethern rode against the army of the south and fought with great courage until he was over-whelmed.

CON: Very moving. Very moving. An uplifting tale which illustrates the respect that primitive society had for the ancient virtue of fortitude. Sister, you're crying. How tender your heart is.
(*CUSACK gives ALI a coin, then exits left.*
CON takes JANET into a corner and gives her an endless kiss. Enter CUSACK past them carrying a cauldron of hot soup and some bowls.)

CUCKOO: Aha! Good. Good.

ALI: I'm famished with all that talking.
(*CUSACK puts down the cauldron and starts ladling out soup.*)
You get the mist from the Shannon here, I should think.

CUSACK: All the time. The walls run with moisture night and day.

ALI: Well, at least you've got walls. Coming from a humble background like our own benighted pedigrees, what would you say there was to choose between walls made of stone, like this monastery, and walls made of sods, like our stinking hovels?

CUSACK: One absorbs, one repels. You get first extras if you can tell me which is which.

FERGUS: Old Bishop Con is wielding his weapon with that sister right now, I bet. It's not what you do but what you say. He has an admirable sense of style when he breaks the commandments like a man who expects a round of applause for having a shit. This is great soup, Brother monk. Who died last week?

CUSACK: Tell me, all of you, are the sore feet worth it? All this way for what?

MAEVE: We know we're forgetting things more and more. The old world is dying on us.

CUSACK: But people will stay the same. You know what I've got so far, after years of work, tramping over the bogs, sitting here with all kinds of children to grandfathers? A poem in praise of thieves and liars and murderers. Why did you bother to remember it? Why did your fathers bother to pass it on?

MAEVE: How do you spend a dark night? There's the rain, the wind, the cows. Now and again there's a frolic or a beast to kill. Make big things out of small things.

CUCKOO: The feat of the javelin and the rope, snapping mouth, hero's scream, spurt of speed, stroke of precision. Games in the night.

FERGUS: Brother monk, think of the size of them Think of the magnitude of the lies and the deeds. It is almost holy, the way our heroes misbehave. I'll have to lie close to this girl tonight to keep her warm. Take that as a warning in advance.

(*CUSACK goes back to his desk. The peasants drink their soup very noisily. He writes for a while. A Gregorian chant from offstage which blends with the slurping of soup. As they finish it they fall asleep, one by one.*)

CUSACK: Good people, if you're ever short of a job, don't
take up monking for a living. In your solitude you will
come hard up against the question – what does the natural
animal mind of man love most? And it has an answer that
will shake your bones.

(*The peasants settle down for the night in a huddle at
CUSACK's feet.*)

There's wisdom in that answer though, painful as the truth
may be. What man loves most he has plenty of. No man is
poor beside this item of his adoration. Blood. Blood. There
is no imbalance in the possession of it.

I have as much as you and the other way about.

CUCKOO: (*Screaming.*) Aaaaah!

CUSACK: What is it, lad?

CUCKOO: Wham! Wham! Wham! Wham! My heart is
going.

CUSACK: A dream. It was only a dream.

CUCKOO: It was real to me, lying here on the stones. My
hands are sweating as if I had been fighting. For a moment
I had forgotten where I was.

CUSACK: You remember me?

CUCKOO: The collector of truths.

CUSACK: The collector of lies.

CUCKOO: There is one I was keeping for another day. If
I tell it to you now, will you give me my fee and ferry me
across the Shannon so I can head for home? There should
be a moon.

CUSACK: Why the hurry?

CUCKOO: I do not sleep easy in this monastery. The stones
are too hard.

CUSACK: It's my bed every night.

CUCKOO: I have the best story of all but it is lying heavy on
my brain. It would help me to discharge it, then I can think
of God and his mercy.

(*FERGUS and MAEVE ARE stealthily embracing and
kissing in the huddle.*

*ALI wakes up and sits with his hands round his knees,
watching them. The chant continues.*)

CUSACK: Is it a tale of lechery? If so, you will have to wait until morning. I suffer enough in the night, alone, my hammer in my hand.

CUCKOO: It is not a story of that kind. Will you hear it?

CUSACK: As long as it is not a story of sleeping, birth or women.

CUCKOO: It is soon told. The men of Ulster saw a boy rowing over the sea towards the strand in a small boat. He had a pile of stones beside him and as he rowed with one hand, with the other he slung shots at the sea-birds, stunning but not killing them. When they had recovered he let then fly into the air again. The king, Conchobor, saw this and was impressed. He told the men of Ulster not to let the boy ashore as he was a worker of miracles. A warrior was sent out to stop the boy beaching his boat. 'Come no further,' the warrior said. 'What is your name?' 'I'll give my name to no man,' the boy replied, 'and you must get out of my way.' 'You can't land,' insisted the warrior. 'I am going where I am going,' the boy replied. 'Even if you had the strength of a hundred men you would not stop me.' With that he slung a stone. It roared like thunder and knocked the warrior headlong. The boy tied his shield-strap round the man's arms and made him captive. So King Conchobor sent his greatest hero, Cuckoo. 'Name yourself or die,' he demanded. 'So be it,' said the boy and cut Cuckoo bald-headed with a stroke of precision. 'The joking has come to an end,' Cuckoo said. 'Now we must wrestle.' 'I'm too small. I can't reach up to your belt,' the boy complained. So he climbed onto two standing stones and threw Cuckoo down three times. Then they went into the sea to drown each other and Cuckoo played foul by bringing to use his terrible barbed spear the *gael bolga* without the boy's agreement. He brought the bowels of the brave boy into a bunch around his ankles. 'You have hurt me badly,' the boy said. 'I have indeed,' Cuckoo said. He took the boy in his arms and carried him to where the men of Ulster were watching. 'I now recognise this as my own son,' Cuckoo grieved. 'Here you are. I have killed him for you.' 'Thank you, said the men of Ulster. And they went home.

(*CUSACK gives CUCKOO a coin.*)

You will remember the ferry over the Shannon. I'm sure there's a moon big enough for rowing a boat.

CUSACK: Take the boat yourself and leave it on the other side. Someone will need it from that direction soon enough.

(*CUCKOO exits.*

CUSACK goes into his cell and starts writing. He looks up.)

Any more dreams from down there?

FERGUS: We're hardly asleep.

CUSACK: What are you doing? – as if I didn't know.

MAEVE: Taking what fun we can from a cold night.

CUSACK: When you get home, will you laugh at me, stuck here in this grave, outlining witless fantasies for the future generations?

ALI: Somebody has to do it. People won't always pass the truth from mouth to mouth. It will have to settle down on paper, close its wings and be caught.

MAEVE: Brother monk, do you know what Maeve looked like? Has anyone ever described her to you?

CUSACK: Only half a picture has emerged, all her activities being concentrated below the waist.

MAEVE: Was she beautiful?

CUSACK: Well, here's what I've got about her so far. A tall, short, long-round-faced woman with soft-hard features and a head of yellow, black hair and two birds of gold upon her shoulder. She wore a cloak of purple folded about her body and five hands' breadth of gold across her back. She held an iron sword with a woman's grip over her head. A massive figure, so a little girl told me, something like her mother, no doubt. Probably a hunchback as well as a whore is my guess.

MAEVE: Many men loved her. That's good enough for me.

CUSACK: Go back to sleep now. Try and dream of something morally improving. Leave her alone now, you lads.

(*MAEVE, FERGUS and ALI SETTLE down in each other's*

arms. CUSACK writes. CON turns.)

CON: All asleep?

CUSACK: Doing their best. Christian floors are hard. (*Pause.*) Your Grace, when I've completed my task and the whole poem has been written down, what is going to happen to it?

CON: We'll keep it safe somewhere. One day the Irish will be amused to remember how fierce and foul they were. They will be able to enjoy their great moment of change in retrospect. (*Pause.*) Cusack, my son, I have news. The exiled king of Leinster, Dermot McMurrough, has invited Henry the Second of England to invade Ireland to help him get back his throne. The English army has already landed.

CUSACK: The treacherous bastard! Sound the alarm! This will have to be resisted! (*Kicks the peasants.*) Wake up you hard-luck heroes!
(*The peasants scramble to their feet drawing weapons which they start to whirl round their heads, slowly at first but building up speed.*)

MAEVE: What is it? What's happening? Why can't we sleep?

CUSACK: The English are invading! They must be stopped!

CON: Quieten down. A message has arrived from Rome. It is a copy of a bull issued by Pope Adrian to King Henry, his countryman, supporting this invasion. See here – (*Shows them the bull.*) '...I agree the English should enter Ireland to extend the boundaries of the church...to restrain the downward course of vice...for the honour of God... salvation of the land...to correct morals...plant virtue'...it's all there in the bull.

CUSACK: Then, if that's the case all the bulls must die! Wham! Wham! Wham! Wham!
(*CUSACK tears up the bull.
The peasants whirl their swords, whamming.*)

End of Act One.

ACT TWO

Sunday, 30 September 1979, 9:20 am.

The yard and despatch room of the north-eastern abattoir, Dublin. The heroes are whirling their swords round their heads, whamming. CUSACK is sitting on the upturned steel tray by the door reading the Sunday newspaper. He is now wearing his blood-stained white coat and hat. CON and JANET stand in a corner. They are wearing their bloodstained clothes.

CUSACK: According to the schedule, your Sunday paper hero, His Holiness the Pope, should be hovering over my old stone cell at Clonmacnois in his helicopter, Mr Sheehan. I can hear the band playing 'You'll Never Walk Alone'. See the faces turned up to the sky in hope. Smell the Shannon flowing behind the old grey towers. I think the answer to the Irish problem will be touching down any minute.

CUCKOO: (*Slowing down his sword.*) Whamwhamwham whamwhamwhamwham.

FERGUS: (*Slowing down his sword.*) Whamwhamwhamwham whamwhamwhamwham.

ALI: (*Slowing down his sword.*) Whamwhamwhamwham whamwhamwham.

MAEVE: (*Slowing down her sword.*) Whamwhamwham whamwhamwhamwham.

CUCKOO: (*Raging.*) Where – are – those – bulls? (*Hacking at the air in front of CON and JANET.*) I'll balance them both.

CUCKOO: On the point of my sword,
skin them in mid-air
and hurl their hides into the sky
to become sunset clouds!
I'll split them-from nose to the nap
on the hairs of the tail!
I'll scatter their bowels.

JANET: (*Screaming.*) Stop it! Stop it!
(*Pause. CUCKOO looks puzzled.*

JANET and CON hold hands for comfort.
CUCKOO prods JANET with his sword experimentally,
smiling.)

CON: Could you see your way clear to stop doing that to her?

FERGUS: The hypocrisy of the man. Why shouldn't he turn a sod where you've been digging so much? (*Pause.*) You're known to each other, aren't you?

MAEVE: Fergus, Ali, I think these two are in love. Remember?

FERGUS: With all my heart. Isn't your wife a great woman to love, Ali? What lucky men we've been.

ALI: Well, Fergus, you haven't had the pain with her that I have; this argument over equality.

MAEVE: That's true. Fergus has never doubted that I'm better than him. (*To CON and JANET.*) Which one of you is the stronger? In Ireland it's always the woman.

CUSACK: True, Maeve. The system was even exported to America.

MAEVE: When Ali and me were married we found that we were level-pegging in everything – power, position, possessions...nearly. We were a fraction out, so there was a furore. I'm a stickler for the final detail, you know.

ALI: A man less wise than your suffering husband might say that you were pedantic. We were equal down to our thumb-rings, our wash-pails, the rams of our flocks, the stallions for our horse-herds, but... I had a bull bigger and better than hers Finnennbach the white – and Maeve did not have the equal of him running with her cattle. There was only one other such bull in Ireland, in Cooley, Ulster.

MAEVE: I offered the farmer who owned it treasure, land, chariots, anything, and my friendly thighs on top of that. The fool said no.

ALI: So we had to go to war to match a pair of bulls. Where else would you hear such nonsense? Who cares about old and overblown cattle? Who wants them? We sold Ireland short with that war.

MAEVE: Oh, go on with you, it was good fun. Thousands upon thousands dead, all for the love of balance in Nature.

What do you say?

CON: Nothing, nothing at all.

FERGUS: It would never have happened if I'd had the taming of her, Ali. If I'd had Maeve from the beginning, as a young girl...

MAEVE: Wouldn't you do as much to be sure that you're getting your proper respect in the world?

JANET: Some us do have to go to extremes to obtain that.

MAEVE: Ach, no one's equal now. They're just all as bad as each other. Don't you think so? I don't feel at home here.

CON: I think people are very confused now, you know, disorientated.

JANET: Yes. One big mess, isn't it?

MAEVE: No room for Cuckoo now. The childhood of Man is over. Bulls, battles, bravado...baloney. Nothing get done for show any more.

JANET: Yes. No style left, no panache. It's all so mundane.

MAEVE: Why did you call here this morning? Eh? Eh? Eh? (*Prods her with her sword.*) Don't lie again or I'll sign my name on you.

CON: Would you leave her alone? (*Pause.*) We were going out.

FERGUS: Into the fields. That was what I saw in the woman's black-ringed eyes. The fields. Flowers, birds. The good old fields.

CON: Yes a picnic.

MAEVE: Ah, you were going to slip off and leave Cusack to it for the day? He said you had a habit of doing that.

ALI: Mr Sheehan, your clerk, of whom we have the highest opinion with the regard to the truth of his tongue, tells us that you often absent yourself for hours on end from your office, that your lunch takes from twelve till half-past three, in fact, that Cusack the clerk runs this place for you. Would that be a fair thing to say?

CON: No I don't think so.

MAEVE: There was an old sacrificial system which used a man and a woman who had played weapon and wound in war, but I can't recall the procedure, the agreed procedure...or the god concerned...

CUCKOO: So, you were going to have a picnic in the fields?

CON: We were.

CUCKOO: After you'd eaten, there'd be some weapon play. Then you'd be at peace, lying in the grass, listening to the herds and flocks. She would be dreaming about children. He would be dreaming about cattle. If I was out there with you, I'd sit apart and dream of war. (*Pause.*) You're more of a warrior than he is, like Maeve. Set aside your shield. We'll have a little hand-to-hand.

FERGUS: Blood on her mouth before she starts. The rings from no sleep already under her eyes. Her skin is beaten to powder.

MAEVE: (*Touching JANET's coiffure.*) And she's wearing a helmet disguised as human hair. Fergus, have you ever known me not take my armour off if I was in for a frolic? A strange one she is; always at the ready.

CUCKOO: (*Stroking JANET's backside.*) I'd fight a thousand men at this ford. No one would cross. My feats of arms would amaze the armies. The river would run red. After that, we would lie in peace in the grass.

JANET: Don't touch me, please. Don't touch me.

CUCKOO: Once a woman and a fool were sent to trick me by Maeve. She thought that the man would not arouse my suspicion, he was so idle, and the girl, Finnabair, would take my weapon. I cut off the woman's breasts and thrust a great stone pillar into her wound. The fool's few brains I knocked out then thrust another great stone pillar up his arse. Those pillars still stand. (*Pause. He resumes stroking her backside.*) They will always be remembered, Finnabair and the fool. Will you?

(*Enter CUSACK.*)

CUSACK: Would you believe it? Would you be able to throw your mind into such convulsions that you could find the angle to credit this I'm telling? In your greatest moment of faith and acceptance of the vicissitudes of life, would you be able to swallow this vicissitude?

(*They keep sharpening their swords.*)

FERGUS: What is it, Cusack? Is it something we've done again?

CUSACK: You take two points a hundred miles apart. One in

Connaught, one in Ulster. You put a white bull in a lorry in Connaught and a brown bull in a lorry in Ulster, then you point them both towards Dublin. Are you with me? From entirely separate directions! A hundred miles apart. What are the chances that at a certain junction half-an-hour to the north-west of the appointed place, these two vehicles should take it into their heads to collide?

FERGUS: Myself, I'd give that story no credence at all.

CUSACK: Right. Now struggle with the news that as I was talking on the telephone to the driver of one of these lorries I could hear the television going in the roadside cafe where the poor lunatic was licking his wounds and spending his hard-earned pennies on a call. The television programme was from Clonmacnois. I heard the commentator saying that the Pope was delayed, held up by the heavy traffic in the sky. Every helicopter in Ireland is fluttering around him, getting in the way.

MAEVE: So we might still make it.

ALI: If they can re-capture the bulls and get them here on time.

FERGUS: More delays can be expected. As soon as the great Druid descends on the monastery there'll be thousands of children to kiss, hundreds of sacred places which cannot be passed without a prayer or a reverence. He'll be hugging the sick, giving blessings till his arm aches.

MAEVE: So, they're both late – the bulls and the Pope. He's held up in the sky. They're held up on the earth. Only destiny will bring them together at the right juncture, random fate. We're in the hands of time itself.

ALI: Maeve, Maeve. Your brain is working. At last, after two thousand years its shifted its base of operations from your friendly thighs. I believe that the Pope, after licking lepers, grazing holy relics with his lips, will hit the old writing-place at exactly the right time, for the miracles have started, here, with you, my queen.

MAEVE: We have news. A couple of liars we have here. These two are not just commercial acquaintances, Cusack.

CUSACK: I know that. They've been at it for a couple of years.

FERGUS: Continuously?

CUSACK: Almost. They're nearly in the same class as you and Maeve.

CUCKOO: (*Thickly.*) Where are the...bulls?

CUSACK: Any minute, Cuckoo.

CUCKOO: I can't hold back much longer. I'll have to fight something. All breezing around in my blood...battle needs... I'm at the ford with my weapon...help me...

FERGUS: Quick, he's ready to blow. Get him something!

ALI: What? What can he hit here?

MAEVE: Give him these useless liars here. Cuckoo, make mincemeat out of these two.

CUCKOO: (*Chanting.*) Slaughter, exile, corpses,
blood, ravens, wailing women,
heads bumping at my belt,
grinning wounds spitting
bones smoking veins death
sings the Warped One! Death!
Beloved Death! Brother!

FERGUS: Will you get him something to hack at? Here, lend me your head! (*Grabs hold of CON and throws him at CUCKOO's feet.*)

CUCKOO: Is this all? It's not enough! A neck like that is nothing but a barley-stalk to slash with a stick. I must have...bulk! Bulk! Bulk!

CON: Don't hurt me...I'll...I'll find something he'll like.

ALI: You'd better be quick. He's on the verge of a major distortion.

CON: I'll get it, I'll get it all right? He'll really enjoy this... (*To FERGUS.*) Will you give me a hand? It's next door...
(*FERGUS exits left with CON.*)

ALI: Calm now, Cuckoo. They're getting you something to play with.

CUCKOO: (*Practising swipes with his sword.*) Give me something to hack in mercy's name! Have you no pity? It's rising up in me... I can't hold on... I can't... Ha! I must hack and hew! Where...where...a target! Wham!
(*CUCKOO takes a swipe at JANET but CON and FER-*)

*GUS have pulled in a full carcase of beef which is hooked
onto the rails on the gantry. CUCKOO connects with the
carcase with a loud clang. He howls and drops his sword.
The carcase gives off a refrigeration mist.)*
Aaah! My hand! My hand!

ALI: What kind of trick was that to play on a man in torment?
Giving him a stone to hack at!

CON: It's frozen. If he'll give it time to thaw he can mangle it
as much as he likes

CUCKOO: My hand is sprained. My elbow is absolutely dis-
located.

MAEVE: *(Touching the carcase.)* As cold as ice. See, it steams but
with winter. What is this thing?

CON: It's a carcase of beef.

MAEVE: Beef? What do you eat it with? A hammer?

CUCKOO: *(Touching the carcase.)* No look at the colour. It's
bleached white. Cold as the grave. Where's the blood?
Where's the bits of hair and fat? This was never alive. It's a
rock, a memorial pillar to some old hero I'm being taunted
with because I was never as good as him. *(To CON.)* My
wrist will remember that. When the sting's gone out of it…

JANET: You'd have killed me without a thought, wouldn't
you?

FERGUS: He was in great need. It had to be let out.

JANET: You useless, gormless, revolting, layabout bastard!
*(JANET kicks CUCKOO in the crutch. He doubles up.
MAEVE, ALI and FERGUS look at the fallen hero in
amazement.)*

FERGUS: That must have been a good pamphlet.

JANET: Dirty, stupid lout! *(Kicks CUCKOO again.)*

CON: Janet, you really shouldn't have done that!

JANET: Oh shut up! I don't care now. Poking people about,
they're going to do this, going to do that. I'm sick of them.
Bastard! *(Hoofs CUCKOO up the backside again.)*

CUCKOO: *(Chanting.)* Now, broken and despairing,
brought low by a woman warrior,
I wish to die. My arm broken
by a dead bull, what hopes

of killing a live one?

CON: I'd like to apologise on her behalf. She's got this temper. It doesn't often show itself...only under pressure, you understand. She doesn't mean what she's saying.

CUSACK: The heroes find that hard to understand. Their lives were all about consequences, Mr Sheehan. You did what you did, then you stood up and took the racket, right on the jaw. You didn't lie, or duck, when the axe came down.

JANET: As soon as this place is surrounded you'll start negotiating for your miserable lives, and blaming everyone else for what you've done. That's what I loathe about you most. You can't accept consequences.

MAEVE: Not at all. Why should we?

JANET: You're children, bloody children. Contemptible! (*MAEVE bursts out laughing.*) You'll look very foolish when all this comes out.

MAEVE: Here you see a great and cunning queen. But I have fools working for me – you know, in cap and bells, for a little bit of fun now and then.

JANET: You're so sly, but so stupid. Why do I let you get on my nerves so much?

MAEVE: Because I understand you so well? You're an ambitious woman, Janet. Probably a drop of my blood in your veins. You know how we Irish have been spread around.

JANET: I'm going.

MAEVE: Cuckoo, your admirer is leaving, so she says.

JANET: Come on, Con. We'll just walk out of here.

CON: Is that all right, everybody? (*Pause.*) Will you be able to manage, Cusack, old son! Lock up after you when you've gone.

MAEVE: So, you're off for your picnic?

CON: If it's all right with you. We won't mention this to anyone.

MAEVE: A drive in the country, a green field, a freshly laundered cloth laid out on the grass...ah. You should have seen my armies at their picnics. Their dishes covered

Ireland. (*Pause.*) If it weren't for the fact that you are about
to offend against the holiest and most time-honoured law
of all men, we might have let you go.

CON: What's that? Tell us and we'll sort it out.

MAEVE: Hospitality, Mr Sheehan, hospitality.

CON: Hospitality?

MAEVE: Look at us. We're starving. The last drink we had
was hours ago. Our stomachs are rumbling. Our mouths
are dry.

CON: You want to share our picnic? Come on then, we'll
all go.

MAEVE: No. We'll have it here. Janet, you go and get it. Mr
Sheehan, Con to his friends, will wait with me.

JANET: What a sadistic bitch you are.

MAEVE: Maybe, but I get even worse when I'm hungry.

JANET: What do you think, Con?

CON: Don't stand there making up your mind. Go and get it!
Quick.

JANET: I think she's bluffing.

CON: Will you stop gabbing and do as they say? Don't
forget, these people have fetched me a crack over the head
already today. I don't want another.

JANET: Come on. Stand up. Walk out of here with me. Dare
them to do what they say.

CON: Not with my neck.

JANET: What you're seeing, Con, within yourself, is how
these lazy, shiftless, evil bloodsuckers get away with it.
If you had the courage to just look this verminous bitch
straight in the eye and say, I'm off.

MAEVE: Off he would be, one way or the other.

JANET: Why should I feed them?

CUSACK: I thought it was your business to feed animals?

JANET: Not political animals.

MAEVE: Would you want we Irish to start eating each other?
Surely not.
(*Pause. JANET looks at CON.*
He nods feverishly.)

JANET: If I forget to say it when I come back – I hope it

53

chokes you.

CUSACK: It doesn't look good for you, Mr Sheehan. Your woman has got impulsive and passionate about the state of her health.

CON: You won't forget to come back, will you, love?

(*JANET exits downstage, waving to CON.*)

ALI: Do you have any doubts about her?

CON: None whatsoever.

ALI: Lucky man you are. Could I say the same, Maeve?

MAEVE: I'd only come back for the chance of a scrap. You've given me all you've got, Ali.

(*Car door slam off. Pause. Everyone is listening. Car engine starting up.*)

CUSACK: Ah, perfidious Albion.

MAEVE: Well, it looks as though we've missed our picnic. Not that it's going to be one for you, Mr Meat Merchant. Where do you want it? Head or heart?

CON: She's forgotten.

MAEVE: Cuckoo, what will you give me to let you have the hacking off of this one's fat head?

CUCKOO: (*Scrambling to his feet, testing his left handed sword-swipe.*) A chariot, a gold chain, two lengths of best purple cloth.

CON: She thought the key to the ignition was the key to the boot. They're easily mixed up.

(*CUCKOO gets into position to cut off CON's head.*)

CON: Or she might have left the picnic at home. She's got a head like a sieve.

FERGUS: Will you keep yours still and stop talking? There're certain forms to be observed in the taking of a head. The victim isn't expected to talk his way through the experience. Try a dignified and heroic silence.

CON: I'm sure Janet doesn't mean you to interpret what she's done as a sign that she's escaping. I think the woman is probably just turning the engine over to keep it supple.

CUCKOO: (*Chanting.*) What strength
in his brains,
what power,

in his blood,
what magic
in his marrow,
make mine.
(Pause. The engine is gunned offstage as if preparatory to
moving into first gear. CUCKOO raises his sword.
The engine is cut dead. Pause. Car door slams.
JANET runs on carrying a picnic hamper and a cool bag.
CUCKOO lowers his sword.)
Shit.

CON: The thought never even crossed her mind.

CUSACK: Old-fashioned terror is dead, but love, even among
the detestable, lives on.

JANET: Did they hurt you, Con darling?

CON: Psychologically I suffered, but the old mind didn't
buckle. It bore up under the strain. I didn't believe
I could die.

CUSACK: See how close you've got to the heroic condition?
You're taking on the form of those who hold you hostage.
When none of us can die, Mr Sheehan, who'll take over
undertaking?
(JANET opens the hamper and takes out a big tablecloth
which she spreads on the floor. JANET and CON start
laying out the picnic.)

JANET: I did nearly go. Sorry, Con, darling. I thought about
it.

CON: Perfectly understandable under the circumstances.

JANET: Do you know, it's a strange thing, but I suddenly
didn't want to leave. *(Pause.)* I have become fond of you all.

MAEVE: Ah.

JANET: This often happens in these cases. We were warned
about it. There is a psychological reason. In the pamphlet
it said that… I hardly dare repeat it.

CUSACK: Wisdom is welcome. I'd like to know what a
pet-food personnel manager comes up with when he's
theorising about life and death.

JANET: It's the adrenalin. We like adrenalin.

CUSACK: Ah. Nothing like it for making friends, is there?

JANET: We get very excited when we are threatened, or we
see anyone else being threatened. Adrenalin flows. We are
addicted to adrenalin.

CUSACK: A natural substance. The alcohol already within us.
Mixes well too. So, you feel better about our intentions.

JANET: We believe you in everything you have said, don't
we, Con?

CON: Er yes...yes yes. Most definitely we do.

MAEVE: What else could you do after seeing Cuckoo's
warp-spasm.

JANET: Yes, that is what persuaded us, isn't it, Con?

CON: Yes. We're ready to eat now, aren't we, Janet?

MAEVE: Taste everything. Everything. Both of you.

CON: Anything you say. You're the guest. The best of service.
(*CON and JANET taste all the articles of food very quickly,
nibbling, breaking off pieces, swigging out of bottles of wine
and beer. Pause.*
MAEVE watches them.
JANET cocks an eyebrow.
MAEVE nods.)

JANET: Well, what a mixture. (*Burps.*) Oh dear. I'm sorry. Is
that an insult in your terms? It wasn't meant to be...

MAEVE: If your food gives us the wind then we'll all suffer
for it. Tell her, Cusack.

CUSACK: Not now, Maeve, not before I'm about to eat.

MAEVE: Now!

CUSACK: When the heroes feasted and their bowels got in
a turmoil, so the peasants reported in their innocence,
hurricanes roared through the countryside, blowing the
roofs off houses... (*Pause.*) You are warned.

JANET: Will you sit there, Maeve? You there Ali, next to your
wife, then you Fergus, this side of me.

MAEVE: Is this the head of the table?

JANET: Of course.

MAEVE: As long as I know. Me and Ali should have been
served the drink first. Don't forget in future. I've had the
legs of serving-men broken for less.

FERGUS: What is this?

CON: A scotch egg.

FERGUS: It must be hard to be a hen over there.

CUSACK: Some prime quality roast beef here, that lovely dark slatey brown, the fat a light gold. It will be delicious. May I pass you a piece of bread to dip in the soup coming soon our of the giant Thermos, Maeve?

MAEVE: What kind of soup is it?

JANET: Minestrone.

CUSACK: The long arm of the Vatican cook.

CON: Would you be after having a gherkin, Cuckoo, old son?

CUCKOO: (*Seeing it.*) Wha! Trophies from the small green giants.

ALI: And where were you going for your picnic, you two lovers?

JANET: We thought we'd go to. Tara.

(*Pause. They munch on.*)

FERGUS: What does the likes of you two want in Tara, the home of the high kings?

CON: Very into history, Fergus, old son. Fascinated. Not much is left there now but…the old vibrations… associations.

FERGUS: So, this banquet was intended for Tara. The new high king and queen. Ireland ruled by meat merchants. As you say, Cusack, good beef.

CUSACK: Know their meat do these two. Fresh, rare, succulent, young. Why shouldn't they take care of themselves?

MAEVE: I'm used to somebody singing my food down. If I don't have music with my dinner I get trouble. Who is it worth asking? None of these boneheads can sing.

CUSACK: C'mon, Mr Sheehan. Agnostic you may be, but you've got a fine voice. I know the secrets you've got, down to the spots on your liver. Give Maeve a song.

CON: Well…

(*Pause. JANET and CON look at each other.*)

ALI: Isn't it true that both of you are members of the Folksong Society, Athlone Chambers, Dundalk Street, every Thursday and Sunday sessions, songs of all nations from Patagonia to the Moscow Underground?

CON: That may be so.

ALI: Then sing for my wife, the woman with the thighs that can sing bass, baritone and treble in one exhalation. She deserves no less.

JANET: How did you know that we sang together?

MAEVE: We get the vibrations. That's why we're so anxious for this earthquake of ours. All we've had is tremors of song, you see. The turf curls up over our heads and the subterranean streams run peuce with sincerity, but nothing changes. Songs are not enough, but one will do for now. (*Pause.*)

MAEVE: Cuckoo, in your experience, is it possible to torture a song from a human throat?

CUCKOO: Maeve, with these bare hands I made a hundred heroes sing higher than larks and lower than moles. Nothing, nothing cannot be achieved with violence.

CON: We'll sing! The Parting Glass? Okay?

CON/JANET: (*Together.*)

Of all the money that 'ere I've spent,
(*In parts.*) I've spent it in good company,
And all the harm that I've ever done,
Alas it was to none but me:
And all I've done
Through lack of wit,
To mem'ry now I can't recall,
So fill to me the parting glass,
Good night and joy be with you all.
(*CUCKOO sobs.*)
If I had money, enough to spend,
And leisure time to sit awhile,
There is a fair maiden in this town
Who sorely does my heart beguile;
Her rosy cheeks,
And ruby lips,
I own she has my heart in thrall,
So fill to me the parting glass,
Good night and joy be with you all.
Of all the comrades that e're I had,

They were sorry for my going away,
And all the sweethearts that e're I had
Would wish me one more day to stay:
But since it falls,
Unto my lot,
That I should rise and you will not,
I'll gently rise and softly call,
Good night, and joy be with you all.
(*They are all crying, sobbing into the food and wine, holding onto each other in the extremes of morbid, sentimental grief. JANET beckons to CON and they start to creep away downstage in the direction of the car. At the last moment MAEVE sees them.*)

MAEVE: Get them! Poets and dreamers, liars and minstrels!
(*FERGUS, ALI and CUCKOO hurl themselves on CON and JANET and catch them just before they get away.*)
Tie them up there so they're on tip-toe. Can you dance as well as sing, you two?
(*FERGUS, CUCKOO and ALI tie JANET and CON by the wrists to hooks on the gantry on either side of the carcase.*)

JANET: Get off you dirty, lousy bastards! Leave me alone! Kick them Con! Kick them in the face like me! Stop it! Heeeeelp! Bastards! Christ!

CUCKOO: (*Chanting.*) Strong tongue
will it talk
in the hour of death?

FERGUS: (*Chanting.*) Breast full of fierce hate
which was once full
of fear. Woman's love
inclining to man's pain.

ALI: (*Chanting.*) After the feast
comes the sacrifice.
We have eaten and drunk.
Let the gods eat and drink.

CON: Cusack, old son. Early retirement, a reasonable pension, call in when you like for a cup of tea and a slab of sirloin big enough to cover the crossbar of your bicycle…

I'm reading your mind now. The indignation of your
friends about your treatment here has impressed me...I've
abused your good nature...

CUSACK: How are we going to approach this, Maeve?

MAEVE: I think we've got to presume that those bulls are
not going to be on hand at the precise moment when your
nephew telephones from Clonmacnois to say that the great
Druid is stepping into your old writing cell. This is all
we've got.

CUSACK: Oh, I agree, I agree. But what's the style going to
be?

MAEVE: I'm a one for disembowelling. Plenty of show.

CUCKOO: Or I could make holes so big that birds could pass
in flight through their bodies with them watching.

MAEVE: I'm almost solid on disembowelling, then
beheading.

FERGUS: What about the Hedgehog?

ALI: Oh, not that. I'm bored with the Hedgehog.

FERGUS: It's a great feat if done well. I've done a Hedgehog
with thirty-seven spears in one man strung up like this,
and I threw every one from a distance of five miles with a
mountain in between.

ALI: Five miles, Fergus? Five miles?

FERGUS: All right then. You've caught me out lying. It was
ten.

CUCKOO: How about the Bladder? I could do the Bladder
for both of them. With one breath of mine down the throat
of each I'd have them inflated to the size of Ireland.

ALI: That's a great boast, Cuckoo. Do you mean each one to
the size of Ireland, or both of them together to the size of
Ireland?

CUCKOO: (*Pause.*) Both, I think.

MAEVE: That sounds the best to me. When we get the
telephone call then you'll do the Bladder on both of them.

CUCKOO: (*Breathing deeply.*) I'd better start stretching my
lungs for this one. It will need plenty of puff to get these
hard cases up that big. Maybe I'll have a little practice.
(*CUCKOO kisses JANET and starts blowing. She bites
him. CUCKOO falls back, holding his mouth which is*

bleeding, yelling with pain. MAEVE, FERGUS and ALI
roar with laughter.)

ALI: You'd better try it first with the man, Cuckoo. He might
go up easier.

JANET: If you kiss my Con I'll bite your balls off you thick
mick bastard!

CON: Janet calmly now – he can kiss me if he likes. It's only
fun…

CUCKOO: You're doubting my strength, the truth of my
boast. Now I've got a split lip I can't do the Bladder, so
that's out, but there's the worst of the lot, Maeve.

ALI: Oh, no, not that!

FERGUS: Cuckoo, what a thought not the…

CUCKOO: Yes, the…

MAEVE: The Sack of the Seven Entrances.

ALI: Whewe! Dare we try it?

FERGUS: Come on! We've got nothing to lose. I'm for it. It's
ages since I've seen that one done. It's a slow thing so let's
start.

CUCKOO: Wham! Wham! Wham! Wham!

CON: Excuse me…

MAEVE: We've alighted on the right flower, us bees. That will
be the kind of honey the gods will like licking. The Sack of
the Seven Entrances.

CON: Excuse me would you kindly tell what exactly is the
Sack of the Seven Entrances?

MAEVE: The Sack of the Seven Entrances? You don't know?
And you up to your ears in folk-lore?

FERGUS: The human body is a sack with seven entrances.
Count them. Nostrils. Ears. Mouth. Arsehole. Weapon or
wound. Taking coin of the realm, the sack is filled to the
brim with money from the seven entrances I have seen it
done only a couple of times. It takes so long that the skin
of the victim goes green from the corrosion of the copper
working in the bowels. The final pieces of silver tarnish
grey in the nose and gold goes dull while blocking up the
fundament, so to speak. Your man dies stiff with riches.
(*Pause.*) Now, we'll be needing some coins.

CON: I've got plenty of change. Here. (*Empties his pockets into FERGUS' hands.*) How about you, Janet?
(*Pause. She glares at him.*)
Be helpful, dear. Swallowing coins. That's all.
(*External telephone bell rings.*
Cusack goes off right.)

CUSACK: That will be Clonmacnois. Everything's getting out of phase.

MAEVE: Where would you like us to start on the Sack of the Seven Entrances? The mouth I think, so they can't sing again.

FERGUS: I'll do the first one. A big silver coin. Is your mouth open, Con?

CON: You want me to swallow a coin? I'll swallow a coin.

CUCKOO: Fergus, the honour of the first stroke in this feat is mine. I claim it and I will not be crossed. Stand back before a better man.

FERGUS: The honour is mine! I claim it for myself!

CUCKOO: A death as ornate as this must belong to the higher hero. Me!

FERGUS: Let Maeve decide.

MAEVE: Ach, fight it out, fight it out. Give us some sport and spectacle. But no codding about, eh? The man killed is the man cured of pride.

CUCKOO: Fergus, my foster-father, no warrior holds you higher than I do. (*Embraces FERGUS.*) I swear by Ulster's god, I'll churn you up like foam in a pool! I'll stand over you like a cat's tail erect! I'll batter you as easily as a loving woman slaps her son.

FERGUS: Cuckoo, my boy, come here. (*Embraces him.*) It is with shame that I view the prospect of killing you. Now you won't see the great Sack of the Seven Entrance or the shudder of the birth-pangs of a new Ireland, as Druid and Death come together in a cleansing. I taught you all I knew, with a few things I kept to myself. Those few things will kill you.

MAEVE: Hurry up. Fergus, if you are dying at any time soon, remember my friendly thighs. Will you dream to be buried there?

FERGUS: For you I betrayed my homeland, Maeve. I put the freedom of Ulster below the freedom of your famous friendly thighs. If either of us die, send our bones to the north.

CUCKOO: For the first coin, Fergus.

FERGUS: For the first coin, Cuckoo.

CUCKOO: (*Chanting.*) You will fall, Fergus,
at an heroic hand
which honours Death
just that fraction
more than a father.

FERGUS: (*Chanting.*) The sun in a bold Ireland
does not shine brighter
than blood. It is Ulster and Ulster.

(*They fight round and round the carcase, and CON and JANET, hacking at each other. Blood leaps from wounds and splashes against the walls, on the floor, over the picnic. JANET starts screaming. CON shuts his eyes. MAEVE and ALI watch with interest. Finally, when FERGUS and CUCKOO are both reduced to bloody, ragged spectres, they kill each other. The room tips. The carcase, CON and JANET slide along the gantry one way, then another. The earth groans and creaks. CUSACK runs on.*)

CUSACK: He's there! He's there! Pope John Paul's in my old cell! We did it! But with no bulls. How?

MAEVE: It was the heroes they wanted! Look, their deaths did it!

ALI: Free, Maeve, free! Now let them go where they want. The old land is dead! Start up the future!

(*The chaos subsides. The carcase, CON and JANET are all jammed up against each other in a corner. CUSACK releases CON and JANET from the hooks. They collapse onto the floor.*)

CUSACK: Two heroes took your places. Think on that for a minute. Old Ireland died for your crimes.

(*Offstage rumblings of two lorry engines. Bawling of bulls. Pause.*)

MAEVE: They're here. Too late. I can smell them. I can feel
    them. Those two old furies together are a terrible power!

ALI: (*Chanting.*) I hear the brown bull of Ulster!
    Dark, dire, devlish, handsome with health,
    horrible, almighty, furiously fierce,
    full of cunning,
    flowing fiery flanks,
    tight, brave, cruel, deep-chested,
    curly-headed skull held on high,
    booming, eyes blazing,
    rough-haired neck, stout and strong,
    snuffling thunderstorms of snot
    through monstrous muzzle!

MAEVE: (*Chanting.*) I hear the brown bull of Ulster!
    Thirty grown men can stand
    on his back in a line,
    a hero to his cows, balls like bells
    swinging, calling them in.
    He is a beast enormous in the brains of men.

ALI: (*Chanting.*) I hear the white bull of the south!
    Though he has white skull, white feet,
    his great body is a true red
    as if blood-washed or dyed
    in a red-running vat
    or trampled in purple flowers and herbs.

MAEVE: (*Chanting.*) I hear the white bull of the south.
    Finnbennach, with his useless tits stuck
    flat against his colossal belly of brawn
    As he gambols with tumbling hair
    and ploughing hooves, his weapon
    scythes the sweet grass, sharpened,
    for slitting heifers and cows.
    Finnbennach smells the future union.
    This roving, red, roaring demon will
    rub his colour off on every hour
    making it dusty with old blood.
    (*Engines are cut. The bulls bawl with sudden force and
    anger.*)

CUSACK: Better late than never. Do we want two

earthquakes, Maeve?

MAEVE: It will be tidier. It would be cruelty to animals to leave them hanging about in a landscape that is too small for them.

CUSACK: Would you be so good as to get them unloaded? (*Exit MAEVE and ALI.*
CON and JANET are holding on to each other.)
The job is here to be done, Mr Sheehan. There's still time to meet the contract. Should we start?

CON: No, there's no need. It's too late. Forget the bulls.

CUSACK: We can't do that. Surely Miss Soames is interested in the beasts she bought? Think of all the arrangements – the health authority, customs clearance, all that. And what a bargain they were. Bottom price beef. The bulls are coming. Old as the hills. Shagged out, but still colossal creatures...tons of old meat hanging on those megalithic bones!...
(*Bawling of bulls, echoing hoof sounds approaching.*)
...heads too heavy with regrets to hold up, dewlaps swinging like melting bells, great scarred bollocks rolling between their knees, all size and shape and show but no substance, no children, no future.

JANET: Keep them out of here! We don't want them! Send them back!

CUSACK: A deal is a deal, Miss Soames. What will the dogs and cats of England do for dinner? We might get the carcases away from the docks before the tidal wave comes.

JANET: I don't care...keep them away! Don't let them see us!

CUSACK: After a lifetime of toil you wouldn't grant these two old Irish monsters a peaceful and humane conclusion. Shame on you. And, for the first time in their miserable, lecherous existences! The opportunity to be useful. Come on the white! Come on the brown! Let's have a look at you, you horny heroes!
(*The sounds of the approaching bulls become very loud and frightening.*
JANET and CON shrink into a corner, covering their ears, terrified.)

Enter ALI in police uniform.
Bull sounds stop abruptly.)
Let me introduce you to the undercover heroes of the
future. An Inspector in the Irish Police Fraud Squad, who
has been working with...
(Enter MAEVE in a smart businesswoman's outfit.)
...a representative of the British Consumers Association.
*(FERGUS gets up off the floor and stands next to ALI
and MAEVE.)*
An official of the World Bank, Agriculture and Animal
Husbandry Division.
(CUCKOO gets up and stands in the line.)
And a member of the European Economic Community's
Meat Products Standards and Subsidies Inspectorate.

CON/JANET: *(Together.)* Aaaah! We're discovered! Deceived
and beguiled!

CUSACK: *(To audience, very fast.)* Within the convoluted and
serpentine wickedness of the human mind would you
think there resided sufficient diabolical skill and energy to
invent a nuclear-powered meat-tenderising machine? As a
further extension of this appalling concept – now working
full-blast in an innocent-looking industrial building in
Birmingham, invented and designed by...

CON: Me! I did it! Shame and humiliation! I want to be
punished!

CUSACK: Would you further toss around in your reeling
imaginations the improbable possibility that geriatric Irish
cattle carcasses are being shipped from Dublin to Holyhead
on Monday mornings to feed this infernal machine. Would
you care to haphazard a guess as to what company and
what agent arranges this?

JANET: Who else but me? I fix it. I forge, fiddle and fantasise
the paperwork!

CUSACK: Now sink deeper into shock and horror as you
torment your brain-cells with the thought that reconstituted
flesh from these ancient Hibernian herbivores is then sold
at centres of the British meat trade such as Smithfield,
posing as top-grade beef!

CUCKOO: *(Chanting.)* Ribs tortured, loins mangled,

shin shattered, rump raped...

ALI: (*Chanting.*) Tripe tattered, tongue twisted,
flank fissured, hide holed...

FERGUS: (*Chanting.*) Brains battered, kidneys crippled,
horns hammered, neck gnarled...

MAEVE: (*Chanting.*) Blood curdled, fat soured,
side smashed, heart broken...

CON: We have discoloured the greenest of green pounds and
undermined the credibility of Irish beef. We confess our
meaty crimes.

CUSACK: Inspector, time to make the arrest, I think. The
job must go on. I have work to do. We're in full swing
tomorrow morning.

ALI: Wouldn't it be nice to round off with the actual story of
the end of the bulls as told in the poem? We've done a lot
of studying for this, you know. One gets involved... How
does it go? Ah...yes... It is soon told.

FERGUS: I think I've got the start. 'The men of Ireland
stopped their fighting and feuding and fretting to see the
two bulls have it out once and for all on the great plain at
Tarbga...'

MAEVE: Tarvga. B is V, remember?

CUCKOO: 'The bulls faced each other The fight began.
Wham! The brown bull of Ulster put one great hoof on the
horn of the white bull of the south. All the day the brown
bull stood there, refusing to move it, holding the white
bull's head thrust into the earth.'
(*CON and JANET start to creep out.*)

ALI: 'A man of Ireland chided the brown bull of Ulster,
saying: "Fight better! Men on both sides have died because
of you!" And he beat the flank of the brown bull with a
stick.'

FERGUS: 'Back came the brown bull's hoof with such force
that the leg broke and wheeeee! The white bull's horn flew
into a mountain nearby!'
(*The four of them are now like children enchanted within
a story.*
CON and JANET are edging towards the exit.)

MAEVE: 'Then the bulls fought each other well into the night
and all that could be heard was furious bellowing and the

crashing of bones.'

CUSACK: Who will ever have their own way with this world?

MAEVE: 'In the morning the men of Ireland saw the brown bull of Ulster going northwards with the white bull of the south impaled on its horns. During the day it fell away piece by piece, the last being a shoulder-blade which blocked a pool.'

ALI: To this day it is called the Pool of the Shoulderblade by the local inhabitants.

MAEVE: Charming.

CUSACK: (*Picking up the black book.*) Your minds have been taken hostage by lies. (*Smiles.*) There is hope for us yet. (*Opens the book.*)

(*CON and JANET exit.*)

CUCKOO: 'But the strength of the brown bull was fading. His wounds were dragging him down. He was almost empty of blood.'

CUSACK: 'Before he could reach home, he fell down and died. And there was peace in the land. Finit. Amen.'

The End.

MY FATHER'S HOUSE

Characters

JOSEPH CHAMBERLAIN

MARY CHAMBERLAIN
his third wife

AUSTEN CHAMBERLAIN
his eldest son

NEVILLE CHAMBERLAIN
his youngest son

BEATRICE CHAMBERLAIN
his eldest daughter

IDA CHAMBERLAIN
his middle daughter

HILDA CHAMBERLAIN
his youngest daughter

IVY
Austen's fiancée

JERICHO
the Bahamian butler

HITLER

MUSSOLINI

ARP INSPECTOR

HOME SUPERINTENDENT

Set in Birmingham, 1906

My Father's House was first performed at Birmingham Rep on 28 October 1991, with the following cast:

JOSEPH CHAMBERLAIN, Dermot Walsh

MARY, Anne White

AUSTEN, Michael Bertenshaw

NEVILLE, Chris Hunter

BEATRICE, Amanda Boxer

IDA, Tamara Ustinov

HILDA, Hazel Maycock

IVY, Juliet Heacock

JERICHO, Ram John Holder

HITLER, Michael Heath

MUSSOLINI, Dick Waring

ARP INSPECTOR, Michael Heath

Director, John Adams

ACT ONE

Pre-set: the hall of Highbury, Victorian Gothic mansion built by JOSEPH CHAMBERLAIN on the southern outskirts of Birmingham. A conservatory abuts the hall stage right. A row of arches backs a living area which is a blend between a spacious sitting room and a tropical hot-house. A grand staircase leads to a first-floor open landing with doors going off. Stage left is a grand piano. There is a telephone on a table by a large sofa.

It is 8 July 1906 at 11 o'clock in the morning. MARY starts arranging the flowers in a vase. BEATRICE enters from left with more flowers and arranges another vase. They work in silence for a while. From the way that they avoid each other's eyes it is evident that they have been having a disagreement. MARY, the wife of JOSEPH, enters in a summer frock carrying a bunch of flowers.

BEATRICE: I spoke hastily. I apologise.

MARY: Oh, don't, Beatrice. It wasn't that serious.

BEATRICE: But don't you think that he's brave?

MARY: I'd rather he had more sense.

BEATRICE: Papa has plenty of sense, Mary.

MARY: How can you say that when the doctor has told him to slow down and all the man does is go faster?

BEATRICE: Going to dinner with Lady Cunard isn't such a steeplechase, is it?

MARY: Up half the night… The drinking…

BEATRICE: Papa doesn't drink so much. Not as much as he used to.

MARY: He shouldn't drink at all.

BEATRICE: What's one dinner?

MARY: It won't be one dinner. That will only be the start. From there'll he'll launch his onslaught on London's most important salons.

BEATRICE: Which he's very good at.

MARY: I think conquest by knife and fork should be left to younger men.

BEATRICE: Lady Cunard is a very influential woman.

MARY: Which I'm not, obviously.

BEATRICE: Papa respects your opinion above all others.

MARY: That's the useful thing about respect. It need not imply agreement.

BEATRICE: Papa is in his political prime. No one must hold him back now, no matter what happens.

MARY: Don't you find it strange that being in one's political prime never seems to coincide with being in one's physical prime. Can this mean that that there is something unnatural about the whole business?

BEATRICE: Mary, be patient. He'll take a rest soon. But these are great days for him. Seventeen miles of people to cheer him through Birmingham for his birthday yesterday. No other politician in the world has that kind of adulation.

MARY: I wonder who goes out measuring these things? Next time it could be his funeral.

BEATRICE: I don't think his health is any worse than the average man of his years. Look at Gladstone. When Papa was fighting him over Irish Home Rule twenty years ago the old boy was well over eighty and still Prime Minister.

MARY: Joe isn't Gladstone. Gladstone could turn off.

BEATRICE: Only because he didn't care. He was a cold man at heart.

MARY: I can see how much help I'm going to get from you. (*Enter IDA and HILDA dressed to go out.*) Where are you off?

HILDA: Reformed women. Smethwick.

BEATRICE: Are you making a speech?

HILDA: Ida is, aren't you? Papa thinks it would be a good idea for her to have a go.

MARY: You sort those women out, Ida. You're the girl to do it.

BEATRICE: Well, this is wonderful news. Ida's going to speak in public! What are you going to say?

HILDA: She's going to thank the reformed women for their birthday present to Papa: Moses found in the bullrushes by Pharaoh's daughter in applique-work, and it will be brilliant and extraordinary because Ida is brilliant and extraordinary and knows the Old Testament so well.

IDA: I've offered to pay Hilda, to do it. But she won't.

BEATRICE: You're turning down a golden opportunity, Hilda. You'd make a fortune in this family if you charged us for standing in on these occasions.

HILDA: Ida has to get to grips with being a Chamberlain. The fallen women will adore her.

BEATRICE: They're not fallen now, Hilda. They're reformed. Don't let Ida get mixed up or we'll lose their support. (*AUSTEN, in blazer and white ducks and carrying a yachting cap, comes onto the balcony.*)

AUSTEN: Ahoy, there! Anyone seen the white whale? (*He runs down the stairs.*) Boating on the Severn. What better way to spend one's time? You look nice, Ida.

IDA: Thank you, Austen. You look nice too.

AUSTEN: Where are you going?

IDA: To make a speech. I'm going to be an orator like my big brother.

AUSTEN: I hope that you'll be better at it than I am.

HILDA: Give her some advice, Austen. You know, things to avoid. How to stand. A few basic gestures.

AUSTEN: Oh, just be yourself, Ida. But don't fidget.

IDA: Do I fidget?

AUSTEN: And don't forget the point that you're making halfway through. I do that, sometimes.

IDA: Oh I won't do that. I've written the whole speech out. I'm simply going to read it like Papa does.

HILDA: He doesn't just read it, Ida. He has it with him to refer to…you know, the odd glance…but he has it firmly in his mind.

IDA: Now I'm frightened. What a fool I'm going to look standing up there reading out this drivel I've put together. They'll boo.

AUSTEN: Ida, in the unlikely event of anyone in the audience having the temerity to interrupt a Chamberlain; barracking, laughing or booing if it comes to that, don't stop talking, whatever you do. Keep repeating the phrase that you're saying when the interruption begins and continue until they get tired, then carry on.

IDA: Oh, God.

AUSTEN: But don't let them stop you at any cost. If you stop, then it's all over. You've lost the initiative and you might as well sit down.

HILDA: Now you've terrified the life out of her. Come on, Ida. You can practice on the way in the car.

IDA: That will make me sick. Thanks for your help, Austen.

(*IDA and HILDA exit.*)

AUSTEN: Is Papa up yet?

BEATRICE: No. Mary wants him to sleep in as long as possible.

AUSTEN: He'd better get up soon. He's got a luncheon at twelve. Thank God I don't have to go.

BEATRICE: I should think Papa can have luncheon in his sleep by now. All they want to do is look at him, after all.

AUSTEN: I offered to stand in for him but he said nothing doing. 'This one,' he said, 'needs the personal touch.' All those old supporters, those faces, year after year. How does he find something new to say to them?

BEATRICE: He doesn't. They like him to keep on saying the same old things anyway, going through the same old rituals. And Papa thinks that's as important as they do.

AUSTEN: So it is, but it's also unbearably tedious. They go on and on at him. I do wish he'd slow down. The last election really took it out of him.

BEATRICE: That's not what he says.

AUSTEN: Defeat need time to be digested. He's still choking on it.

BEATRICE: D'you consider wrecking the Tories was a defeat?

AUSTEN: That's what it's beginning to look like. They hate him now.

(*BEATRICE exits.*

AUSTEN sits down and consults a notebook. The foliage is disturbed.

NEVILLE and IVY enter hand in hand.

AUSTEN looks up.)

AUSTEN: Ah, there you are.

NEVILLE: We've been talking about you.

AUSTEN: Oh, yes?

NEVILLE: I've been telling her about your darker side.

AUSTEN: Good, it's only right she should know.

NEVILLE: And your sciatica.

AUSTEN: She knows about that already.

(*AUSTEN closes the notebook and stands up, giving IVY
a peck on the cheek.*)

Good morning, darling. Has Neville been looking after
you?

NEVILLE: I've been very amusing, haven't I?

IVY: Would you mind if I married Neville instead of you?

NEVILLE: Go on, Austen, say: 'If that's what you want,
darling.' He's such a brick. I've been telling your fiancée
that I have a natural affinity with all wild creatures – which
doesn't include you, I hasten to say – and trying to teach
her a few elementary bird-calls.

AUSTEN: Don't worry. Neville will only be allowed to visit us
once or twice a year, preferably when we're out.

IVY: Well, he certainly knows the difference between
a chiff-chaff and a willow-warbler, I'll give him that.

(*Enter JOSEPH in full morning dress on the balcony.*)

JOSEPH: Where's Mary?

NEVILLE: I saw her going into her room.

JOSEPH: Was she ready to go out?

NEVILLE: I don't rightly know.

JOSEPH: (*Irascibly.*) Well, was she or wasn't she?

NEVILLE: It's hard to say.

(*JOSEPH descends the stairs and goes into the conservatory.
NEVILLE and AUSTEN look at each other.*)

AUSTEN: Bad mood. Watch out.

NEVILLE: Storm cones hoisted. Who's he lunching with?

AUSTEN: Birmingham party faithful at headquarters. Don't
worry, they'll understand him. They have to.

IVY: You know I can't swim, don't you, Austen?

AUSTEN: I'm a trained life-saver. Fancy a few hours on the
river, Neville?

NEVILLE: No thanks. I've got some work to do. Look out for
the bar-tailed godwits. Erik-erik! Remember?

IVY: How does it go? Erik-erik? I'm hopeless.

(*The JERICHO enters with IVY's coat, he holds it out for*

her while she puts it on, then she exits with AUSTEN.)

JERICHO: Will you be in for luncheon, Mr Neville?

NEVILLE: I guess so.

JERICHO: And Miss Beatrice?

NEVILLE: You'd better ask her.

(*Crashing of a door.*

JOSEPH storms onto the balcony and down the stairs.)

JOSEPH: Bloody women always gassing, nagging, moaning, whining, complaining! Nothing getting done! I'll be late. You know how I hate not being punctual. It's the worst thing you can do to waste another's time. Are you punctual?

NEVILLE: Always, sir.

JOSEPH: Punctual punctual?

NEVILLE: On the dot, sir.

JOSEPH: I bet. Very liverish this morning, Neville. I shall be fiery at this luncheon. But they expect that. Want to come?

NEVILLE: Er…

JOSEPH: Useful for you.

NEVILLE: I'm sure it would be, but I'd planned a quiet couple of hours with the orchids. There're signs of distress in the old greenhouse, I'm afraid.

JOSEPH: Oh, they can wait. I want you to come and learn something. It's only the Party faithful. Nothing to overawe you.

NEVILLE: I wasn't worried about being overawed, exactly.

(*MARY enters onto the balcony and comes quickly down the stairs.*)

JOSEPH: Ah, you're ready at last. Neville's coming with us.

NEVILLE: But I'm not properly dressed.

JOSEPH: Then get dressed! Quick march!

(*NEVILLE runs off.*

MARY makes great play pulling on her gloves, adjusting her hat, signalling her displeasure at being rushed so much.)

MARY: Well, thank you for hustling me, Joe. I'm most grateful.

JOSEPH: You look lovely. I'm just going to get my buttonhole.

(JOSEPH exits towards the conservatory.
JERICHO exits right.
MARY shakes her head with irritation, then walks up and
down to compose herself.
Enter BEATRICE.)
BEATRICE: I thought you'd have gone by now.
MARY: Tell me I'm late. Your father is an impossible man.
BEATRICE: You look stunning, Stepmother, as always.
(JERICHO enters with a parasol, which he gives to MARY.
JOSEPH re-enters, pinning an orchid into his buttonhole.)
JOSEPH: Come on, come on. We're late. Bye, Bee. What are
you doing with yourself today?
BEATRICE: (*Quickly.*) Seeing friends.
JOSEPH: Enjoy yourself. Quick, quick, we've just got time.
(JOSEPH ushers MARY off right.
JERICHO follows them.)
(*Off, shouting.*) Tell him to start the car! We're late!
(*Car starting up.*
NEVILLE enters in a hurry, dressed to go out.)
NEVILLE: Where are they?
BEATRICE: They've gone.
(*Sound of car being driven away.*)
NEVILLE: The wretched man has gone without me!
BEATRICE: Lucky you, the mood he's in.
NEVILLE: But he ordered me to go! He said it would be
good for me!
(*He throws the jacket down on the floor.*
JERICHO picks it up, dusts it down, and holds it up for
NEVILLE to put on.)
JERICHO: You'll never get him off your back.
NEVILLE: Eh?
JERICHO: He's left you behind again.
NEVILLE: I can handle my old man.
JERICHO: Ho-ho.
(*Front stage spotlight on JOSEPH making a speech to Liberal*
Unionists.)
JOSEPH: I'm told that we've suffered a huge setback in
the country and we're isolated. The Tories hate me, the

Liberals hate me. What must I do? Should I turn my back
on the British working-man and the Empire and give my
support to Free Trade? Time and again during my career
I have sacrificed party unity and my own aspirations –
and I am an aspiring man, I readily confess to cherishing
the unity of the British Empire. And Birmingham, our
home ground which is the powerhouse of the Empire, the
hub of its strength. Made in Birmingham. Yes, we're all
Made in Birmingham here! and no new-fangled coalition
of Liberals and Fenians and Socialists will change that
because we're more radical than any of them. The voters
will come to realise that as this government sinks beneath
a task that is far too great for it. Can you see them dealing
with Germany? With those Prussians who envy our great
empire? This nation will have to be held together like
the Germans are, but not with their mindless form of
discipline, but in the discipline of democracy. (*Pause.*) On
this, my birthday, seventy years young, I woke thinking
about a lot of things. Many adventures, challenges,
battles lost and won, but most of all about this city of
ours. Birmingham to me is the most beautiful place in
the world. Some aesthete would deny this and say, 'Oh,
no, Venice, Athens, Paris is better,' but not to me. We
have the moral leadership of a great nation. Our work on
health, on housing, on the nuts and bolts of civic life, is
streets ahead. During my time as mayor we parked, paved,
assized, marketed, gas-and-watered, and improved this city
till it did not know itself, and so its special beauty to me
was born. I was only saying to my younger son, Neville,
this morning, that I wished the Press and my political
adversaries would let me choose my own epithet with
which they can insult me. 'What would that be?' he asked
'Why,' I replied, 'I'd like to be known as the only British
statesman who learnt his trade in the sewers.'
(*Laughter.*)
'And who saw off the rats.'
(*Laughter. Pause.*)
And who are those rats? Who undermines our city? Who

undermines our army and our navy? Who undermines our empire? And, what is worst, who undermine the British working man? Isn't it the rat of compromise? The rat of dishonesty? The rat of coalition government which feeds upon the corpse of hung parliaments? And the rats of recession, unemployment and poverty. (*Pause.*) Fellow-workers, you know me and you know my record. No matter what office I have held, no matter what the sacrifice, I have fought to keep Britain strong and great, and her empire intact. My reason? I believe it is a force for good in the world's future. And whatever binds the empire together, be it steel or money, or ideas, finds favour with me. This Birmingham of ours is a great imperial city! When I hear the rifle-bolts rattle in Germany or Russia, I tell myself – that doesn't frighten Birmingham. We probably made the weapons they're waving about! And we know how to use them!

(*Cheers.*)

But, my friends and fellow party-workers, I must end on a serious note. These have been happy days for me. You have given me a birthday to remember. But there were people not at the feast. Thousands and tens of thousands of men cannot find work or bread for their families. I do not blame them if they complain loudly and are dissatisfied with the conditions in which they live. But you are only mocking their wretchedness when you offer them political reforms which will not fill their stomachs, or a social revolution which will plunge them deeper into misery than before. Those are the people who have the ear of Joey Chamberlain. Those are the people for whom I fought this last election. And when this absurd cocktail of a government is poured down the drain of history, they will be the people who go forward with our Liberal Unionist party into power!

(*Applause. Cheers. Blackout.*

Lights up on NEVILLE in shirtsleeves playing a Beethoven sonata from sheet-music. He is learning the piece and makes a number of errors, cursing under his breath.

BEATRICE sits on the sofa reading a pamphlet.)

NEVILLE: *(Making a mistake.)* Oh, God, damnation blood and hell!

BEATRICE: Do shut up, Neville.

NEVILLE: I must get it right, RIGHT! Mein Gott, what a dumkopf! Mein fingers are liverwurst! Beethoven, dear chap, I must apologise.

BEATRICE: Why is it so important?

NEVILLE: I want to play it for him tonight.

BEATRICE: Any particular reason?

NEVILLE: So he can criticise. It's the only thing that makes me happy; being pulled to pieces by Papa. What are you reading?

BEATRICE: An article.

NEVILLE: An article. Don't tell me anything, will you?

BEATRICE: I thought you were playing the piano?

NEVILLE: I'll be good enough after a few stiff scotches. He'll be dazzled, the old philistine.

BEATRICE: He's not a philistine. He's a very civilised man.

NEVILLE: Don't get me going. Tell me what you're reading.

BEATRICE: It's a very stupid piece of feminist propaganda and most ill-written. The woman knows nothing about the subtleties of power.

NEVILLE: Ah, the Chamberlain girls go about it a different way.

BEATRICE: Of course. In this house, I am not treated as an inferior.

NEVILLE: No more than anyone else. If I were a woman I'd be on the streets…let me rephrase that… I'd be agitating for the vote. But I'm no lady so I don't agree with it. *(Plays the piano.)* Beethoven would not have supported it, but then he was deaf and more than a bit mad, n'est-ce pas?
(Enter JOSEPH and MARY, having returned from the luncheon.)

JOSEPH: That sounds good, Neville.

NEVILLE: Just messing about. You forgot me.

JOSEPH: Yes, sorry about that; but I mentioned you in my speech.

NEVILLE: Thanks a lot. How did it go?

JOSEPH: Very well. (*He sits down next to BEATRICE.*) They were absolutely splendid to me, as usual, the dears. What's that you're reading?
(MARY starts looking for something.)
NEVILLE: Rabid feminist tract. Atrociously badly written.
BEATRICE: It's not. To be honest I think it's quite well argued once she's made her a priori statement, which one either believes or doesn't believe. (*Looks at JOSEPH.*) I simply don't wish to be anything like a man. I prefer to be kept separate out of pure self-interest.
JOSEPH: A wise attitude. Maleness has no advantages, rest assured. In my dreams I'm a houri who lives in a harem with no speeches to make or meetings to attend. I suck sherbert and torment the eunuchs.
(MARY finds a ledger and opens it, leafs through, searching the pages for something.)
NEVILLE: But if the women did have the suffrage, which way would they vote?
JOSEPH: Answer him, Bee.
BEATRICE: I'd vote for you.
NEVILLE: But I mean generally. What do women want out of life? Are they naturally authoritarian? Liberal? Do the distinctions in masculine politics coincide with theirs? Enormous doubts exist.
JOSEPH: Women are family creatures, used to sharing.
NEVILLE: Then I'd expect them to be Communists.
MARY: (*Reading.*) Here it is. I knew that it rang a bell. You do try to get away with murder, Joe.
JOSEPH: What have I done now?
MARY: Do you remember when we all sat round a couple of weeks ago and gave this play of yours whatever it's called…a reading?
JOSEPH: 'The Game of Politics'? My comic masterpiece? Yes, I remember. It worked rather well. Lots of laughs. Neville was especially good with all the accents.
NEVILLE: If I fail again as a business man, Papa, I can always become an actor.
MARY: You used a speech from the play as part of your real speech this afternoon. Why did you do that?
JOSEPH: Waste not, want not.

MARY: Are you confused about what's real and what isn't?

JOSEPH: Of course not. Don't be ridiculous.

MARY: I'd like to feel that you have the distinction clear in your mind. Life is difficult without it.

JOSEPH: Why do you have to be so serious about everything? I wrote the play for our amusement. It will probably never see the light of day outside this house so what does it matter?

MARY: It shows what you think of your audience and yourself. It's all a game. So, you play with your life and you play with ours. Is that why you want to be Prime Minister? To play games? You can play games here, at home. C'mon, let's go and play billiards, let's play ping-pong.

BEATRICE: Mary dear, you're putting your case far too strongly. Papa wrote the play to show us the lighter side of politics. I, for one, thought it was very good.

MARY: When we'd finished reading it I was left with a nasty taste in my mouth. It made me think: all this hard work, all this devotion he gets, all this loyalty and love, and he's able to mock like this. How? Why? Something's wrong in the way he looks at things.

JOSEPH: What, exactly? What are you trying to say to me?

MARY: You're willing to risk your life for a joke like some buccaneer in a boy's story. The play's got out of hand, Joe.

(*HILDA and IDA enter and overhear.*)

IDA: Don't talk to Papa that way! It's hateful!

MARY: I'll talk to him any way I want to! He's my husband as well as your sainted father! He doesn't scare me.

IDA: You must stop attacking him! We all have to stick together now. So stop it!

(*Pause. MARY is suddenly aware that she has gone too far, but she refuses to retreat because in her heart she believes what she has said is true.*)

MARY: Don't get so upset, Ida. I talk to your father this way sometimes to keep sane. This isn't an easy family to live with all the time, you know. I'm sure you gave a wonderful speech at Smethwick.

JOSEPH: (*Shakily.*) If there is ever a genuine welfare system in this country, I will have to be given a major share of the credit for getting it going. Is that playing games?

MARY: No, it's blowing your own trumpet.

JOSEPH: Why shouldn't I blow my trumpet? A better life
for the working-people of this country? Is that nothing?
I appeal to my honourable friends. My achievements in
arousing the public conscience to the conditions and wages
of our lower classes are considerable, are they not?

IDA: Hear, hear!

HILDA: May I ask the Prime Minister if it is his intention to
introduce a bill for Imperial preferences during the course
of this Parliament?

JOSEPH: My honourable friend from the back bedroom
alludes to an election pledge that countries of the British
Empire throughout the world will be granted preferential
treatment both in import and export tariffs, in order to
foster trade between the colonies and dominions and the
mother country. Thus will the British Empire secure its
future prosperity.

(*BEATRICE, HILDA, IDA, NEVILLE and JOSEPH
create the strange, male sound of the House of Commons
digesting information.*

HILDA stands up, her hand in the air.)

BEATRICE: (*As the speaker.*) Hilda Chamberlain!

HILDA: Does the Prime Minister not concede that such
preferences will damage British relations with our trading
partners outside the Empire and create international
tensions at a time of volatile and dangerous shifts in
European alliances?

JOSEPH: I am grateful to the honourable member opposite
for raising this question. Does she not accept that a British
Empire that is economically strong and competitive is a
stabilising force in terms of world trade? If it is a shambles
then chaos and confusion will govern the marketplace.

(*More male rumbles of agreement and disagreement.*)

BEATRICE: Ida Chamberlain!

IDA: Oh – er. My question to the Prime Minister is…
(*Whispering to NEVILLE.*) I haven't got one.

NEVILLE: Ask him about South Africa.

IDA: What about South Africa?

BEATRICE: Come on, Ida.

NEVILLE: Ask him about the native franchise. Will the Africans get the vote under the terms of the peace treaty of Vereeniging?

IDA: I can't pronounce that. Never mind. (*To JOSEPH.*) In the peace treaty with the Boers...

(*HILDA, BEATRICE and JOSEPH start to boo.*
HILDA shuts here eyes.)

...the Boers the Boers the Boers the Boers...

BEATRICE: Order! Order!

IDA: ...the Boers the Boers...

HILDA: You can carry on now, Ida.

IDA: Oh! (*Opens her eyes.*) You've stopped. Yes the Boers... will the natives get the vote?

JOSEPH: The member for the bedroom overlooking the kitchen courtyard is perfectly aware that this is a question which cannot be answered at this time as His Majesty's government is still in negotiation on this issue. It is not a simple matter.

(*JERICHO enters.*)

JERICHO: A deputation from Lichfield, sir. They've driven over in a charabanc to wish you a happy birthday.

(*Horn sounds off.*)

They've had a good time of it so far, sir.

JOSEPH: Thank them for their trouble. I'll come out and see them right away, bless their hearts.

IDA: No, Papa, you mustn't. You don't know who might be there.

JOSEPH: What do I care? They're only people.

IDA: It could be an ambush.

JOSEPH: Have we got a charabanc full of Fenians out there.

JERICHO: No, sir. It's an outing of old ladies from Lichfield.

JOSEPH: Will the Speaker adjourn the House? Go and keep them happy, Ida, until I'm ready to step out.

IDA: Oh must I, Papa?

JOSEPH: Yes. It will be good practice for you.

(*IDA and JERICHO exit.*

JOSEPH checks out his appearance.)

NEVILLE: What will you say to them, Papa?

JOSEPH: I'm thinking about that.

NEVILLE: Women with time on their hands seem to idolise you. I wonder why? I shouldn't put too much effort into charming them, Papa. They don't have the vote.

BEATRICE: Don't keep them waiting too long, Papa.

JOSEPH: (*Holding on to his good humour.*) What are you getting at Neville? Everyone is important to me. We all affect and influence each other. These women have brothers, nephews, pupils perhaps.

HILDA: He's teasing us, Papa. We're used to it.

BEATRICE: Could it be that our little brother is jealous? Loyalty seems to appal him. Perhaps you're feeling left out because it's not your birthday, Neville. Don't worry. Yours will come round.

JOSEPH: Half the time I don't know what's going on in this establishment. (*Pause.*) Let me say this, Neville, outside are fifty or sixty fellow beings who support me. They are my friends, even though I do not know them personally. I have the sense to know that I need my friends.

(*Horn toots outside.*)

Do you understand?

NEVILLE: Yes, sir.

BEATRICE: (*Picking a thread of JOSEPH's jacket.*) I think that you've made them wait long enough, Papa. If you don't go now they may drive off.

JOSEPH: Oh, I expect they've found Ida interesting enough. Come, Mary, let's go and meet some real people. (*Exits with MARY left.*)

HILDA: That was a mistake, Neville. We don't mind you making jokes at our expense but Papa does.

BEATRICE: Speak for yourself, Hilda, I, for one, am beginning to find it tedious. If the smart business person in ship's bunks will help to find a chap who will measure up to Papa, I'll marry him: tomorrow. Do you accept that challenge, know-all?

(*Snap blackout.*)

*Lights up on AUSTEN in a dinner suit sitting on the sofa
and reading a newspaper. It is past midnight.
IDA enters to the balcony in a dressing gown and descends
the stairs.)*

IDA: Austen.

AUSTEN: I thought you'd gone to bed.

IDA: I can't sleep. I keep seeing all those women. I didn't say
anything, you know, but it didn't seem to matter.

AUSTEN: That's what is called heart-warming enthusiasm.

IDA: Joe Chamberlain's daughter. That was enough. It's very
strong, isn't it, that feeling a crowd gives off? I've always
been with Papa at these meetings before and he's been
the focus of attention. But when one is the target of it, it's
different. I felt quite alarmed.

AUSTEN: I'm always alarmed by it.

IDA: Hilda says that some people have a natural magnetism.

AUSTEN: I expect she's right.

IDA: I hope Papa doesn't ask me to do too many of these
appearances. I'm not sure that I enjoy them very much.
(*Pause.*) Could you convey that to him somehow?

AUSTEN: Very well.

IDA: Thank you, Austen. (*Kisses him on the cheek.*) Good night.
(*IDA goes back up the stairs to the balcony and exits.
AUSTEN starts to read his newspaper again, putting his
feet up on the sofa.
NEVILLE enters from the conservatory carrying an orchid
in a pot. He is dressed for dinner but he has loosened his
tie. He creeps up on AUSTEN and stands over him.*)

NEVILLE: Get your dirty feet off my sofa, boy!
(*AUSTEN reacts immediately, sitting bolt upright and
clutching the newspaper, fooled by NEVILLE's mimicry
of his father's voice.
NEVILLE laughs at him.*)

AUSTEN: Don't do that!

NEVILLE: Got you, didn't I?
(*NEVILLE walks round and puts the orchid on the floor
in front of the sofa and sits down beside AUSTEN who
pointedly resumes reading the newspaper.*)

Where's Papa?

AUSTEN: Gone to bed.

NEVILLE: He should stay in bed for a week.

AUSTEN: But he won't.

NEVILLE: (*Touching the orchid with his foot.*) This Grand
Monarch isn't going to make it. Papa will go peuce when it
conks out.

AUSTEN: Well, you can tell him.

NEVILLE: I've done all I can for it. No human being could
do more. Just another failure. (*Touches it again with his foot.*)
Wretched plant!

AUSTEN: Don't keep kicking the poor thing. Orchids are
delicate.

NEVILLE: Why are you sitting up so late?

AUSTEN: I had to wait for a call.

NEVILLE: Secret stuff?

AUSTEN: Not in your line, Neville. Westminster gossip. The
coalition government is crumbling. Once the Socialists and
the Liberals have torn each other apart, Papa will be in
with a chance.

NEVILLE: I thought he wanted you to be Prime Minister.

AUSTEN: Har-har.

NEVILLE: Austen, I'm shocked! Are you implying that Papa
doesn't mean what he says?

AUSTEN: Oh, do shut up and be serious.

NEVILLE: And here's me, innocent as ever, imagining that
you think Papa is the oracle.

AUSTEN: For me to become Prime Minister would be
distinctly second-best for both of us. If he sits tight things
can still go his way.

NEVILLE: This government is barely six months old, has a
big majority and everyone seems to love them. No one's
interested in Papa these days.

AUSTEN: One crisis and Campbell-Bannerman's coalition
will collapse. The Tories can only form a government if
they deal with us. Two thirds of their MPs are against Free
Trade.

NEVILLE: It's an odd way for an old man to choose to spend
his final years.

AUSTEN: What he wants is any politician's dream, any politician who is worth his salt, that is.

NEVILLE: You're such an old humbug, Austen. When you've been a Cabinet Minister you've moaned all the time, 'I'm exhausted', 'I can't stand all the lying and hypocrisy', 'It's driving me mad', all that grizzling we had to put up with. Now, suddenly, it's all marvellous.

AUSTEN: Yes, when you're out of office it does seem marvellous.

(*Enter MARY in a dressing-gown.*)

MARY: Nothing to go to bed for?

NEVILLE: Nothing as far as I'm concerned. Austen may have Ivy up his sleeve.

AUSTEN: Cut that out.

NEVILLE: He thinks that's a bit strong. Better not talk about it. D'you know, Mary, I can remember that when you married Papa, at odd moments I used to forget that you were my stepmother and team you up with Austen in my imagination. Why not? You were the same age.

AUSTEN: You really are the limit.

MARY: We've had this exchange before, Neville. May I ask why you choose to revive it now?

NEVILLE: Well, Austen's leaving. He actually is going. That's made me think. What have the last fifteen years been all about?

MARY: Do they have to have been about anything?

NEVILLE: Oh, yes. We've all been together in a kind of zoo. All we think about is whether the chief animal, the main attraction is happy to share our captivity. But the chief animal is the zoo-keeper in disguise.

MARY: Over these dreadful years, I've found that ignoring you in this mood is probably best.

NEVILLE: Quite right. If I had a bag handy I'd tie it over my head. But why did you marry Papa? For his money? His reputation? You know what people say? That Papa went to America to find a suitable wife for Austen, found you, and decided to keep you for himself.

MARY: Once you leave, Austen, everything will change;

and not before time. There's been something amiss in this house for the last few years. Our lives have been out of balance. Haven't you felt that? If Joe was a real man he'd have thrown Neville out by now.

NEVILLE: I'll go into the jungle and find a missionary to talk to. Ah, a cannibal. Good day, sir. Would you like my father for dinner?

MARY: He'll need to be tenderised.

(*NEVILLE goes into the foliage but remains in view.*)

NEVILLE: (*To a plant.*) Why did she do it? So young! So beautiful. She could have had me. And what's an American doing in Birmingham?

AUSTEN: Neville! For God's sake!

MARY: Don't shout at him. In many ways I think Neville's the one who's kept us sane. Without him it would have been a house of cards.

AUSTEN: We've all remained together because it was necessary. We had to stick with it in order to push the cause forward as far as possible. It was in all our interests, after all.

MARY: Does that mean that your marriage to Ivy is a signal to your father that the cause, as you call it, the Chamberlain machine, has reached its limit? (*Pause.*)
Well, that's a silence that I'm glad Joe can't hear, though I think he should. Nothing will make you change your mind about getting married?

AUSTEN: Why do you ask?

MARY: Some men flunk it. Now and then you make me nervous. It's difficult to know what's going on inside you, Austen.

AUSTEN: D'you think Ivy will make a good wife?

MARY: Now I'm even more nervous. Haven't you made up your own mind?

AUSTEN: I'm not sure that Papa approves in his heart. But it's too late now. I can say that I love her. I'm certain of that.

MARY: Well, I'm glad that you can put out that statement. No woman will ever be good enough for you as far as your father is concerned. That's something that you'll always have to deal with, I'm afraid.

AUSTEN: (*Pause.*) Is Papa asleep?

MARY: No. He's lying there worrying whether he got his speech right today.

AUSTEN: With that audience I would say that it would have been impossible to have got the speech wrong. He could have recited nursery rhymes and they'd still have loved it.

MARY: You know your father, Austen. He likes to feel that everyone understands the way his mind works. Good night.

AUSTEN: Good night.

NEVILLE: Good night, great an' gracious chamberlady, good night.

(*MARY goes up the stairs, onto the balcony and exits.*)

AUSTEN: She's so patient with you.

NEVILLE: I know. It drives me mad.

AUSTEN: If Papa knew for a moment the way that you talk to her you'd be finished. Can't you be a bit more gentle with her these days? You take the joke too far sometimes.

NEVILLE: Why shouldn't I? You know as well as I do that he only married her to torment us; to show how he could get a woman of our age and make us both jealous. If she hadn't been so good about it life would have been hell for everyone.

AUSTEN: I was never jealous.

NEVILLE: Liar.

(*JOSEPH wanders from right to left along the balcony in his dressing-gown. He pauses a couple of times to listen, then exits.*)

AUSTEN: There are plenty of women.

NEVILLE: Whores. You'd never go near a whore. You'd be terrified of the clap.

AUSTEN: I wonder why this orchid has got into this state? It looks as though something has been sitting on it.

NEVILLE: I was in love with Mary for years.

AUSTEN: Oh, yes?

NEVILLE: I told her about it. She was very decent, as well as patient.

AUSTEN: That's character for you.

NEVILLE: Did I tell you that I discussed the matter with a

Franciscan friar? An Anglican one, of course. He advised me to find a way of sublimating it. That's why I took up fly-fishing.

AUSTEN: I shall miss living with you.

NEVILLE: Can you imagine what it's going to be like once you've gone? You're deserting me. I'll be stuck here with him and all his women. D'you realise what's in store for me? When you've gone and he has to admit that he's come to the end of all the work he's done on making you into a political tool, he's going to start on me in earnest. Life is going to be absolute hell.

AUSTEN: Papa's always got your interests at heart. The trouble with you Neville is you resent that somehow.

NEVILLE: To be honest, I couldn't care less if he does die.

AUSTEN: Why d'you insist upon saying things you don't mean?

NEVILLE: I do mean it. He's had his three score years and ten, hasn't he? He's done a lot in his life. There must be more than enough for his conscience to deal with by now.

AUSTEN: (*Indignantly.*) What d'you mean by that?

NEVILLE: All those soldiers killed in the South African War.

AUSTEN: Don't be such an innocent.

NEVILLE: Someone must be responsible. Isn't it his duty to accept the blame? He claims the credit for the victory often enough.

AUSTEN: You're such a child. Try to think at the right level.

NEVILLE: I had a strange idea today during Papa's triumphal procession through Birmingham for his birthday. What's all this about? I asked myself. He thinks he's God. That Rolls-Royce is a donkey. This is Jerusalem. The crowd are going to start throwing palms beneath his feet.

AUSTEN: What a ridiculous thought to have.

NEVILLE: And I suddenly realised that I was the son of a megalomaniac. It made me feel quite odd.

(*JERICHO enters from left.*)

JERICHO: I am going to bed shortly. Is there anything I can get you before I finish?

NEVILLE: You know me. I'm the man who has everything. Don't you remember me lying on the beach in the

Bahamas sunning myself?

JERICHO: Mr Joseph is wandering around.

NEVILLE: Thanks for the tip, Jericho. Did he seem to have any sense of purpose?

JERICHO: I can't say that he did. He's been going all over the house, looking in this room, looking in that room, muttering to himself.

NEVILLE: Aimless wandering, would you say? The kind of behaviour one might expect of a man with a lot on his mind?

JERICHO: Maybe he's looking for something?

NEVILLE: What, for instance?

JERICHO: Something he's lost.

NEVILLE: Fifty thousand pounds.

JERICHO: A good, round sum, Neville. I thought we had that plantation in profit till the day you told me we'd have to go into liquidation. The sisal plants were certainly growing.

NEVILLE: But no one wanted to buy the stuff, did they? I was just telling my brother here that he'd better pull his socks up. Losing my father fifty thousand was failure on a much grander scale than anything he managed as Chancellor of the Exchequer. It impressed Papa no end.

JERICHO: Yes, Mr Neville. I can remember the look on his face when you showed him the accounts for the Andros plantation. Wow! Thunder over the bay. He wasn't pleased with you at all.

NEVILLE: Great days, Jericho. Have you been in the study for interrogation with the rum bottle lately?

JERICHO: Not for some time, Mr Neville. I reckon your father knows everything there is to know about you so far. He seems to be up to date. I went to the market and what did I see? Limbo, limbo like me.

NEVILLE: (*Sings.*) Politician telling lies to prove his integrity. Limbo, limbo like me.

(*JERICHO exits.*)

That man worked shoulder to shoulder with me on an island of Papa's commercial illusions, growing the raw material for old rope. Know why he's so happy here? This house is the island of Papa's political illusions. When you jump out of the frying pan into the fire at least you don't have to adapt.

AUSTEN: You're the one with the illusions.

NEVILLE: What about? Listen, at my postmortem they'll find Andros written on my heart. And the reward for my failure? He puts me into a company making ships' bunks. Ugh! That's cured any illusions that I ever had, I can tell you.

AUSTEN: When I hear you sounding off like this I can understand why Papa has kept you out of politics.

NEVILLE: Doesn't attract me. I've watched you making yourself ill with it. I've seen him eaten up with insane ambition all his life. He's warped this family.

AUSTEN: I don't want to hear any more. You're just saying the first thing that comes into your head.

NEVILLE: But it is coming into my head, isn't it? Ever thought why?

(AUSTEN takes a cigar from a box. He is upset by what NEVILLE has said and it shows. He cuts the cigar and lights it.

JOSEPH steps forward from the foliage.)

JOSEPH: I'll have one of those, if you please.

AUSTEN: Papa. We thought you were in bed.

JOSEPH: I'm not.

AUSTEN: I'll have to open a new box.

JOSEPH: Do so.

(JOSEPH sits down on a sofa next to NEVILLE.

AUSTEN exits right.

NEVILLE sits absolutely still, looking ahead.)

That orchid doesn't look too chipper.

NEVILLE: No, sir.

JOSEPH: Are you going to put it out of its misery or persevere?

NEVILLE: Persevere, I think, sir. I'll put it in a cooler corner.

JOSEPH: Why does it look so crumpled. Has someone sat on it?

NEVILLE: It could be the cat.

JOSEPH: Ah, the wicked cat.

(AUSTEN enters with a new box of cigars. He tears off the wrapper and offers the box to JOSEPH.)

Thank you. The first one out of a fresh box always has the best flavour. Atmospherics, Neville. Atmospherics are very important. *(Holding the cigar out to AUSTEN.)* Will you do the honours?

(AUSTEN takes the cigar, cuts it then lights it for JOSEPH. He takes a deep lungful and blows it out.)

Ah, delicious. Smoking is the only exercise I get.

(Pause. NEVILLE is very tense.

JOSEPH lets him sweat.)

Any news?

AUSTEN: Harry did ring, sir, but he had nothing to tell us. Apparently they're still hanging together somehow.

JOSEPH: Did I come into it?

AUSTEN: Only in a general way.

JOSEPH: People talking behind my back, Neville. One gets used to it. *(He reclines, putting his feet over NEVILLE's lap and puffing on his cigar.)* You don't mind, do you?

(NEVILLE mutely shakes his head.)

Austen, I think it's time that your brother went into politics. I've been noticing lately how certain basic skills which one requires for that high calling have been developing in him. I've heard things which have encouraged me to believe that he has that tigerish instinct to go for the throat. Also, if the circumstances are right, he can be candid to the point of cruelty. That is an essential quality in any politician who might aspire to become a statesman. What do you say, Neville?

NEVILLE: I haven't thought about it very much.

JOSEPH: Well, it's time you did. You're a Chamberlain. I thought we'd start you off on the city council, then you can be mayor when you've gained some experience.

NEVILLE: My understanding, sir, is that I will need to be elected.

JOSEPH: Of course you will. But you can leave that to me. *(He laughs and gets to his feet.)*. What a good day I've had. And the night hasn't been bad so far. An excellent family dinner, followed by a moment of illumination about

Neville, a fresh cigar… Pity you missed my speech, Neville.
I love the sight and smell of a good crowd. It gets me going
like nothing else I know. But I prefer the ones which are
hostile to me at the beginning, the ones I have to coax.
There's something strange about the way I can make them
come round, don't you think, Austen?

AUSTEN: I have always stood a little in awe of it, sir, and I
wish that I had it myself.

NEVILLE: (*Getting off the sofa.*) I think I'll go to bed now, sir, if
you don't mind.

JOSEPH: I do mind. Sit down. We have things to talk about.

AUSTEN: Do you need me, sir? If it's something private…

JOSEPH: When will you get it into your head that we're a
team!

(*NEVILLE subsides onto the sofa.*
JOSEPH offers him a cigar from the box.
NEVILLE takes one. He cuts it and lights it for himself.
JOSEPH paces up and down in a state of sustained
indignation and excitement.)

It's time that we three sorted ourselves out. There's been
too much groping in the dark for my liking. There's nothing to be frightened of, I can assure you. But this is our
moment, do you understand? I'm not going to hold office
under any other man again. I've done that. I've fought a
war for someone else, and let him take the credit when I
won. From now on we act as a family and we keep for-
mation. The time will come when we are all in the same
cabinet, I promise you.

AUSTEN: What portfolio had you in mind for me, sir?

JOSEPH: Chancellor.

AUSTEN: To be frank, sir, I wasn't too happy when I was
Chancellor for Balfour.

JOSEPH: I'm not Balfour. I'm your father.

AUSTEN: I'd be hoping for consideration as Foreign
Secretary, sir.

JOSEPH: No, no, I'll be doing that myself.

AUSTEN: Prime Minister and Foreign Secretary? Good Lord,
that would be an immense workload!

JOSEPH: I must do it myself. I don't want any bungling
in foreign affairs. Everything in eastern Europe is on a

hair-trigger at the moment.

AUSTEN: (*Abashed.*) Well, I'd try not to bungle, sir.

JOSEPH: (*Aware of the slight he has given.*) No, of course you'd be a fine Foreign Secretary but the most important thing in my life is Tariff Reform which is Exchequer work, and I'd need the best man I could find. But what about Neville? It will take us a couple of years to get him into the House as an MP, I'm afraid. A junior minister would be all I could offer at first.

NEVILLE: Oh, that's all right, Papa. Anything will do.

JOSEPH: (*Leaning over NEVILLE.*) Tell me, is there any more horrible man in the universe than your father? The answer is no, as far as you're concerned. But there are worse than me out there, Neville, and you'd better learn how to deal with them or they'll eat you alive.

NEVILLE: I'm not sure what you're talking about, sir.

JOSEPH: Yes, you are. I heard what you said about me a little time ago. I know you're squiffy and a bit overexcited, and I know that you didn't mean it, but you said it.

NEVILLE: Only to shock Austen, sir. I like shocking Austen.

JOSEPH: That's all very well, as long as you remember that there will be people who will like shocking you. See now, you've depressed your big brother. Come on, Austen, brighten up. You're going to get married and escape from this madhouse. Soon you'll have a little place of your own. Won't that be nice?

AUSTEN: No matter how busy I am, sir, I will never neglect my family.

JOSEPH: Or Birmingham, if you want to stay alive in national politics. Always court her, woo her and, if necessary, seduce her. Do you understand what I'm saying?

AUSTEN: Yes, sir.

JOSEPH: Give her what she wants, as I have done. Make her grateful. Whatever they give you, Austen, lord this or that, the earl of what you like, remember Birmingham. It paid for this house, for your education, for the clothes on your back and the food in your mouth.

AUSTEN: Yes, sir.

JOSEPH: Now I'm going to count sheep. Good night.

AUSTEN: Good night, sir.

NEVILLE: Bless you, fader. Go rest on your virtuous couch.

(*JOSEPH laughs lightly and shakes his head.*)

Sleep the sleep of the just, O King.

(*Pause. NEVILLE gets us then lies full-length on the sofa in imitation of his father, his face pressed against the place where his head had rested.*)

He'll never make prime minister if he keeps using that hair-oil.

(*Blackout.*

Lights up on JERICHO, the butler, feather-dusting the plants. He pauses, goes to the piano and accompanies himself as he sings a limbo calypso.)

JERICHO: Mr Neville is a devil, his Papa believe...

Fifty thousand gone make anyone grieve...

Mr Austen hasn't cost him such money and strife...

Obediently surrendered his intended wife...

Three sisters, no misters, for matrimony.

They only love Papa, none better than he...

I want somebody limbo like me...limbo like me...

(*Leaves the piano and resumes dusting the plants. To audience.*)

Mr Joseph likes to keep these healthy. They've been collected from all over the Empire. When one dies because it's too cold or it just gives up the ghost, Mr Joseph gets down in the mouth for a few minutes as if he's been confronted with personal failure. Now and again when Mr Neville has had a difficult or frustrating time at the factory, or gets to feel a bit defiant or frisky, he urinates on the plants. But I keep saying to him: that won't kill them. They thrive on it. (*Picks up the dying grand monarch potted orchard and sniffs it.*) Well, I can be wrong.

(*NEVILLE enters in a long coat and sits at the piano.*)

NEVILLE: Stop doing that now.

JERICHO: Has to be done, Mr Neville. Your papa's orders.

NEVILLE: The dust gets in my throat.

JERICHO: Are you going to play the piano?

NEVILLE: No, I'm about to levitate taking it with me.

JERICHO: What are you going to play?

NEVILLE: Beethoven. You'll hate it.

JERICHO: I've got jobs to do. (*Exits left.*)
(*NEVILLE practises on the piano.*
BEATRICE, HILDA and IDA enter carrying presents.
They hang up streamers.
NEVILLE slips into a musical flourish of 'Happy Birthday'.)

NEVILLE: Well done, girls. On time for once.

BEATRICE: Don't play that yet. You'll spoil the surprise.

NEVILLE: What did you get him.

HILDA: A cane. Can't you tell?

NEVILLE: I thought it might be a bar of rock.

HILDA: Now I feel awfully silly. It's got a silver top in the shape of a duck. He'll think it's ridiculous.

NEVILLE: No, he won't. When he knows who it's from he'll see deep meanings in it. What did you get him, Bee?

BEATRICE: Cigars. Havanas. Big ones.

HILDA: You are wicked. It's a good job Mary agreed to stay in her room. She wouldn't be pleased.

BEATRICE: He'd smoke cigars whether I bought them for him or not. He adores cigars and I adore him, so why not?

NEVILLE: You know, the old boy seems to be wandering around in a bit of a daze, don't you think? He doesn't cotton on so quickly.

HILDA: He cottons on fast enough when he needs to.

NEVILLE: Strange to see him at all vague.

HILDA: We should have all gone away on holiday together for his birthday and not let him get involved with all this municipal junketing. I honestly don't think he's enjoyed it much.
(*Enter AUSTEN and IDA with presents.*)

NEVILLE: Ah, the would-be Foreign Secretary is late. Black mark.

AUSTEN: Sorry. Seeing someone off. Everything running to plan, Neville? You've got it all organised?

NEVILLE: Like clockwork. I bet no once can guess what I've bought him.

HILDA: We know better than to even try. Come on, tell us.

NEVILLE: An example of the taxidermist's art: a stuffed bulldog.

HILDA: A stuffed bulldog! What a monstrous thing to buy anyone.

NEVILLE: I thought he could kick it when he's angry.

IDA: Neville, you're mad. He'll think you're pulling his leg.

NEVILLE: No, he won't. He knows the way I think. I can't stand giving him what everyone else gives him.

BEATRICE: He's coming. Start, Neville!

(*NEVILLE starts to play 'Happy Birthday To You' on the piano as JOSEPH enters in his smoking jacket.*)

JOSEPH: Oh, no! Not again!

NEVILLE: This is our party, Papa. So just relax and be very happy. It's all going to be wonderful fun, just like the old days.

JOSEPH: So many parties! Did ever a man have so many?

IDA: We need you to ourselves sometimes, Papa.

(*Pause. JOSEPH nods.*)

JOSEPH: That's true. We must always be able to get together.

HILDA: No matter what happens.

JOSEPH: Well, I am knocking on a bit. Not many birthdays left, perhaps.

AUSTEN: Nonsense, sir. You've got a long life ahead of you.

JOSEPH: A politician's ambition, let me say, a *real* politician's ambition is to see his policies made flesh in his lifetime. These presents will all be wonderful, and I will treasure them all because they are from you, but the big present… ah! Who can give me that?

NEVILLE: My present is quite big, actually.

JOSEPH: You're all so good to me. I wonder sometimes if I deserve you. (*Pause. He tries to control his feelings.*) I don't know what it is with me these days but I keep wanting to weep. Not like me, not like me at all.

BEATRICE: (*Going to comfort him.*) Papa, it's all been a bit too much.

JOSEPH: (*Moving away from her.*) No! Please don't touch me or I'll start. I'm sorry, Bee, just give me a moment.

BEATRICE: Should we leave it and all come back later?

JOSEPH: No. It makes me very happy to be with you. It's terribly difficult to explain. It wells up inside me. I don't even know why. In the old days I could manage anything.

BEATRICE: Of course. We've seen you perform miracles.

JOSEPH: Being so easily upset is discomforting for everyone. I apologise to you all. Age does get on one's nerves, I'm afraid.

BEATRICE: May we give you our presents now?

JOSEPH: I've been given many presents over the last few days but these are the most precious ones I will receive.

BEATRICE: Wait until you see what Neville's bought you before you say that!

NEVILLE: Oh, Bee, don't spoil it.

BEATRICE: Austen's first.

(*AUSTEN gives JOSEPH his present.*)

AUSTEN: It's something I thought you might enjoy. Bags I read it after you.

(*JOSEPH takes the wrapping off.*)

JOSEPH: Austen always buys me books, and they're always good ones. (*Holds it up.*) Doctor Livingstone, I presume?

AUSTEN: It's a first edition of his 'Missionary Travels' in mint condition. I thought it might remind you of your travels in South Africa.

JOSEPH: Thank you, Austen. I'll give it a good read. Not a lot of jokes I should think.

AUSTEN: Don't be too sure of that, sir. The old boy had quite a sense of humour, I believe. Considering what he was faced with out there, he probably had to have.

JOSEPH: And what's the big present you've bought me, Neville?

(*JERICHO enters with the nursery tea.*)

NEVILLE: You haven't got one of them, I'm certain. Oh, look, here's our special tea.

JOSEPH: Well, where's this present then? I can't wait to see what it is.

NEVILLE: (*Starting to stand up but finding himself too scared.*) Wouldn't you like a piece of jam and bread?

JOSEPH: Is that what you've bought me?

NEVILLE: No, sir, I've bought you a stuffed bulldog.

(*NEVILLE stands up and walks round the piano. He is wearing a pair of lederhosen.*
IDA laughs nervously. The rest are silent.

NEVILLE takes a school cap out of his pocket and puts it on his head.)
I'll go and get your present. It's not a stuffed bulldog at all. It's a cravat.

JOSEPH: I don't care what it is. (*Pause.*) Are you trying to tell me something by making yourself look ridiculous?

NEVILLE: Just a bit of fun, Papa.

JOSEPH: You've hurt me very much, Neville. I don't know how I bred a son as insensitive as you are. Go and change.

NEVILLE: Yes, sir! (*He marches out.*)

HILDA: Don't be too upset, Papa. You know what Neville's like. He goes too far sometimes, but he means no harm.

JOSEPH: Well, he's certainly done that today. What a damned-fool thing to do. He's spoilt everything.

BEATRICE: No doubt he'll be feeling very ashamed, Papa.

JOSEPH: It's a bit late for that. I think I'll take a walk in the garden to cool down. He has managed to make me very angry, I'm afraid.

(*JOSEPH exits right through the conservatory. Pause.*)

JERICHO: Shall I pour the tea, Mr Austen?

AUSTEN: Yes, why not? (*Looks at the tray.*) My God, look at this, a complete nursery tea with all the trimmings. Welsh Rarebit, Sausages, Jelly and Blancmange. Oh, Neville, Neville, you wicked fellow.

JERICHO: And there is Battenburg cake, Mr Austen. Notice that.

AUSTEN: Yes, so I see. Neville has an eye for detail. We can look after ourselves, I think.

JERICHO: Thank you, Mr Austen. Enjoy the spread. (*Exits.*)

BEATRICE: Well, Austen, you're the professional politician. Here's a breach to heal. Those two won't talk to each other for a good long time after this piece of silliness. I doubt if Neville will come out of his room tonight.

NEVILLE: (*Appearing from the foliage.*) Don't speak too soon! The prodigal returns, mit trousers!

IDA: Well, I hope you're pleased with yourself.

NEVILLE: Oh, do be quiet!

BEATRICE: Well, you've upset him terribly. There were tears

in his eyes.

NEVILLE: (*Interested.*) Where there, really?

HILDA: Don't encourage him. I'm not surprised Papa
wonders about Neville's feelings for him sometimes. You
are very ambiguous, you know.

NEVILLE: Nonsense. Where's his sense of humour?

BEATRICE: You can't make jokes like that.

NEVILLE: Of course you can. People do it all the time.

BEATRICE: Oh, I do wish you'd try to grow up. (*Pause.*) Give
him some credit, Neville. He loves you very much.

AUSTEN: I disapprove of the bulldog, and all that, but I have
to say, in Neville's defence, one can't keep a long face
all the time. Papa himself can be quite savage when he's
making jokes at an opponent's expense during a Commons
debate, for instance.

IDA: Yes, but this isn't the House of Commons. This is his
home.

NEVILLE: Rubbish! This is his House of Commons. His
Westminster. We've had three women in Parliament for
as long as I can remember. Do you think that you three
haven't had an impact upon British politics, just because
the debates have been here, at home? This hasn't been
a home at all. It's been a test laboratory for his bloody
rhetoric and ideas.

AUSTEN: I think you're completely wrong. He's a wonderful
father because he's always credited us with having minds
of our own.

NEVILLE: He's used us. What natural growth has he
allowed? None at all. Will you do that to your children?
Make them midget politicians? God, how ghastly.

IDA: Don't you dare ever say such a thing to Papa. I'd never
forgive you.

NEVILLE: If I did, he wouldn't understand, so it wouldn't be
worth it. But I resent having to shoulder his burdens.

HILDA: That's what families are for.

NEVILLE: That's what this family is for. Look at us! Most
sons and daughters are free by now, living on their own, or
with wives and husbands, but he's got us here. Why is that?
What's the matter with us? Are we freaks?

BEATRICE: Well, you may be a freak, but I'm not.

NEVILLE: Haven't you noticed that when our birthdays come round they're pretty muted affairs? Not a lot to celebrate, is there? A touch of unease, hm? Happy forty-fifth, Bee? Forty-forth, Austen thirty-eighth, Neville? Thirty-seventh, Ida? Thirty-sixth, Hilda? What, still under Daddy's wing? God, it makes me cringe.

IDA: No one has had a more exciting life than we have. We've been at the centre of everything.

NEVILLE: Don't you know why we're still here? Haven't you worked it out? This is Joe Chamberlain's real party. Cheap labour and utter devotion. D'you know, he's just told me, directed me, to become a city councillor. It's my job, my duty, to look after his interests. What about my life? Perhaps I don't want to be a politician. Perhaps I want to be a taxidermist!

(JOSEPH enters, smiling. He goes over and puts an arm round NEVILLE's shoulder.)

JOSEPH: Sorry, my boy. Forgive me. I don't know why I went off the deep end like that.

IDA: Bravo! I'm so glad you've made up. Here's my present.

JOSEPH: Are we friends again, Neville?

NEVILLE: Of course, Papa. We have never been enemies, have we?

JOSEPH: It's good to have a torment in the house. Mischief is a necessary spice. And I mustn't be allowed to get too pompous. *(Unwraps IDA's present and produces a small revolver.)* Well, Ida, this is a most unexpected present, I must say.

IDA: Careful. It is loaded. I put the safety catch on.

JOSEPH: It's beautifully made. Birmingham Small Arms, of course.

IDA: Promise you'll carry it about with you. The Irish…

JOSEPH: Just let them dare have a go at me now.

IDA: See if it works

JOSEPH: Oh, it will. Made in Birmingham. But I'll check. Slips nicely into my pocket and no one would guess that it was there. I'd better shoot it through one of the open ceiling lights to be safe. Oh, beware Fenians! Joe's coming.

(*Exits via conservatory.*)

NEVILLE: Thanks, Ida. I think you've probably shortened my life.

(*A shot off.*)

IDA: Good. It works. What a loud noise it makes for such a small thing.

(*Enter JOSEPH with the revolver, laughing.*)

(*Going to him.*) I hate it when you're in danger. People are being assassinated all the time. I want you to always defend yourself. Promise me you'll keep it in your pocket

JOSEPH: There, there, my lovely girl. No one can kill me.

NEVILLE: Oh, come on, Ida, no waterworks today.

JOSEPH: Leave her. It was a beautiful thought. Now, what's that you've got for me?

(*HILDA hands him her present.*)

HILDA: You have to guess.

(*Laughter.*)

JOSEPH: What would you say it looks like?

IDA: I know. I went out with her to buy it.

(*JOSEPH tears the wrapping-paper off the silver-mounted cane. He holds it up, then rests his weight on it.*)

JOSEPH: Why, it's got a duck's head. Quack-quack. How charming. You know the riddle: what has four legs, then two legs, then three? Mankind. Baby on all fours. Man, upright. Old age, stick.

HILDA: Let me have it back, Papa.

JOSEPH: You're taking my present back? What have I said?

(*He hands HILDA the cane.*
She gives the knob a twist and draws out a long blade. The cane is a sword-stick.)

Good God! What bloodthirsty daughters I've got!

HILDA: We decided that you had to be able to protect your life.

(*JOSEPH takes the swordstick off her. He has the revolver in his other hand.*

NEVILLE picks up a parcel from behind the sofa and gives it to JOSEPH.)

NEVILLE: Here's your present, Papa.

JOSEPH: Not so big, is it?

(*JOSEPH tears off the paper. Inside is a hangman's noose.*

Aghast, he dangles it from his hand.)
Neville, what are you doing to me today?

NEVILLE: It's a kind of cravat, isn't it? And everyone keeps
saying that you're killing yourself. I've had it in my
cupboard for years.

JOSEPH: What for, for God's sake? Were you in despair?

NEVILLE: It's the first piece of rope ever to come from the
sisal we grew on the plantation. I made it up like this for
Austen when he was dying to be Home Secretary.

JOSEPH: By why such a cruel thought?

NEVILLE: To remind him that he'd have to sign
death-warrants.

JOSEPH: The Home Secretary is a great officer of state, not a
hangman. He carries out the law, you fool.

NEVILLE: (*Obstinately.*) He also has to sign death-warrants
and I knew that Austen hadn't thought about it.

AUSTEN: I had, actually.

JOSEPH: (*To NEVILLE.*) Oh, God, what am I going to do
with you?

NEVILLE: Grow old in peace.

JOSEPH: Peace? What d'you mean, peace?

NEVILLE: Don't you know what it means?

JOSEPH: No. You tell me.

NEVILLE: In Joe Chamberlain's Birmingham peace is a dirty
word. Peace is bad for business. Peace is unemployment.
Peace is poverty.

BEATRICE: Don't let him say any more, Papa. Please!

JOSEPH: This is a democratic household. Let him have his
say.

NEVILLE: All the family's interests in armaments explosives
even metal ship's-bunks...would get a boost if YOU
became Prime Minister and provoked Germany into a trial
of strengths.

AUSTEN: For God's sake, Neville, hold your tongue!

JOSEPH: No! Go on. Tell me more. I'm learning things about
myself.

NEVILLE: War is madness but that wouldn't stop you with
your pathetic parliamentary party of seven MPs – which
includes you and Austen – power-broking this country into

another slaughter.

(*BEATRICE, HILDA, IDA and AUSTEN erupt into a howl of rage and disgust. It is so powerful and vicious that it shakes NEVILLE but he holds his ground, whispering.*)

…another slaughter…another slaughter… another slaughter…another slaughter…

HILDA: Traitor! Liar! We've had enough of you!

IDA: Shame on You! Get out! Get out!

BEATRICE: You're a disgrace to the family.

(*The volume and force of the outcry against NEVILLE is so loud that MARY and IVY run onto the landing.*)

MARY: Good God. What's going on?

NEVILLE: Another slaughter…another slaughter…another slaughter…

(*JOSEPH puts the noose round NEVILLE's neck and draws it tight, cutting off the whispered repeats. Silence.*)

MARY: Joe! What are you doing?

JOSEPH: Nothing, nothing. Only the end of a children's party. We've been playing Hide and Seek and Neville's just been found.

(*NEVILLE locks eyes with his father, then looks down. He exits as the lights fade to blackout.*)

End of Act One.

ACT TWO

Highbury. The next evening.

JOSEPH and AUSTEN sit reading newspapers. NEVILLE stands by the foliage, staring into space, smoking a cigar. JERI-CHO enters and stands close to him.

JERICHO: Mr Neville hasn't said a word all evening. Not a joke. Not a crack. I know the signs: guilt and fear. But the man struggles to stay cool. And he can do that like no one I've ever seen. Once, in Andros, when we were out in the fields, I was bending over examining a drain when I heard bees. When I looked up I saw this big swarm which had settled on Mr Neville's head. He stood there, still as a stone, with the bees covering him from the neck up. 'Don't move, Mr Neville,' I said. Any other man I know would have panicked and run off, getting the bees wild. But not him. He just stood there, the bees in his eyes, up his nose, in his ears, his hair. 'Come and stand under this tree,' I told him. 'Follow my voice. Go slowly. If they sting, do nothing.' And he obeyed, inching his way after me until he was under a branch. I told him to stop there and wait. After a little while the bees lifted from his head and went onto the branch. That's an instinct built into them; to hang on to what's above. When we talked about it as we walked back, I said that it was a useful lesson in Nature. He hadn't been stung to death because he'd stayed cool, waited, listened and obeyed. He just laughed in that grim way he sometimes has. 'What thoughts were going through your head when those bees were all over you?' I asked him. But he wouldn't tell. He just spat on the ground.

NEVILLE: Got to get out.

JERICHO: Buzz buzz.

NEVILLE: No, no. No guts left. I was a different man in those days. I could take him on in my head at least. But not now. He's got my balls nailed to the shed door.

JERICHO: Stay cool. Think it out.

NEVILLE: I can't help provoking him. Every time I do it I
    come off worst. So why do I do it?
JERICHO: Well, you should have left home long ago, Mr
    Neville.
NEVILLE: Yes.
JERICHO: You left home once.
NEVILLE: Did I? Wasn't the plantation just this place
    somewhere else? And equally unmanageable. And he sent
    me!
JERICHO: Mr Neville, you can't think that way. If you do
    then everywhere is Highbury. That's a nightmare.
NEVILLE: Perhaps it is. Perhaps I always have to come back
    with my tail between my legs, and nothing achieved. I
    have to go before he destroys me utterly.
JERICHO: No time like the present, Mr Neville.
NEVILLE: If I get a place of my own, will you come and
    work for me?
JERICHO: No. I need a Mr Joseph in my life. He's got me
    addicted.
    (*JERICHO exits left. Sound of birds fluttering in the
    conservatory.*
    JOSEPH half looks up.)
    Better see to that.
    (*NEVILLE exits right to conservatory. More fluttering
    and banging.*)
JOSEPH: Go and open a window, Austen, and let that damn
    thing out, whatever it is.
    (*AUSTEN gets to his feet. The fluttering stops.*)
AUSTEN: Seems to have stopped of its own accord.
JOSEPH: No, it will be sitting on something and doing
    damage. Sort it out.
    (*AUSTEN goes to the conservatory and meets NEVILLE
    coming out.*)
AUSTEN: Neville's seen to it, sir.
JOSEPH: What was it?
NEVILLE: A buzzard. It had broken a wing, I'm afraid. I had
    to put it out of its misery.
    (*Sound of breaking glass.*)
JOSEPH: Good God. Not again! I thought you'd seen to it?

(*NEVILLE and AUSTEN run off right.*
MARY enters from left.)
MARY: What was all that noise?
JOSEPH: They've gone to look. Something about a buzzard
  in the conservatory.
  (*NEVILLE enters from the conservatory, wiping blood*
  off his hands.)
NEVILLE: It was its mate. Must have seen it from the air
  and come crashing down through the glass not knowing
  something was in the way. Mad mad bird. Austen's gone to
  bury them in the garden.
JOSEPH: I thought that all hawks were supposed to have
  superb eyesight.
NEVILLE: Even birds of prey get old, Papa.
JOSEPH: Do they, indeed?
  (*JERICHO enters with NEVILLE's gladstone bag, hat*
  and coat, puts them at NEVILLE's feet, then exits.)
NEVILLE: Papa, I'm leaving.
JOSEPH: Oh yes? (*Pause.*) Where are you going?
NEVILLE: I don't know. Friends, maybe. It doesn't matter.
  Anywhere!
JOSEPH: Ah, that kind of leaving. Let me talk this through
  with my son, Mary. There's a routine we have to go
  through.
NEVILLE: I'm not going to discuss it with you. You've stifled
  me for long enough.
JOSEPH: Stifled you? Explain.
NEVILLE: Goodbye, Mary. I'll be in touch. Thank you for
  everything you've done for me. My own mother could not
  have been kinder.
JOSEPH: Nobly said, Neville. And thanks for reminding me
  about your poor mother at the point when you're shaking
  the dust of my house off your feet.
NEVILLE: Yes, your house. We've never been allowed to
  forget that!
JOSEPH: But you can't shake my blood out of your body.
  You walk out of here a Chamberlain, and a Chamberlain
  you'll stay.
NEVILLE: Sentimental nonsense! I'm my own man, damn

you!

JOSEPH: Go on then, if you're going.

(*NEVILLE hesitates.*)

What are you waiting for?

NEVILLE: A sign.

JOSEPH: What kind of a sign?

NEVILLE: That you understand. (*Pause. He starts to shake, covers his face with his hand.*) I'm not ungrateful, Papa.

(*JOSEPH signals to MARY that she should leave him alone with NEVILLE. First he takes the case out of NEVILLE's hand and gives it to MARY to take with her. He puts an arm round NEVILLE's shoulder and leads him to the sofa.*)

JOSEPH: Sit down, Neville.

(*NEVILLE shakes his head.*)

Tell me what the matter really is.

NEVILLE: I can't leave you in such a helpless position.

JOSEPH: (*Laughing.*) What? I'm not in a helpless position.

NEVILLE: Yes, you are.

JOSEPH: How absurd you are, Neville.

NEVILLE: You're never going to be Prime Minister.

JOSEPH: Yes, I am. You'll see.

NEVILLE: I'm not a politician, Papa, but I can see that this last election has done for you. The people who've been cheering you in the streets haven't been saying, 'Joe for Prime Minister,' they've been saying, 'thank you for what you've done for Birmingham. '

JOSEPH: I know that.

NEVILLE: The Liberals have hated you for twenty years for splitting the party and stopping Irish Home Rule, which is now a festering wound. And they hate you for keeping the Tories in for those twenty years by dividing the Liberal vote. Now the Tories hate you for splitting them at this last election on the tariff issue. You brought their twenty years of rule to an end at one blow. The Irish Republicans loathe you, and with good reason, and the Socialists are suspicious of any capitalist turned radical. To them you're still just a screw manufacturer.

JOSEPH: I don't think there's anyone you've left out Neville, except my own party. Why do they hate me?

NEVILLE: You're not a party man, Papa.

JOSEPH: Like all the major figures in British political history, one might say. (*Pause. He weakens for a moment, staring at NEVILLE, shaking his head.*) My own son. Abuse from my own son.

NEVILLE: It is not abuse. It is the truth.

JOSEPH: Oh, don't talk to me about truth. Talk to me about getting things done.

(*MARY re-enters.*)

MARY: D'you mind if I come back in? I don't want Neville to mangle you too much.

JOSEPH: Can't you leave us alone?

MARY: No. I don't want you getting into another temper. D'you understand that, Neville?

NEVILLE: Yes.

JOSEPH: God almighty, Mary, stop treating me as if I were made of some volatile substance that's going to blow up at any minute. What's the matter with getting into a temper over things that matter?

MARY: What are you talking about?

JOSEPH: Neville pities me because I'm so well hated. He's astonished how much his father is loathed and detested up and down the land. People look at him in the street and say: 'Isn't that Joe Chamberlain's boy, God help him?'

NEVILLE: You see what I'm up against, Mary? I said none of this, really.

MARY: Well, your father has a right to feel unloved on his birthday, even when he's been deluged with affection. The older you get the more isolated life becomes, eh, Joe?

NEVILLE: One can't say anything without it being taken the wrong way. We won't talk any more, Papa. I don't want to upset you again.

JOSEPH: You won't upset me ever again. I've been thinking about your attitude, Neville. And you're right. The bastards do all hate me, but that makes it easier for me to deal with them. I've got the killer instinct, you see. What I hadn't realised was that I'd passed it on to you.

NEVILLE: I haven't the faintest idea what you're talking about.

JOSEPH: You hate me, so you attack me. You go for the throat.

NEVILLE: The ankles, Papa.

JOSEPH: Austen can't do it. But you can. I've kept you hidden away too long, Neville. You could be my secret weapon.

NEVILLE: Papa, I'm awestruck at the perversity of your thought-processes.

JOSEPH: This family needs a tiger to lead it, not a labrador like Austen.

MARY: Are you talking about a family, or a dynasty?

JOSEPH: Oh, don't be so damned smart, woman! Someone has to manage a democracy or it starts to consume itself. What would you have? That we domesticate every aspect of life until it's one long orgy of bloody babies and birthdays?

MARY: Thanks for the remark about babies, Joe. I don't recall that we've been troubled with them, or had you untypically forgotten a human weakness in my case?

JOSEPH: I apologise, Mary. That was most insensitive of me. But could I have a few moments alone with my son?

MARY: I've gone once and come back.

JOSEPH: I know. I'm asking you to go again.

NEVILLE: Don't bother, Mary. I don't mind if you hear. Papa, I'm going to be cruel again. It's not killer-instinct. Just me struggling to get away. Look at me now. Another grand exit coming to nothing. I have to use the last ammunition I have. (*Pause.*) Papa, I deliberately bungled the plantation. I overspent, I drove the whole project into bankruptcy.

(*Pause. JOSEPH looks at NEVILLE.*
NEVILLE waits.)

Why? do I hear you ask?

JOSEPH: No, you don't.

NEVILLE: I made it fail because it was for you!

JOSEPH: I knew that. You had to get all that infantile rebellion out of your system.

NEVILLE: God damn and blast you!

JOSEPH: It was an expensive way to do it, perhaps, but absolutely necessary. Neville, there comes a time when

every man has to forgive his father and I think in your case, it's about overdue. But I can help. (*Rings a bell.*)
Division! Division! All members down here!
(*HILDA, IDA, BEATRICE enter, then AUSTEN and IVY.*)
No, not Miss Dundas. I mean no harm. You're not quite family yet my dear.
(*She turns to go, hurt.*)
Hold on. There is something that I would like to discuss with you a little while later. Don't go too far.
(*IVY exits, giving AUSTEN a look.*)
Sit down all of you.
(*They find places to sit, except AUSTEN and NEVILLE who remain standing.*)

IDA: What's all this about, Papa?

JOSEPH: You'll see. The house is in session. (*Pause.*) Because, in a week or so, Austen will be leaving us, I have been feeling that this marks the end of an epoch. We have all been together for a long time. Once one goes, well, then the dam is breached. You will all go in time. Mary won't, I hope. This house has always been a sacred place to me. Everything that I hold dear is represented. Much of what goes on in the heart of a parent is mysterious, as you will have observed. However, everything has its span… (*His voice breaks.*) Excuse me… (*He takes out a handkerchief.*)

NEVILLE: He's got his notes written on that.

BEATRICE: Neville!

JOSEPH: Neville always has to have his little joke. What I want to tell you is that I have decided to retire from public life.

IDA: I don't believe you.

JOSEPH: It's a good time to go.

BEATRICE: What about the premiership? Don't you want it now?

JOSEPH: Not to die for it.

BEATRICE: Papa, you don't know when or how you're going to die any more than anyone else. Isn't this just scaremongering? Most politicians in their prime are well over sixty. And you still lock so young; certainly not like someone ready to retire.

JOSEPH: They've got me frightened, Bee. They're saying that I can't do it.

BEATRICE: I say you can do it. All those who say Joe should fight on say 'aye'.

HILDA: Aye.

IDA: Aye.

BEATRICE: Aye.

(*JOSEPH looks at AUSTEN who smiles as if to say 'do you need to ask', then at MARY and NEVILLE who stay silent.*)

JOSEPH: Looks like I have the casting vote. You stern daughters of mine, Greek tragedians to the core, haven't convinced me that I have to embrace destiny, I'm afraid. What's the fuss about? It's a thankless job, being PM. Why should I shorten my life for it? Neville's right. My ambitions are hollow.

NEVILLE: Is that what I said?

JOSEPH: And so many things have changed. The family is falling apart.

AUSTEN: Don't say that, Papa!

JOSEPH: I have to. How will I absorb it all if I resist and carry blindly on believing that everything is just the same. I'm going to be alone.

HILDA: You won't be alone! You'll never be alone, Papa. I'll be here, Ida will be here, Neville, Bee, Mary... How many do you want?

JOSEPH: No, no. I believe everyone should think about the future in a different way.

BEATRICE: But, Papa, we're so close. We depend upon one other enormously. It will never break up.

AUSTEN: I'll be back often, sir. Just because I'm getting married it doesn't mean that I'm not part of the family.

JOSEPH: I've made up my mind. It's all over.

HILDA: Well, I think it's outrageous of you. What's made you suddenly be so defeatist?

(*JOSEPH looks across at NEVILLE.*)

Neville? Oh, Papa, come on. Neville was only being stupid.

JOSEPH: He made me think. Neville sees into the centre of things, sometimes. I'm an old man, a violent old man according to you all. That is shameful. At seventy? Rushing around, talking about war, relishing conflict? What's happened to my gardens? My plants? Isn't that enough?

BEATRICE: No it isn't, and you know it.

JOSEPH: Then it should be. Ought a man of my years run an empire? It's a nonsensical idea. So, there we are. I give up, I give my ambitions the coup de grace. That was all I wanted to say. You can all go about your business now.

NEVILLE: Are you going to make an announcement to this effect?

JOSEPH: Yes. Everyone in the world knows it's my seventieth birthday and they'll understand why I've chosen this moment to retire. It will be seen as perfectly natural. Does that satisfy you, Neville?

IDA: But it's not natural, is it? It's not natural at all. It's not you, Papa. You're a fighter. You don't give into anyone, most of all yourself.

JOSEPH: Thank you Ida, always my loyal supporter.

IDA: More than that. You live a great deal of my life for me. I live through you, Papa. I do things through you. When you accomplish something I share in that.

JOSEPH: Austen must have that role now.

IDA: (*Flaring up.*) Austen isn't you!

BEATRICE: All right, Ida don't raise the temperature. Austen does his best.

IDA: I don't know what I'll do with myself. Where will I go? There's nowhere.

JOSEPH: This isn't all going to happen immediately, Ida, my darling. There'll be plenty of time for you to adjust. Don't forget, there's the whole world out there.

IDA: I don't want the whole world. You're the one who's always wanted the whole world. Why can't you just keep doing that?

(*Pause. JOSEPH stands up, adjusts his jacket.*)

JOSEPH: Well, I'll leave you all to discuss it. See you at dinner. I'm going for a stroll in the garden with my beautiful wife whom I hope I have made very happy. (*Exits*

119

left through the conservatory.)

NEVILLE: He doesn't mean a word he says. He has no intention of retiring.

IDA: Yes, he does. Yes, he does. And it's your fault you fool.

NEVILLE: Do you think that I could achieve what the whole Liberal Party and the Tory Party failed to do – to break the great Joe Chamberlain? He broke them! By changing his mind, going back on his word, shifting his ground, he's brought them all to the verge of destruction at one time or another. And if he chooses he can do the same to me, or any one of us, and he knows it. Sometimes I think he's broken us already.

(*Pause. They all look at him.*)

AUSTEN: You have to withdraw that.

BEATRICE: And apologise to Papa. We'll leave you to think about it. Try to face up to yourself for once.

(*General exit except for NEVILLE.*
JERICHO enters.)

JERICHO: Short trip, Mr Neville?

NEVILLE: They ganged up on me. He was brilliant, as usual.

JERICHO: You're staying, then?

NEVILLE: The Chamberlain show goes on. I'll be glad to get back to my office, shut the door and hypnotise myself with accounts.

(*The telephone rings. JERICHO answers it.*)

JERICHO: Highbury, the residence of Mr Joseph, Mr Austen, Mr Neville for the moment, Mrs Mary, Miss Beatrice, Miss Ida and Miss Hilda Chamberlain...yes, sir...I'll get him.

(*JERICHO winks at NEVILLE and exits left.*
NEVILLE puts the telephone receiver down the front of his trousers.)

NEVILLE: Big Joe Chamberlain, the molten core of the earth, speaking. What is your question? What is left undone in my life? Well, let me see: I've made a highly competitive screw, won a war single-handed, built a university with the most rampant tower in the Midlands. Oh, it can be see for miles!... Been married three times...sired five dwarves... Yes, yes, we can safely say that the only active volcano in Birmingham is still erupting and terrifying the local inhabitants. But there is still something left outstanding and you're talking to it.

(*JOSEPH enters.*

NEVILLE quickly pulls the receiver out of his trousers and gives it to him.

JOSEPH stares at the telephone, puts it to his cheek, wrinkles up his nose when he finds it warm, then speaks into it, keeping it away from his mouth.)

JOSEPH: Harry? Sorry to keep you waiting no, not at all. You're not interrupting anything. All the celebrations are over. Back to work...yes, very pleasant...the family were wonderful, making a great fuss of me... Did he really? ... Well, that's better than a kick in the teeth, I suppose...

(*IDA and HILDA come onto the balcony and listen, smiling.*)

...yes, I take your point, but I don't want anything you do to overlap with my efforts at Lady Cunard's. It's too obvious. Wait a couple of days and the mention it to him...of course, then we can make a move...well, even if it doesn't work it will sow a little dissension in the ranks. That shouldn't be too difficult. I reckon that 102 Tory MPs are with me against Free Trade. All we have to do is keep stirring them up. (*Pause.*) Yes, Austen will be in touch...and Harry, I'll be looking for a seat on the council for Neville shortly...he's more than ready...oh, yes, he's keen, very keen...exactly, a chip off the old block... Good night, Harry. (*Puts the phone down.*)

(*During the phone call IDA and HILDA have descended the stairs, AUSTEN has entered from left and NEVILLE has entered from the conservatory. IDA goes to JOSEPH and kisses him on the cheek.*)

Just tying up a few loose ends.

IDA: I'm so glad, Papa. (*Exits.*)

JOSEPH: Have you got anything to say to me, Mary?

MARY: Joe, all I can do is wait and see. There isn't a move you make that hasn't got more than one meaning.

JOSEPH: I've made my intentions perfectly clear. Now, I'll have a word with that Dundas girl.

MARY: What are you going to say to her?

JOSEPH: Only a chat. I've been meaning to do it since she arrived. Don't look so nervous. I know how to deal with young women. Will you ask her to come to me?

MARY: Be careful, Joe. Don't queer Austen's pitch again.

(*JOSEPH gives her a frown, then looks away.*
MARY comes over and kisses his cheek.)

Don't worry. I'm glad you did. (*Exits.*)

JOSEPH: (*To himself.*) Women, women, women.

(*AUSTEN enters with IVY.*)

AUSTEN: Is this to be a private interview, Papa?

JOSEPH: Yes.

AUSTEN: Ivy is quite anxious.

JOSEPH: She has no cause to be. (*Pause. He looks hard at AUS-TEN.*) I'd like to make a start.

(*AUSTEN exits unwillingly, giving IVY a last look.*)

Sit d own.

(*IVY sits where he indicates on the sofa.*)

I feel a great affinity with you, Miss Dundas. Mary was your age when I married her. She brought a lot of beauty and freshness into my life at a time when I was in sore need of it. But, Austen. (*Pause.*) Austen. A sweet and noble soul.

IVY: Yes.

JOSEPH: A good man in a vile world. One of Nature's genuine innocents. (*Pause.*) Do you know much about men? Are you strong?

IVY: (*Flustered.*) I think so…fairly…

JOSEPH: I don't want Austen to be hurt.

IVY: All I'm doing is marrying him.

JOSEPH: You're a lot younger than he is. (*Pause. He sits next to her on the sofa.*) 'What a hypocrite,' you're thinking. But I had had two wives before and I was no innocent. Both of them died in childbirth. I killed them, in a way. That was my nightmare, nonsense though it sounds. Er…women must be strong… (*He seems confused.*) Sorry…are you able to follow me? (*Sharp cry of surprise.*) Wha…wha…oh… (*Holds out a hand to her.*) Hold!

(*IVY is terrified, but she takes his hand. Pause.*)

Is this sofa propped up on anything

IVY: Not that I can see.

JOSEPH: It's n…n…not on a tilt?

IVY: No, I don't think so.

JOSEPH: Look.

(*He releases IVY's hand.*
She stands up and examines the sofa.)

IVY: There's nothing the matter with it.

JOSEPH: Sit down.

(*IVY obeys.*
JOSEPH reaches for her hand again.)
Someth...some...uh...very odd...hell! (*He touches his mouth.*)

IVY: Are you ill, Mr Chamberlain?

JOSEPH: (*Clinging to her.*) No...musn't...oh, God...here we go... (*Puts his head on her breast.*) Hold me. Don't let go.

IVY: I must get you some help.

JOSEPH: (*Violently.*) No!

IVY: Please let me. I don't know what to do.

(*She struggles to release herself.*
JERICHO enters. Pause.
JOSEPH looks at him and snarls.)

JOSEPH: Get out! No men!

IVY: He needs a doctor.

JERICHO: Do you need your doctor, Mr Joseph?

JOSEPH: No.

(*He lets go of IVY.*
She gets to her feet, upset and shaken.)

JERICHO: Do you still want me to get out?

JOSEPH: No. You'd better stay. Can you see if this sofa's st... (*Pause. He takes a deep breath.*) Standing unevenly.

JERICHO: (*Bending down to look at the bottom of the sofa.*) No, it's standing steady like it should. Did something happen? Did the sofa misbehave?

(*IVY whimpers, nearly in tears.*)

JOSEPH: I apologise for having upset you, Miss Dundas. Yes....perhaps Joey's had a visitation. Wasn't prepared for it. Don't worry, my dear, it's all going away now.

IVY: May I go to Austen?

JOSEPH: Soon. When I've got my breath back. Whew. It's passing, thank God. (*Laughs.*) Must be something I ate. No matter, the angel's flown on.

IVY: (*Recovering her composure a little.*) Are you really feeling better?

JOSEPH: Oh, yes. Much improved. Hm. (*Touches his mouth.*)

IVY: Are you certain?

JOSEPH: Please…don't be concerned…had this on and off all my life. A childhood complaint.

JERICHO: Mr Joseph, don't be proud. You need looking at.

JOSEPH: I forbid you to mention it to the others. See? It's left me. I'm all right.

(*Pause. He stands up shakily.*

JERICHO takes his arm.)

Thank you, Miss Dundas… Ivy… (*Smiles.*) Our secret?

IVY: I'm sorry but I have to tell your wife.

JOSEPH: No!

(*IVY runs out.*)

JERICHO: Better sit down again, Mr Joseph. What hit you?

(*JOSEPH sits down with JERICHO's help.*

JERICHO sits down beside him.)

JOSEPH: A moment of weakness. Now listen to them.

(*Slow fade to blackout as the family run in and stand around JOSEPH, staring at him. Lights up on JERICHO frontstage.*)

JERICHO: He lied to them, of course. It was his word against that of an inexperienced young woman who had held him in awe until she found his head on her bosom. That was never mentioned. Miss Ivy said that he'd been ill. He said that he had been playing optical games. Everyone knew the truth, him most of all. It was a warning which he chose not to heed, and no one could heed it for him.

(*The telephone rings.*

JERICHO answers it, listens, covers the mouthpiece.)

It's the Palace. Frequent callers. Mr Joseph has always turned down offers of elevation to the peerage and that kind of thing, but now, with an obituary in mind, a corner of the Abbey, he might think again.

(*AUSTEN enters.*)

AUSTEN: Who's that?

JERICHO: Buckingham calling Birmingham.

AUSTEN: Give it to me. Hello Austen Chamberlain speaking. I'm afraid that no such invitation has arrived… Yes, the postal services under this government are not really up to scratch, are they? …Well, I can ask him but I'm fairly

certain that he has an appointment on that day. Yes, I'm
sure that the Sultan of Sokoto would like to meet him but
my father is a busy man...
(*JOSEPH enters.*)
JOSEPH: Is that for me?
(*AUSTEN holds out the telephone.*
JOSEPH takes it and begins to speak soundlessly.
AUSTEN stands by looking anxious.
As the telephone call continues MARY appears on the
balcony and listens.)
JERICHO: Mr Joseph will squeeze the Sultan of Sokoto
into the diary for his raid on London, somehow. This old
Islamic ruler from the middle of nowhere grows a lot of
peanuts. Mr Joseph will tell him that if the Nigerian peanut
price is not protected the American peanut will drive it out
of the market place. Then he will talk about a guaranteed
price for Nigerian peanuts on the London peanut exchange
no matter what they cost to produce, which is the only
scheme that would have saved Chamberlain.
JOSEPH: (*Still on the telephone.*) Thank you yes, I've got all
that. Goodbye. (*Puts receiver down.*) The Sokoto region is
vast, apparently. Huge potential.
AUSTEN: Yes, sir.
MARY: Is there any space left in your schedule to take me to
the opera, Joe?
JOSEPH: Er – Thursday night? Anything that you'd
particularly like to see?
MARY: Oh, I just want a little light entertainment. Is *The*
Twilight of the Golds on anywhere? (*Exits.*)
JOSEPH: I think we'll take Neville to meet this Sultan as well.
It's about time that he started learning how to deal with
people at this level.
AUSTEN: Am I to go as well, sir? I thought that in view of the
wedding being so close...
JOSEPH: Austen, you *always* accompany me when it's
anything to do with foreign relations, and for a reason that
you understand. What language does he speak?
AUSTEN: I think that it will be Hausa, but I'll check.
JOSEPH: Write out a few useful phrases that I can learn. You
know the kind of thing: 'Hello, how are you?' 'Good Luck!'

'How's your father?' They like it when they can see that you've taken some trouble.

AUSTEN: I'll do that, sir.

JOSEPH: You can come back to Birmingham with Neville straight after the garden-party. I won't have any further need of you for the rest of the week.

AUSTEN: I do wish that you would cancel this visit, sir.

JOSEPH: Et tu Brute?

(JOSEPH laughs and takes AUSTEN's arm. They exit left together.

JERICHO enters.)

JERICHO: On the night before they went to London, Mr Joseph came to the pantry and we had a glass of rum. In fact we had half a bottle. I could see that the man was excited by the trip, as if he anticipated squaring up to his most dangerous political adversary. We talked a bit about sons and how to bring them up, but that wasn't the thing on his mind. There was no room for children where he was headed. When he left I went to bed and lay there thinking for a while. 'That man knows what's coming,' I said to myself, 'and the strange thing is, he's not afraid.'

(Blackout.

Dragging sounds in the darkness.

Lights up on AUSTEN, NEVILLE, BEATRICE, HILDA, IDA and IVY as they drag large canvas sacks on stage between the plants.)

BEATRICE: Would you believe anyone could get so many birthday cards?

NEVILLE: I hate doing his mail. It's like living in his armpit. You've always got something to moan about, haven't you, Neville? How did you get on at the banquet?

HILDA: Yes, tell us about the Sultan of wherever-it-was. Carve him up.

NEVILLE: I never got to speak to him. Papa did all the talking, as usual. Surprising what he knows about peanuts if pressed.

IDA: What was this old sultan like?

NEVILLE: He was short, fat and kept laughing at nothing. To

be honest I thought the man was inebriated.

HILDA: How dreadful. Did you have a good time as well?

NEVILLE: Austen did. He knows what it's all about. I just
found it all a bit pointless, people just floundering about
gassing.

IDA: And Papa was all right?

NEVILLE: Going full steam ahead from what I could see. By
the time we left held agreed to make a couple of speeches,
attend a few meetings, and take over the universe. Mary
was getting madder and madder but to no effect. He just
carried on, regardless. Watching him operate at these
affairs is quite fascinating. He collars someone, sucks what
he wants out of them, digests it in a flash, then moves on to
the next like a snake in a top hat.

IDA: Don't call him a snake.

NEVILLE: You have to be a snake to be a politician. Ask
Adam.

*(They undo some of the sacks and empty the mail onto
the floor.*

BEATRICE hands out pads and pencils.)

BEATRICE: Let's make a start. There's loads to get through.
When you open an envelope enter the name and address
on your list and grade the sender: A is for top people who
will get a personal, hand written reply from Papa; B is for
party workers and useful acquaintances and they'll get
a standard, printed letter which Papa will sign; C is for
ordinary people. Papa has a card for them; and D is for
children who get a picture postcard of the university tower.

NEVILLE: Bee, wouldn't it be better if each of us kept four
lists instead of one? Then we wouldn't have the job of
compiling lists of all the As, Bs and so on at the end.

HILDA: Very good at the paperwork, our Neville. One of
Nature's bureaucrats.

NEVILLE: God, I have to be good at something!

AUSTEN: Is it to be four lists each then?

BEATRICE: I think so. We mustn't stifle Neville's innovative
urges, must we?

IDA: Beast! *(Tears up a letter.)* How absolutely foul and cruel!

BEATRICE: Don't tear up the bad ones, Ida. It will waste

time.

NEVILLE: Bee, you haven't got this at all organised, have you? Forget lists. All we need is a pile for As, a pile for Bs, Cs and Ds, and a pile for the furnace. Here, put them in the middle and we'll all sit round to cut down the to-ing and fro-ing.

(*NEVILLE arranges the sacks and puts people in place.*)

AUSTEN: Postmaster-General for you in the cabinet on this showing, I should think, Neville.

NEVILLE: The thing I can't stand about you politicians is the amount of time and energy that you waste.

AUSTEN: That's called democracy.

NEVILLE: Oh, rubbish! Everything is excused by blaming it on democracy. There's nothing democratic about confusion. Common sense and good, efficient business practice would do wonders for Westminster, as far as I can see. But you wouldn't dirty your hands with that, would you Austen? You'd rather be in the Carlton Club talking about the rear quarters of racehorses from which all wisdom in England emanates.

AUSTEN: Come on, Neville. Ivy's here, remember. She's not used to that kind of talk yet.

IVY: I don't mind. Do you spend all your time in the Carlton Club?

AUSTEN: Of course not. That's all part of Neville's Birmingham business man's private mythology. Since he started making ship's bunks he's been positively anti-establishment, poor fellow. Not a good word to say for anyone. But if you did get the call, Neville, and had to choose a cabinet post, which one would you prefer?

NEVILLE: Oh, something to do with health or housing, one of those practical, boring ministries. I'd leave all the flash stuff to you.

IDA: Would you say Beatrice Webb was a B for a useful acquaintance or a C for an ordinary person?

HILDA: I think old girlfriends must be A or furnace.

BEATRICE: She's a socialist which merits the D for children but put her in A and let Papa decide for himself.

IVY: All this for one man? It's incredible. To arouse all this feeling in people. How does he do it?

BEATRICE: Leadership. People look up to him so they write to him.

NEVILLE: The more leadership we accept the more we lessen ourselves.

BEATRICE: Oh, do be quiet, Neville. Where did you pick that up from, you old parrot?

NEVILLE: A thought I had after we came back from London. When he's not here this damned house doesn't make any sense.

HILDA: The Italian ambassador?

AUSTEN: Has to be A. All ambassadors have to be A, even if it's someone we don't like.

IDA: I wish they'd ring.

BEATRICE: Mary's very good. If there was any trouble she'd let us know right away.

HILDA: He'll be all right.

IDA: Of course he will.

BEATRICE: He has enormous inner resources, but I do hope Mary isn't undermining him too much now she has him to herself. Good Lord, here's one from that self-important little know-all, Winston Churchill. I must say, I don't know why Papa rates him so highly.

AUSTEN: Steady on. Winston's a good friend of mine.

BEATRICE: What is it about him that Papa admires so much?

AUSTEN: The man has courage, talent and brains. And he's a fighter.

NEVILLE: Everything we're not, eh, Austen?

AUSTEN: You speak for yourself. I can fight if I need to.

NEVILLE: Have you got courage, talent and brains, though?

(*The telephone rings.*

AUSTEN answers it.

NEVILLE rips open a letter.)

AUSTEN: Mr Chamberlain's residence…yes I see…is that serious?

(*IDA covers her ears.*)

Well, if it was best coal we ordered I suppose we might as well wait…no, we have very little but it's summer and we

wanted to stock up at the lower price... thank you.
(*AUSTEN puts the telephone down.*
HILDA pulls IDA's hands from her ears.)
HILDA: It's all right. It was the coalman.
(*AUSTEN goes back to IVY and sits beside her, opening letters. Relieved that the telephone call was not what they feared, they find a mood of strange gaiety.*)
Oh, I've got an A.
(*NEVILLE gives an a note on the piano.*)
(*Sings.*) A A A A A!
BEATRICE: (*Sings.*) But I've got yet another boring C!
(*NEVILLE gives a C note.*)
ALL: (*Singing.*) Boring C C C C C!
IDA: (*Sings.*) And yet another C.
AUSTEN: (*Sings.*) And another C. When will it end?
IVY: (*Sings.*) C again!
BEATRICE: (*Sings.*) At last, a D!
IDA: (*Sings.*) A run on D.
HILDA: (*Sings.*) No, we're back to good old C.
AUSTEN: (*Sings.*) Cs of the world unite!
NEVILLE: (*Sings.*) I see said the blind man!
IDA: (*Sings.*) The see of Canterbury!
HILDA: (*Sings.*) I must go down to the sea again, to the lonely sea and the sky.
IVY: Would you say an A? (*Shows a letter to AUSTEN.*)
AUSTEN: Er let's see (*Looks at the letter.*) No, I'd say (*Sings.*) a B.
IVY: (*Sings.*) B?
AUSTEN: (*Sings.*) Definitely only worth a B.
BEATRICE: (*Sings.*) A C from Selly Oak!
HILDA: (*Sings.*) A C from Edgbaston!
IDA: (*Sings.*) A D from dear old Broad Street!
NEVILLE: (*Sings.*) A C from Saint Mary's.
IDA: Eeeeeee!
NEVILLE: You can't have an E, Ida. We haven't got an E category. Play fair.
IDA: This Envelope is Empty!
(*Laughter. The telephone rings. Pause. They look at each other. NEVILLE answers it.*)

NEVILLE: Neville Chamberlain speaking.
> (*Pause. They continue sorting the mail in silence.*)
> (*Low, into the telephone.*) Yes I see of course we will…yes, I'll get that done…yes, I've got that straight…do tell him that we all love him…
> (*They stop sorting the mail.*)
> …tell him not to worry. Everything will be looked after at this end…God bless…Cheerio…
> (*He replaces the receiver.*
> *They are all sitting, looking up at him.*)
> Papa's had a stroke.

BEATRICE: Oh, God!

IDA: I knew it, I knew it!

NEVILLE: He's paralysed down his right side.

IDA: (*Hysterically.*) He'd rather be dead! I know him. He'd rather be dead. He'll leave us.

HILDA: Stop that! What does the doctor say?

NEVILLE: Papa can't speak properly so I couldn't talk to him, but I gather from Mary…well, it's too early to tell what damage has been done.

AUSTEN: Is his life in danger?

NEVILLE: They don't know. Mary sounded so angry, I couldn't get all that much sense out of her.

AUSTEN: (*Sharply.*) I think whether his life is in danger or not is a question to which we must have an answer. I'll ring.

NEVILLE: Please don't. Mary was on the verge of being out of control, she was so indignant.

BEATRICE: Well, the main thing is, he isn't dead.

IDA: I must go to him.

NEVILLE: No, we must stay here. Mary says that Papa has given her instructions. We are to stay put until he calls us.

HILDA: He can't be that bad if he's still bossing Mary around, can he?

NEVILLE: God knows what's going on down there.
> (*The telephone rings again, NEVILLE snatches it up.*)

NEVILLE: Neville Chamberlain speaking! Yes! Hello, Mary…yes…yes, I've told them…

BEATRICE: Let me speak to her.

NEVILLE: (*Waving her away.*) Yes! If that's what he wants

then that's how it will be...obviously, we'd like as much information as you can give us...yes, yes, when you have a moment...well, you wouldn't expect him to be any different, would you?...Yes, don't worry...I'll look after everything... Ring again when you can... Cheerio. (*Replaces the telephone receiver.*) He's being difficult.

BEATRICE: Well, that's promising anyway.

NEVILLE: He doesn't want his political enemies to get any advantage out of the situation.

AUSTEN: Yes, I was just thinking about that.

NEVILLE: He wants us to go to London one by one as if nothing had happened. We mustn't go as a group and we mustn't talk about it to anyone. That's absolutely essential. He's very ill and he won't be seen in public for a while. If we are asked why, we have to say that he's got gout.

IDA: Gout! That's stupid! What's he playing at?

HILDA: Who's going to believe that?

NEVILLE: Anyone who knows his drinking habits would. Anyhow, that's the only information people are going to get.

AUSTEN: Papa's right. We must keep it a secret for as long as we can so it doesn't jeopardise his chances.

BEATRICE: He'll recover, you'll see.

AUSTEN: I'd better go down first. There's a lot to attend to.

NEVILLE: No, he wants you to stay here with Ivy and prepare for your wedding. He's very determined to be there but that only gives him eight days to get back on his feet.

HILDA: Eight days? You don't get over a stroke in eight days!

NEVILLE: Ordinary mortals don't, but we're dealing with Joe Chamberlain. He's worried that it will be noticed if he's not at the wedding.

IDA: Did he say that?

NEVILLE: He did. I'm afraid he still thinks he can be Prime Minister, which is, of course, nonsense.

AUSTEN: (*Pause.*) Do you think so? (*Pause.*) I expect you're right.

NEVILLE: Well, you can't do that job if you're half-dead, can you?

HILDA: Shut up, Neville.

IDA: How can you stand there and say things like that?

NEVILLE: He wouldn't want me to pity him.

(*IDA starts crying.*)

BEATRICE: Try to keep it down, darling. It's a terrible time, I know, but we must deal with it sensibly.

HILDA: Oh, let the woman cry, for God's sake! Her world has fallen apart, hasn't it? Isn't that worth crying about? I wish I could join her.

AUSTEN: Papa isn't dead, Hilda.

HILDA: He's as good as dead. Papa paralysed? Can you imagine that? All his wonderful energy choking inside him.

NEVILLE: Steady on! Whatever you do, don't let him hear you say that.

HILDA: (*In an outburst.*) What d'you take me for? Am I the one who's attacked and tormented and contradicted him? You should be ashamed, but you're not because the only person you care about is yourself. I'm disgusted with the way you've been behaving. He's probably had a stroke because of you!

BEATRICE: Hilda! That's a horribly unfair thing to say. You mustn't put a thought like that into Neville's head. Please, take no notice... I'm sure that she didn't mean it.

HILDA: I did. And Austen's no better, standing there waiting to step into Papa's shoes. But you'll never get near him, not within a thousand miles. Look at you, a useless pale imitation. By God, we must mourn Joe Chamberlain. Neither of you two are half the man that he was. You just haven't come up to the mark. If I'd had the chance to be his son and model myself on him I'd have made a better job of it. (*Pause.*) I'm sorry. I don't know what I'm saying. Forgive me... I should be crying but I can't...I'm so wretched... I love him so much...if I could have the stroke in his place I would... (*Weeps.*)

AUSTEN: Sorry, but I can't bear this.

HILDA: You should be able to bear it, damn you! Papa can even when he's at death's door.

BEATRICE: Sssh, Hilda, darling. It's just rotten luck. It had to happen now, of course! If he'd got through the next couple of weeks he'd have stood a chance, poor man. He'll get better. Let's look on the bright side.

HILDA: (*Furiously.*) There isn't a bloody bright side!

AUSTEN: I must postpone the wedding. I can't possibly get married under these circumstances.

HILDA: Oh, get on and marry the girl. Who cares? I don't.

IDA: I'll never get married now, I swear. It's unthinkable.

NEVILLE: Papa insists that you go ahead with the wedding, Austen.

AUSTEN: You see? No one mentions Ivy. Is anyone worried about her?

IDA: That's your job, isn't it? You brought her here so you look after her. We've got other things to think about now.

AUSTEN: Poor Ivy. She'd be better off staying out of this family. If I broke it off I'd be doing her a favour.

(*IVY runs off.*
AUSTEN goes after her with NEVILLE.
Music. Lights dim.
Enter JERICHO pulling a mail sack. He drags it to the sofa and delivers it to BEATRICE, HILDA and IDA.
The sack moves. They open it and bring their stricken father out and sit him on the sofa.)

JERICHO: Mr Austen did get married but his father was one of those not at the feast. Mr Joseph did not recover. He remained half-paralysed and he had lost the power of speech. But this did not stop him standing for Parliament when the next election came round – it was all the standing he could manage – and the people of Birmingham put the shell of their hero back in his seat. When he appeared at the House of Commons to take the oath of loyalty as the member for West Birmingham, he had to have help.

BEATRICE: I, Joseph Chamberlain, swear by Almighty God, that…

HILDA: I will be faithful and bear true allegiance to…

IDA: His Majesty King Edward, his heirs and successors as a chorus according to law. So help me God.

JERICHO: With Mr Neville it was a time of change. Now that his father was an invalid he found it easier to obey his wishes. By 1914 he was a Birmingham city councillor and well on the way to becoming Lord Mayor like his father before him.

BEATRICE: Are you ready for your daily briefing, Papa?

(*JOSEPH nods.*

MARY enters to the landing dressed in mourning with white sheets folded over her arm.)

MARY: This house has had its day. We can't stay here any longer.

BEATRICE: We now have more details of the assassination of the Archduke Ferdinand in Serbia on June the twenty-eighth.

MARY: We have to move.

BEATRICE: I must say, Papa, that it has all the makings of 1914's biggest love-story.

(*MARY paces slowly up and down hugging the sheets.*)

The Archduke had married someone who was not suitable and, as it has turned out, is the reason for his downfall. Because he had fallen for a woman who was selfish, vain and desperate for the limelight, he took a decision which would kill him, and her, as it happened. Do you want to hear more or might it prove too upsetting.

(*JOSEPH nods and signals by mime that he wants a cigar.*)

Get him a cigar, Hilda.

(*HILDA selects a cigar from the box.*)

The Emperor, the Archduke's father, was extremely displeased with having this featherbrained embarrassment as a daughter-in-law and he issued a protocol that she should never appear at the Archduke's side on state occasions. But it seems that Ferdinand was so besotted with his wife, whom he thought beautiful beyond measure, though opinions differ here, that he found a way of getting round his father's commandment.

MARY: Joe, let's spend more time in London. Let's travel; go to France, Germany, Italy, see the sights. It'll be good for you.

BEATRICE: As a field-marshal of the Austro-Hungarian Empire, the Archduke had the right to take his wife with him on all ceremonial military inspections. So, on his wedding anniversary she accompanied him at a review of imperial troops which were occupying Sarajevo.

MARY: (*Throwing down a sheet.*) Cover the furniture. We're going.

BEATRICE: On the fatal day, one person had already thrown a bomb at the Archduke's car which had missed the mark, but, such was his desire to show off his wife, that he insisted upon continuing with the procession.

(*HILDA lights a match waiting until the gases have burnt off, then gets the cigar going.*)

His chauffeur took a wrong turning into a cul-de-sac. (*Suddenly increases the pace.*) Trying to reverse out. Schoolboy jumps onto running board. Bang! Through the Archduke's heart! Bang! Through the floozy's head! Blood everywhere! People screaming! Chaos, Papa! Mayhem! (*Pause.*) I hope you didn't find that too disturbing.

(*JOSEPH smiles and holds up his hand for the cigar.*
HILDA puts it to his lips, then takes it away.)

Only a little puff, Papa, Not too much at once. Isn't it shocking that the assassin was a schoolboy?

(*JOSEPH mutters.*
BEATRICE leans forward to hear.)

No, you may not hold your own cigar: and no, the schoolboy was not wearing short trousers.

MARY: (*Throwing down another sheet.*) C'mon, help me, will you? Let's get out of this old place. It's so gloomy, so oppressive. You need sunshine, Joe, flowers, music. (*Sings.*)
You are my honey honeysuckle
I am the bee –

BEATRICE: Give him another puff, Hilda, then you can finish it yourself.

(*HILDA puts the cigar between JOSEPH's lips and gives him a puff.*
IDA puts his socks and shoes back on then collects his nail parings.)

Austro-Hungary is mobilising against Serbia. Russia is mobilising against Austro-Hungary. Germany is mobilising against Russia. Where will it end? Will we be involved?

(*JOSEPH smiles and nods.*)

But are we ready to fight?

(*JOSEPH smiles and shakes his head.*)

MARY: (*Throwing the last sheet down.*) For God's sake, Joe, let's go to the Mediterranean and forget all about Birmingham! I'm going to pack.

(*MARY exits to her bedroom.*

JERICHO enters and helps BEATRICE, HILDA and IDA to cover the furniture, then the sisters exit.)

JERICHO: Mr Joseph died that day. Maybe it was the excitement. No one bothered to measure how many miles of people lined the streets of Birmingham for his funeral. Everyone's mind was on the Great War that was coming. Behind him, Mr Joseph left two sons who loved peace at all costs, and a city that became a boom town as the guns began to open up in Flanders. Seven years after that great blood-letting, Mr Austen had his chance to be himself in the Mediterranean. Ahoy there! Anyone seen the white whale?

(*Enter AUSTEN in yachting white and cap.*

MUSSOLINI runs on in a pair of trunks with a towel round his shoulders. He runs on the spot for a moment as he dries himself.)

MUSSOLINI: Mr Foreign Secretary, I like to be loved. I like to be friends. To have you with me on my yacht is a great pleasure. You know every day I receive sacks and sacks of letters from women all over Italy who want to make love to me. My secretary writes back and asks for a photograph. Then, if she looks good, he arranges an appointment, usually in the afternoon. I like love in the afternoon, don't you?

AUSTEN: It's as good a time as any, I suppose. But about Germany –

MUSSOLINI: Do you know, Mr Chamberlain, every one of those women gets pregnant. There are now thousands of little Mussolinis running around in Italy.

AUSTEN: Really?

MUSSOLINI: And they will all grow up naturally, not in my direct shadow but in the sunshine of my leadership. We believe that this is the best kind of influence over the young.

AUSTEN: What do you think of my proposals for the Treaty of Locarno?

MUSSOLINI: I agree.

AUSTEN: You have no alterations or amendments?

MUSSOLINI: If Germany invades France then Italy will invade her.

AUSTEN: Ah. What my text actually says is that if Germany invades France then Italy will invade Germany.

MUSSOLINI: Isn't that what I said?

AUSTEN: The terms of the treaty have to be precise. No government must be able to misunderstand or misinterpret them. If we leave it at 'If Germany invades France then Italy will invade her', then it could be taken to mean 'If Germany invades France then Italy will invade France'. Do you see my point?

MUSSOLINI: What a strange way of thinking you have. I am not a pedantic man. I follow the general thrust of what people say.

AUSTEN: Nonetheless, and with the greatest of respect. Sir, I submit that the distinction that I am making is a vital one.

MUSSOLINI: (*Angrily.*) When will you get it into your head that we're a team? It's time that we three sorted ourselves out. There's been too much groping in the dark for my liking.

(*A big crash of breaking glass from the direction of the conservatory.*)

Go and open a window, Austen, and let that damn thing out, whatever it is. (*Exits.*)

(*AUSTEN runs to the conservatory.*

More breaking glass. The flapping of wings. Pause.

HITLER enters from the conservatory.

NEVILLE enters from left in a dark coat and hat, carrying a gladstone bag. He is now grey: the man who went to Munich in 1938. He sees HITLER and halts.)

NEVILLE: Pardon me.

HITLER: No, pardon me for springing this surprise.

NEVILLE: I didn't think that you'd be here. Is this my room?

HITLER: After our brief meeting at the airport I became

impatient to know you better, so I came on ahead to see your reactions to what we have prepared.

NEVILLE: (*Bemused.*) You seem to have gone to an awful lot of trouble.

HITLER: You recognise it?

NEVILLE: Highbury?

HITLER: Yes, yes! Highbury. Your father's house. We went to great pains to get it accurate. Every detail.

NEVILLE: I can see that. What can I say? This is most unexpected.

HITLER: Gothic. It's something we Germans understand.

NEVILLE: Of course.

HITLER: Can you spot something that is not quite right? You seem ill-at-ease.

NEVILLE: No, it's a bit of a shock, actually. I was anticipating something quite different.

HITLER: Well, as a politician you are accustomed to having your expectations proved wrong, no doubt, but not always as pleasurably as this. I don't know about you, but I feel at home here.

NEVILLE: I just need a little time to get used to it. (*Pause.*) May I ask, with respect, what your purpose was, Herr Hitler?

HITLER: Would you accept an act of friendship?

NEVILLE: Always.

(*Pause. HITLER walks amongst the foliage, stroking the leaves.*)

HITLER: And the plants are exactly the ones that you used to have. To find some of them was not an easy task. We had to scour Germany. The temperature in this room is kept controlled. Let me take your bag.

NEVILLE: No thank you. I'm a little chill.

HITLER: The German people are very pro-British at the moment, thanks to the enormous gamble you've taken in coming here to Munich.

NEVILLE: That's very gratifying.

HITLER: Do you wish to unpack? Don't let me get in your way.

NEVILLE: No, no.

HITLER: I hope you will be comfortable here.

NEVILLE: Thank you.

HITLER: Already I feel that there is trust between us.

NEVILLE: Do you?

(*Pause. NEVILLE is unnerved and indignant at the Highbury replica.*

HITLER sits down on the sofa and pats the place beside him.)

HITLER: Come and sit down.

NEVILLE: I'll stand for a while.

HITLER: Is it too much for you? Are you taken aback? Disorientated?

NEVILLE: Fatigued, perhaps.

HITLER: Ah, the journey.

NEVILLE: Yes.

HITLER: The journey forwards to Munich, or backwards to Birmingham?

NEVILLE: Why have you done all this?

HITLER: To make you feel at home. (*He whisks the sheet off the piano.*) Same model, same make – German, of course – same tone. Play! Play!

NEVILLE: I don't understand.

HITLER: I want these talks between us to have a chance. Everyone tells me that they are of crucial importance to the future of Europe. So, what is a little interior decoration, a few sticks of furniture compared to that? It is nothing, the least I can do for you.

NEVILLE: I wish that you hadn't. It's thirty years since I lived at Highbury.

HITLER: This was a very famous room in British politics! So much went on here. So much debate, so much decision

NEVILLE: Would it be too much of an inconvenience if I asked to be put in different quarters?

HITLER: But why? Don't you like it?

NEVILLE: Let us say that I appreciate the thought but the reality is too disconcerting.

HITLER: You find your own home, the place where you lived so happily in the bosom of your family, disconcerting?

NEVILLE: Yes.

HITLER: Incredible. Then all this has misfired?

NEVILLE: I'm afraid so.

HITLER: Give it a chance. Relax into it. I know that you are suffering from the tension of these times, but try to forget, just for a few hours.

NEVILLE: (*Raising his voice.*) I find this room very disturbing and I want to be moved!

HITLER: Disturbing? How can it be disturbing? I am giving away an advantage, some would say. Instead of feeling insecure in a strange country I want you to be surrounded by things which are familiar to you. I will confess the real reason why I have done this. To make ours a contest of equals. If we come to an agreement over German claims to Czechoslovakia then I don't want you to have been at a disadvantage, playing away.

NEVILLE: Will that make the difference between Germany's a hundred and fifty divisions and our fourteen any smaller?

HITLER: Ah, now you have started bargaining. That is for tomorrow. This evening I planned for acclimatisation. By the way, you have to mention French divisions, Soviet divisions, Czech divisions on your side, but we won't go into that now. Let us agree not to bring up the subject of war and the Sudatenland Germans again tonight. I had planned this part of your visit as all pleasure. Surely you want to get to know me better, too?

NEVILLE: Of course. And, even in this short time, I have.

HITLER: But you would never have done this much for me? No, I think not. It would have been an audience with the King, a banquet with a lot of old defunct aristocrats, and, if I was lucky, you'd have taken me fly-fishing. I was told that you were a man of soul, Mr Chamberlain. My friends, the Astors, know you well. A sensitive, shy but spiky fellow, they told me. Nostalgic. That was the key word.

(*Pause. NEVILLE shakes his head and sighs.*)

Are you nostalgic, Mr Chamberlain?

NEVILLE: This was all very misguided, Herr Hitler.

HITLER: I deal with things as they crop up. I have a policy

but personalities matter. Mine is a soldierly spirit, and to any soldier dreams of home are everything. I sympathise with your yearnings.

(*HITLER whisks the dustsheet of the stage left end of the sofa to reveal JOSEPH CHAMBERLAIN, monocle in place, staring belligerently and arrogantly.*
NEVILLE steps back, horrified.)

Isn't it good? Uncanny what they can do. You know this figure, of course, from your visit to Madame Tussaud's to see your father's waxwork. When they changed their display of great British statesmen in recent history we picked him up cheap.

(*NEVILLE approaches his father and sits beside him. He touches the waxwork's cheek. Music.*
JOSEPH turns and takes NEVILLE's head in his hands, kissing his brow, then resumes his fixed stance.)

Are you all right?

NEVILLE: Is this an attempt to drive me out of my mind?

HITLER: Certainly not. Our idea is to drive you into your mind. Yours was a formidable family, Mr Chamberlain. From small beginnings in screw-making in Birmingham your blood produced three world-class statesmen. This interests me greatly because I am thinking of founding a dynasty myself. I have found a suitable woman and I am about to make a start. What I would like from you tonight is advice on how to manage the whole business. I assume that the important thing to get right is internal political structures within the family... Are you feeling all right?

NEVILLE: Herr Hitler, I am your guest...

HITLER: My honoured guest. Is something the matter?

NEVILLE: Whatever your motives are, and, if you insist, I am compelled to believe that they are such as you have described, I would still much prefer another room.

HITLER: There are no other rooms in Munich tonight. The whole city is booked out. Everyone has come to see you! The screw-maker! Now, I have another surprise for you.

(*HITLER rings a bell and JERICHO enters with a tray of drinks. He is now seventy-seven and white-headed.*)

JERICHO: Don't think me a traitor, Mr Neville.

NEVILLE: Is it you, Jericho? I thought you'd gone back to the Bahamas.

JERICHO: I did, Mr Neville, but I couldn't stand the weather.

NEVILLE: (*Whispering to him.*) Buzz – buzz time again.

HITLER: We found him in a boarding-house in Ramsgate. He has provided us with many of our intimate insights into what forces have gone into making you the man that you are. From him we have learnt all your foibles, Mr Chamberlain.

JERICHO: They dragged it out of me, Mr Neville. Shining lights in my eyes. Keeping me awake for days. Electric shocks in private parts.

NEVILLE: This is monstrous!

HITLER: All I seem able to do is disappoint you. I thought that you might find all this good fun.

NEVILLE: Sir, you are trespassing on my innermost concerns.

HITLER: Have a drink. Whisky, isn't it? With the same amount of water. Your old slave will serve you.

JERICHO: Your usual, Mr Neville?
(*NEVILLE refuses the drink.*)
Mr Joseph would have known how to deal with him.
(*JERICHO exits.*)

HITLER: Now, when I have these sons I'm planning, how do I make them into fighting men? Give me a few hints, if you will.
(*NEVILLE does not reply.*)
Nothing to say? Come on, my boy, you can think of something. No? Never mind. Let's talk about Czechoslovakia.
(*An air-raid siren starts to wail.*
Slow fade.)

The End.

DAVID POWNALL

THE VIEWING

Characters

BESS

IAN

GUEST

JOANNA

MARION

FRED

Set in London, the present

The Viewing was first performed at Greenwich Theatre on 1 February 1987, with the following cast:

BESS, Priscilla Morgan

IAN, Greg Crutwell

MR GUEST, Graeme Garden

JOANNA, Abigail McKern

MARION, Lavinia Bertram

FRED, Jonathon Newth

Director, Alan Strachan

ACT ONE

The present.

The living room of a large commodious old house in north London. Originally this was two rooms but they have been made into one by having the separating wall removed; a free standing open spiral stairway leads to the first floor from upstage left. There is a door stage right which leads to the hall and kitchen. The room is full of furniture, carpets and pictures. Small statues, bric à brac, clocks and plants occupy all available space, there is no overall design but the contents of the room harmonise to say 'family'. A television set stands downstage left, its back to the audience. There is a telephone, a big fireplace stands on the left with an ornate fender. Only the spiral stairs have a modern feel, having a slender, delicate sweep to them. As the lights fade up BESS is sitting in an armchair reading a newspaper. Enter IAN, her grown-up son, from stage right door carrying a sports bag that is stuffed to the point where it cannot be zipped up.

IAN: Hi, Ma.

BESS: (*From behind the newspaper.*) Hi. How did you get on?

IAN: (*Throwing down the sports bag.*) We won. It was a walkover, embarrassing.

BESS: Put your dirty things in with the washing it you want them done.

IAN: Hardly worth it. I didn't get touched. I just stood on the wing. In fact I did less work than the spectator.

BESS: Another big crowd?

IAN: I think it was the referee's mother.

BESS: I'd have your things washed if I were you. I wouldn't want a son of mine to play football smelling badly. No one would pass you the ball. Why are you back so soon?

IAN: Oh, I get fed up with them. It's always the same. They get really witless, all that beer-swilling…I don't know. I think I might give up playing soon.

BESS: Hm.

(*Pause. BESS continues reading the newspaper.*

IAN takes a new football out of his sports bag.)

IAN: I've got to get this signed by the whole Liverpool football team for the Christmas raffle.

BESS: Hm-hm.

IAN: They think I can fix it because Fred's so famous.

BESS: Hm-hm.

IAN: *(Bouncing the ball.)* I'm changing sex.

BESS: Hm-hm.

IAN: There's smoke pouring out of the kitchen.

BESS: Hm-hm.

IAN: Am I talking to you or chewing a brick?

BESS: *(Putting the paper down.)* You should have stayed out with the lads. It's Saturday night, isn't it? I thought all lads went out with the lads on Saturday night? It's a good ritual. All for it myself.

IAN: Will you ask Fred if he can arrange to get this thing signed for me? Use his influence with the BBC or something.

BESS: You ask him.

IAN: I don't like asking him for anything.

BESS: He knows that. Perhaps you could give him a nice surprise.

IAN: *(Putting the ball in the fireplace.)* I'll leave it here to remind you.

BESS: *(Lifting up the paper.)* It can stay there until you swallow your pride and ask him yourself.

(IAN sits down on the arm of her chair.)

IAN: I met a man at the club who offered to let me buy into his business. He'd heard that I had some capital and was looking for a promising investment. Know *what* he does, Ma? He breeds snakes. The market for snakes is booming. Young women carry them around in their handbags, or they wear them on their heads. Believe it?

BESS: In this city, son, I would believe the news that Adolph Hitler is alive and well and running a record company.

IAN: It's rude not to look at people when you're talking to them. And you should wear your reading glasses.

BESS: You're quite drunk, aren't you?

IAN: Yes. What do you expect? Six-nil. Mad celebration.

Songs in the bar. Heroes one and all. (*Pause.*) Stupid sods. (*Pause.*) Where's Fred?

BESS: He had to go up to Cambridge.

IAN: That's his story. I reckon he's got another woman somewhere. Nuclear adultery is on its way in, you know.

BESS: Cut that out, please.

IAN: Fred's getting tired of you.

BESS: You hope. He's at a meeting. He'll be home about seven.

IAN: We can sit and talk as if we were normal people. Ma, we can actually communicate! This is a very strange sensation. Alone with my old Ma. But what's this? Her ears are pricked. Fred may be early. A helicopter has brought him. Delirium! (*Pause.*) She is waiting for Fred. That means Fred is here in her mind. When he arrives he will merely occupy his place in the present that Ma has kept warm for him all day in the future.

BESS: I am not waiting for Fred.

IAN: What are you all dressed up for then?

BESS: Someone is coming to look at the house.

IAN: (*Jumping up.*) Not that again! I can't stand it! Shits snooping about. None of them are genuine buyers. They just come in out of the fucking rain.

BESS: Stop saying that. You know I hate it.

IAN: Don't show them my room, please.

BESS: I'd avoid it if I could, but it is supposed to be part of the house.

IAN: But this has been going on for months. We've had hordes of them traipsing through – oh, I'd change that, I'd tear that up, wouldn't it be nice if they'd put in gas fires, what wallpaper!

BESS: We have to sell this week, Fred's bridging loan on the new house is costing him a fortune.

IAN: You dirty old speculator, give me that. (*Takes the paper out of her hands.*) Houses. Houses. Big houses. Bigger houses. It's all you think about these days. You drool over this kind of stuff.

BESS: (*Snatching the newspaper back.*) You'll find it interesting one day if you ever get up the courage to buy somewhere.

IAN: Is that all I need – courage?

BESS: You'll feel heroic when you pay the rates, mate.

IAN: If you do manage to sell it to someone, I won't leave. I'll barricade myself in.

BESS: Why don't you buy it off us?

IAN: Buy my own house? I'm part of the bloody brickwork! Besides I couldn't live here alone. I'd go mad.

BESS: Get married. Make it into flats. Turn it into a commune if you like. I'm sure all the lads from the pub that never closes would like to live together, wouldn't they?

IAN: You don't want to leave here any more than I do. Nor does Joanna. It's the one intelligent opinion she's got, the prat. (*Pause.*) Ma we were very happy here. Once.

BESS: So what? I'm a peasant. I'd be happy anywhere. And don't call your sister a prat. I don't know what a prat is but I don't like the sound of it.

IAN: Don't let Fred make you sell the house. Cancel it.

BESS: We've already exchanged contracts on the new place. We can't go back on it.

IAN: Come off it, Ma. Fred's got more money these days than he knows what to do with. Have two houses.

BESS: But what he's got he's earned. More than can be said of some people.

IAN: Dad wanted me to enjoy his money. He hadn't, poor sod.

BESS: He didn't want you to become a lay-about because of it.

IAN: He should have left it to you, I suppose. Knowing what you do now – the real joy of living with Fred and his warped mind – would you still do my old Dad down? Ah, so, sorry, I remember. That is an unfair question to ask any woman who has proved that she has no taste and is living with the consequences.

BESS: When we do manage to sell the house you really must find somewhere of your own to live.

IAN: I took that flat with Connie, didn't I?

BESS: You came home for your dinner most nights.

IAN: She couldn't cook to save her life. Ma, I like living here. This in our house – the house I was born in. We don't need a bigger place. What's the point of moving just because of

Fred's tax problems? Let Fred move! Have two houses and
let him live in the other one...

BESS: Don't have a bath or anything until this man has gone,
will you?

IAN: I will. I'll flash him and frighten him away, the bastard!
Ma, this is your house...

BESS: It is Fred's house and my house. From the beginning
we have done everything together, and we'll carry on that
way whether you like it or not.

IAN: Well, I don't. And no good will come of it. Dad will be
very choked off with all this. He watches over me, you
know. He's determined I'll keep you on the straight and
narrer.

(*Front door bell ringing.*)

BESS: Go upstairs. If you so much as...

IAN: (*Running up the spiral stairs.*) I'm going to use all three
toilets and piss on the floor in every one of them.

BESS: Don't act the goat. Try and be helpful for a change.

(*IAN exits.*

BESS goes to answer the door via the stage right exit.)

IAN: (*From upstairs off.*) God almighty, what's this? Dry rot?
Woodworm! Subsidence! The place is a death-trap!

(*Enter BESS with GUEST. He wears a coat and carries
a briefcase.*)

(*From the top of the spiral stair as if calling up to someone.*) Yes,
Alf, I'm afraid we'll have to tell the old lady that the whole
fucking roof needs fucking redoing, the wiring will have to
be fucking torn out, the fucking guttering is fucking lethal
and the waste-disposal unit is fucked solid.

BESS: My son is training to be a comedian.

GUEST: (*Opening his arms to the room.*) Ah! Wonderful!

BESS: This is the living room.

GUEST: There are some houses that have a positive effect as
soon as you step through the door. Something hits you and
holds you. I felt that just now as I came in.

IAN: (*Peering down from the top of the stairs.*) Ma, there's no hot
water again. The immersion heater isn't working. And the
whole central heating system is buggered into the bargain.

BESS: (*Calmly, to GUEST.*) Yes, I felt the same thing when I

155

first came here.

IAN: (*In a huge stage whisper.*) Ma! One of the legs of my bed has gone through the floorboards again.

BESS: It had been empty for a long time when we first looked at it nearly thirty years ago, even then it felt warm, lived-in...

IAN: Ma!

GUEST: Your son has a problem, Mrs Turner.

BESS: It's all right. He doesn't go with the house. Ian! Now stop fooling around! Leave us alone! (*Pause, she turns back to* GUEST.) He doesn't want us to move.
(*IAN withdraws.*
GUEST puts the briefcase down.)

GUEST: It is because he loves the place. That is understandable.

BESS: Yes.

GUEST It has been a happy house. That would not put us off buying it, Mrs Turner. I know that times occur in life when people have to move in spite of strong attachments.

BESS: Ian will get used to the idea.

GUEST: This room speaks volumes. Some people do not need to write about themselves. It is done for them by the environment that they create around them. This room has great tranquillity, Mrs Turner, but it is a tranquillity that hums with life.

BESS: Yes, it has. Originally this was two rooms. We knocked them together to make a double aspect.

GUEST: London has lost a lot of walls that way.

BESS: (*Pause.*) Yes. The disadvantage is the television. It dominates everything, even in a room this size. Sometimes I've thought of those folding doors in the middle.

GUEST: Having light at both ends is a good principle.

BESS: It gives an impression of space which we enjoy.

GUEST: The house lies east-west. The sun rises on the back of the house and sets on the front. Only at noon is this house in shadow.

BESS: Yes.

GUEST: There are a lot of plants in this room.

BESS: One of my interests. I grow things from pips.

GUEST: Do you talk to your plants?

BESS: No. I don't like one-sided conversations.

GUEST: The front of the house is noble.

BESS: In the depths of winter it sometimes appears austere to me, but that may be my mood.

GUEST: You're not a moody person.

BESS: No. We had all the skirting-boards replaced two years ago.

GUEST: Austerity and nobility are often found in the same nature.

BESS: Yes, I think you could be right.

GUEST: It's a very good price you're asking.

BESS: Oh. Is it?

GUEST: To be able to assume that people have got so much money.

BESS: The price is negotiable. Offers will be considered.

GUEST: I am very impressed Mrs Turner. This is a beautiful room. A lot of care and time has gone into it. There must be many stories behind all these things.

BESS: A fair number. Would you like to see the kitchen?

GUEST: (*Taking off his coat.*) Although every article, every painting, has its place, they are all disturbable. That capability…re-arrangement potential, is very important. Your furniture reflects an intensely personal choice. It is full of character.

BESS: Well, it's something we've worked on, you know. Saving up for pieces we specially like.

GUEST: It is precious to you. Would you mind if we waited a few minutes for my companion? I value her opinion in a matter like this. If that is acceptable, Mrs Turner, I'm quite happy to wait here and enjoy the feeling that this room gives me.

BESS: Of course. Take a seat.

GUEST: (*Sitting down.*) Thank you. Your son has been drinking.

BESS: A little. May I offer you something?

GUEST: No, thank you. How old is he?

BESS: Twenty-four, I'm afraid.

GUEST: Some children take longer to grow up. You are a well-built woman.

BESS: I hope the same goes for the house.

GUEST: It was constructed by good craftsmen, and an experienced architect. No-one cut corners in those days. It was all quality.

BESS: That is what you're interested in, Mr Guest, I hope.

GUEST: A house is many things. It is the people who have lived in it. The time that has passed. Suffering and history. Discipline as well. The daily round. All these signs and shapes of existence remain within.

(*Enter JOANNA in a student nurse's uniform.*)

JOANNA: Hello, Ma.

BESS: This is my daughter, Joanna. Mr Guest is looking at the house.

JOANNA: Hello. Is Ian home?

BESS: He's upstairs somewhere.

JOANNA: I'll leave you to it. If you want me I'm in the kitchen having something to eat. (*Exits by the door right.*)

BESS: She's on afternoon shift. She always comes home starving.

GUEST: Hardly a beauty. No virgin either.

(*Pause.*)

BESS: Are you sure that is what you wanted to say?

GUEST: She puts no price on herself. The girl has no dignity. All her sexual activities have taught her nothing of value. That is not the way to enjoy one's youth.

BESS: It's probably better if you take yourself off now, Mr Guest. You're making me angry, I'm afraid.

GUEST: You should have guided her.

(*Front door bell rings.*)

That'll be for me. Don't worry, I'll get it.

(*GUEST leaves the room.*

BESS runs over to the spiral stairs and shouts up.)

BESS: Ian! Ian! Come down here right away!

(*Enter JOANNA.*)

JOANNA: Do you want a cup of tea?

BESS: I've got to get rid of this man.

(*Enter GUEST, with a young sharp-looking woman.*)

GUEST: Marion, this is Mrs Turner and her daughter. Isn't this a marvellous house? I was saying to Mrs Turner that it has great natural warmth. So much has gone on here.

BESS: Hello. Joanna, do me a favour will you? Go up and ask Ian to come down.

JOANNA: (*Calling.*) Ian! Get yourself down here! Ma wants you!

BESS: No, I've already shouted. He'll have those headphones on.

JOANNA: I've got something under the grill...oh, hell, it'll be burning! (*She runs back to the kitchen.*)

BESS: (*To GUEST.*) I have to go upstairs...

GUEST: I was complimenting Mrs Turner on her china and pictures. And these little statues, aren't they true to life? They must be of considerable value.

BESS: Ian! Damn you!

GUEST: Mrs Turner, the asking price for your house was one hundred and eighty-seven thousand pounds. (*He puts the briefcase on the table and opens it.*) It's an outrageous price but I am going to pay it. (*He unloads piles of bank-notes onto the table.*) You will want to count the money. How much is in each bundle?

MARION: Ten thousand pounds sterling.

BESS: You shouldn't have done this.

GUEST: To pay for the house, Mrs Turner

BESS: I hate to tell you but this isn't how it's done.

GUEST: It is the advertised price.

BESS: It must be done through a solicitor in the proper manner.

GUEST: Do you want to sell your house or not?

BESS: Of course I do.

GUEST: Mrs Turner. I want the house. I meet your price. Here is the cash. It is what you need. Take it. Marion has made out a receipt. All you need to do is sign it and we have an agreement.

BESS: I'm sorry but I can't...this is something I can't manage.

My husband will have to talk to you.

GUEST: No doubt he will be home soon.

BESS: Well, perhaps...I don't know. He mentioned seven. Mr Guest, are you English?

GUEST: No. These bank notes, Mrs Turner. Would you like to have them authenticated?

BESS: Have you ever bought a house before?

GUEST: I haven't had to.

MARION: The man who built this house ninety-seven years ago had fourteen children. Two died in infancy. One died of scarlet fever at the age of six. Three of the sons were killed in the Great War. All the rest died in their completed age, exhausted.

BESS: Could you put all that money away? I don't want Ian or Joanna to see it lying around. I find it faintly obscene, don't you?

MARION: (*Re-packing the money in the briefcase.*) The original owner was called Ronald Pike. He was a baker who perfected a certain kind of large-scale oven for bread. This house was the pride of his life, but his spouse was a cause of great unhappiness. Her mind was out of balance. However, Mr Pike loved her and cared for her. He bred his children by her and all those that survived into maturity had minds in harmony. Why would your children be frightened of money, Mrs Turner? (*Puts the briefcase next to BESS.*)

BESS: Would you like to go for a walk perhaps and come back in an hour or so. My husband will be back by then, I'm sure.

GUEST: We have the rest of our house to look over. That will fill in the time.

BESS: (*Pushing the briefcase away.*) I haven't accepted anything yet. Please don't try to suggest that I have. This is still yours.

(*Enter JOANNA.*)

JOANNA: I'll go and get Ian now. (*Aside.*) What kind of state was he in when he got home?

BESS: Don't bother, Jo. Stay with us. My daughter is training

be a nurse and hopes to specialise in geriatric care when she qualifies. You should see the books that she has to read. And the hours she has to work.
I couldn't cope with it at all.

GUEST: We've bought your house. Are you pleased?

JOANNA: Well...Ma will be pleased, and Fred. I've never lived anywhere else so I feel a bit different about it, I suppose.

GUEST: Why do you want to be with old people so much, Jo?

BESS: In this country we tend not to ask such direct questions until we know each other better. That sometimes takes years.

JOANNA: It's all right, Ma. It's a good question. Why would anyone want to be with old people? They're selfish, very demanding, ungrateful. Some of the time.

GUEST: Do you imagine that you will be doing good? These people are dying. Their lives are over. People who are closer to that condition themselves are better equipped to deal with them.

JOANNA: That's what Ma says.

GUEST: Then you should listen to her. Let the dead bury their dead.

JOANNA: But I want to help. I've got a lot of energy and patience. Not many brains I'm afraid. What else could I do? Paediatrics? That's worse. You can't talk to them. They haven't had a life. The old people tell you stories...

BESS: I'm just going upstairs for a moment. (*Goes up the spiral stair.*)

JOANNA: (*Who has hardly broken her thought.*) ...They're interested in what you're doing, your boyfriends, whether you're happy or not. The men's wards are horrible. Everyone's so crude. Some of the nurses get a really hard time. I've known girls give up nursing altogether after working in the men's wards. It destroys their confidence you know. Not being taken seriously...
(*The telephone starts ringing as BESS makes a call from an upstairs extension. Pause.*)

MARION: Geriatrics are essentially parasitic forms. They

sustain themselves by feeding off younger organisms.
People like you, Jo.

JOANNA: I know. I like that about them. It means I can give
them something.

GUEST: Your mother is ringing for help.

MARION: Perhaps you give too much. Your youth only lasts
a short time. When you are old yourself you will regret
that you spent so many of your best years in the shadow of
degeneration and decay.

GUEST: Jo, suffering is not to be sought after. Choose your
friends wisely. Find health, good spirits in the company
you keep. The young man whom you mate with more than
the others is a bad match.

MARION: Ronnie is his name.

GUEST: He's a fool. He's got good health, a quick mind, fine
prospects but he wants to suffer. He refuses to take
a job. Pretends to be a brother of the poor. He is none
of these things by nature. If he finds life so painful why
doesn't he end it? Efficiently this time.

JOANNA: You've been to   the hospital, you must
have…

GUEST: Before him there was a stream of incompetents,
addicts, idiots, fools… What are you trying to do? Mother
the impossible? You are what you are, Jo. Your father's
daughter. There's no need for you to give succour to
failures and men who make cause out of hating the world.
(*BESS comes down the stairs.*)

BESS: Ian will be down in a moment. As I thought he was
listening to some music.

GUEST: Pretending to. He was listening to silence. Something
he misses in his life.

BESS: Well, he had a cassette in his machine.

GUEST: It was blank.

JOANNA: I want to talk to you, Ma, alone.

BESS: There are too many things happening at once. Can't
yours wait?

JOANNA: (*Drawing her aside.*) Did you happen to tell them
anything about Ronnie?

BESS: Ronnie? I never tell anyone about Ronnie if I can help it.

JOANNA: Then these two are from the hospital. They're
patients who've seen our ad for the house in the
newspaper.

GUEST: We'll just go and have a look at the kitchen and
the laundry. And to look at the garden. I'm very fond of
gardens.

BESS: Hold on a minute, please.
(*IAN comes down the spiral stairs.*)
Ian, take Mr Guest and show him round. He'd like to see
the kitchen...the dining room?

GUEST: Yes, I'd like that.

BESS: And the garden.

IAN: What about the cellar? We've got a gigantic cellar, Mr
Guest. Have you got the key, Ma?

BESS: It's hanging up in the spice cupboard.

IAN: Follow me. We tried growing mushrooms in the cellar
once. Some of my experiments in wine-making are still
down there. Ever tried wheat and raisin brandy, Mr Guest?
(*IAN ushers GUEST and MARION out.*)

BESS: They don't look very ill to me if they're patients. Or
are you talking about the psychiatric ward?

JOANNA: We don't have a psychiatric ward.

BESS: Jo, these people would not be in a National Health
hospital. That much I know. They're far too wealthy.

JOANNA: Were you ringing Fred just now?

BESS: Yes.

JOANNA: They guessed. We could hear the phone ringing
down here.

BESS: Well, they can see that I'm nervous. In fact, I think
they're trying to make me nervous. It'll be half an hour
before Fred gets home.

JOANNA: What are you going to do? Call the police?

BESS: I can't do that. They haven't done anything except
offer to buy the house. It's a genuine offer, Jo. They know
so much about the place, about us. I've got a feeling we've
been researched.
(*Pause.*)

JOANNA: Are you going to accept their offer?

BESS: What does it matter to us where the money comes from?

JOANNA: Our old house? Sell it to freaks?

BESS: Whoever we sell it to can have it on the market again within a week and sell it to the Mafia for all we know. We can't afford to worry about selling it to the right person.

JOANNA: I think that's awful.

BESS: We have to be practical. Once it's sold it's sold. Finish.

JOANNA: Don't talk about it. If you're going to do it, just do it and don't involve me. I'm moving out anyway.

BESS: Where are you going?

JOANNA: Oh, don't worry. I'm not going to live with Ronnie. I wouldn't be seen dead in that hole he lives in. I'll go into the nurses' quarters.

BESS: Could we talk about this tomorrow?

JOANNA: Nothing to talk about. I can't stand the thought of loonies living in this house. I'd rather keep that kind of thing in the hospital, thanks.

BESS: Or with Ronnie.

JOANNA: Yes, or with Ronnie. Where d'you think I got the strength to deal with people like him, and the patients? From here! This is my home, Ma! My home! You sold out Dad. Now you're selling out his house. You're destroying everything I have.

BESS: Jo, don't… I didn't sell anyone out.

JOANNA: You'd do anything for Fred. So have we, remember? Ian and me. We've put up with him because he was what you wanted. And we were taught to do that by Dad. Your Ma's fallen in love with old Fred. There's nothing I can do about that. Men get prone to cancer when they retire. Some people get the same way when they lose faith.

BESS: No more now, love. You've got it all wrong, as usual.

JOANNA: My Dad was ten times the man that Fred will ever be.

BESS: Of course he was. That's probably why I thought he didn't need me any more.

JOANNA: Bullshit.

BESS: You're losing the argument again.

JOANNA: Stop saying that. It's childish.

BESS: You are, and you know it. Listen, if Fred left me, and
you left me and Ian, I'd get over it. I'd find a way to be
happy without any of you. I'm strong. When I leave this
house it just becomes like all the other houses in London.
I'll walk past it without a thought.

JOANNA: My, you are a tough old lady.

BESS: Tougher than you'll ever be if you go on as you are.
Sometimes I think you're a real drip. Any little crisis a bit
of pressure and whoosh! You're off.

JOANNA: Can't stand criticism, can I, Ma? Not me. When
the matron, the assistant matron, the ward sisters, the
doctors, the housemen, the patients get at me I just
collapse. Nobody ever has a go at you except me and Ian.
Fred daren't or you'd kick his balls off.

BESS: You should be on your own.

JOANNA: I am.

BESS: It would be better for you. Teach you some real
independence. But I suppose you'd end up in some
snake-pit with Ronnie or some other no-hoper.

JOANNA: Thanks for nothing.

BESS: The first job of any parent is the creation of the
independent child. In that I appear to have failed.

JOANNA: Who taught you that? Fred? (*Goes towards the spiral
stairs.*)

BESS: Don't   go. I might need your help.

JOANNA: What do you want me to do? Throw them out? I
can do that. I'm trained to chuck people around. (*She sits
down and picks up the newspaper pretending to read it.*) Bitch.

BESS: I am, I am. Thank you for staying.
(*Telephone rings.*
BESS answers it.)
Hello…oh, thank God it's you…no, I won't bother to
explain, just come home as soon as you can. No, it's not a
disaster, not exactly, all right? …Some people are here and
they want to buy the house…yes, I know that's good. Fred,
but they keep insulting us…yes, no, not abuse no…well,

not too bad but bad enough...no, they're not aggressive
except, yes, they are serious about the house but...
(*Enter IAN quietly.*)
...we can manage, I don't think they're dangerous but it's
not funny, that's all... Where are you? What are you doing
right over there? Well...hurry up...bye... (*Puts the telephone
back on the cradle.*)

IAN: (*Holding up a key.*) Don't give it another thought, Ma.

BESS: You haven't locked them in the cellar.

IAN: No-one can get out of there. I know that from when Jo
used to lock me in.

BESS: (*Snatching the key off him.*) You cretin. D'you think
anyone is going to buy a house when they've been treated
like that?

IAN: You're not still going to sell it to them, are you?
(*She is rushing out right when GUEST and MARION
enter.*)

GUEST: Will you be taking the stove with you when you go,
Mrs Turner?

BESS: Yes.

GUEST: Good. Most of the fittings as well?

BESS: All the fittings!

GUEST: The lock of the cellar door needs attention. Now we
are going to examine the garden. Are there any special
features that we should look out for?

BESS: It's a very ordinary garden full of flowers and trees.

JOANNA: Don't forget that you'll be taking the garden
furniture, Ma. You see, her first husband made that with his
own hands.

GUEST: I'll try it out. I like hand-made things.
(*GUEST exits with MARION.*)

IAN: Ma, I know that lock. I've known it all my life. It was
okay. You couldn't force it.

BESS: Oh, be quiet. Don't try to be so helpful when you don't
know how. All I want you both to do is be here, stay with
me until Fred arrives. Then he can sort them out.
(*IAN goes to the French windows.*)

IAN: He's sitting in Dad's garden seat, I hope the green stuff comes off on his trousers.

BESS: Ian, we have to be cute. Do what I'm doing. I'm saying to myself: they're crazy but they're customers, they're customers.

IAN: The cheeky sod, he's picking our apples!

BESS: I think I've worked out who they must be.

IAN: He's giving his girlfriend one and he's having one. That'll set their teeth on edge.

BESS: I think they're mediums.

JOANNA: Here we go. Why don't you ask them to do your horoscope? You're a sucker for all that stuff.

BESS: Mediums have to buy houses don't they?

IAN: Mediums can't pick locks.

BESS: What about that man who could bend spoons?

IAN: If you look at them from a good distance and pretend that you've never met them or know that they're a pair of nutters, they look rather comforting. I'd like him as an uncle – visually. I can't imagine them in bed together.

BESS: She may just work for him.

IAN: They're coming back in.

BESS: Do anything to keep them amused. Don't talk about us though. Find something else…what's in the newspaper?

JOANNA: Houses.

BESS: No, in the news. Something we can discuss.

JOANNA: South Africa… Common Market repayments…

BESS: They don't seem like Common Market members to me. What is their accent, d'you think?

IAN: For a moment I thought they sounded like Australians.

BESS: If they're Australian mediums we have got a problem.

(*GUEST and MARION enter eating apples.*)

GUEST: Many pleasant hours in that garden, I should think, Mrs Turner. Your apples are ready.

BESS: They're cookers.

GUEST: I have a taste for bitter   things. No sign of your husband yet?

BESS: He did ring, I told him that you were here and he is coming home as fast as he can. What do you think of the Common Market?

GUEST: It is a good idea but it must not be allowed to get in the way of a World Market. (*Sits down.*) Also it encourages excess. That I disapprove of.

IAN: All it's done here is put up prices.

MARION: Why should that worry you?

IAN: I have to pay them.

MARION: In your father's will he left you two hundred and fourteen thousand pounds. You have that invested at between twelve and sixteen per cent in various stocks that respond to the rise in the cost of living. If we define a rich man as someone who lives off the interest on his capital, you are a rich man. Prices don't affect you.

BESS: Have you ever been to South Africa?

GUEST: Yes.

BESS: What's it like?

GUEST: Any other place. Did you know that there is cyanide in apple seeds?

BESS: No, I didn't. I will avoid them in future.

GUEST: We would like to see upstairs now.

BESS: None of the beds are made.

GUEST: We don't want to sleep.

IAN: I'll take them, Ma.

GUEST: No, thank you. You showed us the cellar. Jo, will you show us round?

BESS: (*Going to the foot of the spiral stairs.*) You'll have to excuse the mess that was there… I think…I'd rather you didn't, you know.

GUEST: It's Teresa's day off. Making the beds is the first of Teresa's tasks when she comes in the morning. The second is to clean the bathrooms.

BESS: (*Climbing the stairs.*) Do you remember at what point in her schedule she steals from my stock-cupboard?

GUEST: Come, come, Mrs Turner – you don't begrudge the poor woman a few items of food for her children. You know what an idle man her husband is. Comfort the needy.

JOANNA: (*To MARION.*) Aren't you going upstairs?

MARION: No. I'm going to stay down here and talk to you.

(*GUEST and BESS have exited.*)

JOANNA: Are you mediums?

MARION: There is a presence in this house. It is stronger than the others who have lived and died here. The man had a very high intelligence.

IAN: Why do you want to buy this house?

MARION: Don't you want to talk about your father?

JOANNA: We try not to. It upsets Fred.

MARION: Ah. It would. A brilliant man, Fred. As brilliant as your father. It must have been a difficult friendship for them. Competition at work creates envy and suspicion. Your mother had the feeling that she always belonged to both of them simultaneously, but your father never understood that. With him it was all or nothing. He could not share.

IAN: Did you know Dad? Go on, say you were his mistress. I'd love that.

MARION: Commuting from London to Cambridge every day is an onerous routine. It takes an hour's fast drive in a car from the gates of the Cavendish Laboratories to your front door. No man should be expected to do that twice every day. Sixty-two miles up in the morning, sixty-two miles back at night. It's too far.

IAN: Fred doesn't do any driving.

MARION: But in the old days your father used to drive him up and down every day. Fred used to have his breakfast here with you. Often he would stay for dinner. He went on family holidays with you. (*Pause.*) Didn't everybody love Fred in those days?

JOANNA: Don't answer any more questions, Ian.

IAN: I don't need to. She knows all the answers. Some nights she'd go to the big bedroom, some nights to the small bedroom.

JOANNA: Ian!

IAN: We used to listen. In fact we used to have bets which one she'd go into. Aha! You're from the News of the Screws. Sex in the Nuclear Age. Cold science. Hot pants. This is all gossip you've picked up in the pubs near the lab, isn't it? We've got something to worry about, Jo. They're reassuringly sordid.

MARION: It must have been very bewildering for you as children. Your loyalties must have been put under severe pressure.

IAN: We were all just good friends. Uncle Fred was one of us. Isn't that right, Jo? They played cribbage and sexual roulette.

JOANNA: You promised never to talk out of school.

IAN: What's the point? She's got all the information anyway. I bet it's Fred who's been shooting his mouth off. He wants some showbiz glamour for his image. The New Scientist who breaks all the rules. They'll give him a Nobel Prize yet.

(*GUEST comes down the stairs carrying a pillow across two hands.*)

BESS: (*From upstairs off.*) Mr Guest, you haven't seen the other bedrooms yet.

(*GUEST lays the pillow on the coffee table. He handles it as if it were contaminated.*)

GUEST: Here it is.

MARION: It thou shouldst mark iniquities who shall stand?

BESS: (*Looking down.*) What are you doing with that? You're not supposed to remove things while I'm showing you round... God in heaven, what I have to put up with! I'll be glad when today is over.

(*BESS comes down the spiral stairs.*
MARION and GUEST stare at the pillow.)

Bring that back up here at once! This is disgusting! Can't you behave properly for a change?

(*BESS is now in a temper. She strides over to the coffee table and goes to take the pillow.*
MARION holds her arm.)

You mustn't touch our things.

GUEST: And my world, Mrs Turner?

(*MARION releases BESS's arm.*
BESS turns away.)

His pillow. See, it bears the mark, carries the imprint of his proud, sinful head. This is where Fred dreams. This is where he generates destruction.

(*Pause. They stare at the pillow.*
BESS turns back.)

BESS: They'll have to go. We can't have this in our own home.

GUEST: No, we can't have this. In the mind in the head that lies on this pillow, we can't have this, it is too much to bear. Fred seldom sleeps. His rest is tormented. But he cannot see that he has gone too far. I must butt in.

BESS: Get them out of here! I don't care what you do but get them out!

GUEST: This is not a pillow any more. It is an anvil of sin. But I am the smith and I swing the hammer.

IAN: What did Fred do, exactly?

BESS: Nothing! Don't you start now, Ian!

GUEST: You know that your father was Fred's best friend – and his working colleague at Cambridge. Together they laboured over some of the deepest secrets of the created universe. But your father knew when to hold back. He did not plunge on into knowledge regardless. Your father had a horror of pride. I don't need to tell you, Ian, that Fred glories in it. (*Pause.*) Ask your mother what Fred has done. She is closer to him than anyone. What has Fred done, woman?

BESS: Nothing! He's a wonderful man…he's not proud…he hates pride…

GUEST: Your father sheered away from the logical conclusion of his research, he refused to be part of it any more. But Fred pressed on, gathering all the energy of that accursed place and its ambition into himself. At the same time he usurped your father's place here, in the man's own home, in his bed. He took your mother's love.

IAN: Is that what you call it? Love is not love which alters when it alteration finds.

GUEST: Fred was a conqueror. Nothing stood in his way. Where his mind went he felt his body could follow. He was master of everything he laid hands on.
(*The door right opens and a man wearing dark glasses enters. By his side is an Alsatian guide dog on a harness lead.*)

BESS: Fred!

(*IAN walks across the room and runs up the spiral stairs as BESS greets FRED.*)

FRED: Take the dog off me someone.

(*JOANNA takes the guide dog off him.*)

Evening, Jo.

JOANNA: Hello, Fred. We have some visitors.

FRED: Yes, your mother told me.

GUEST: My name is Guest, Fred.

FRED: Sit down.

GUEST: I am sitting down.

BESS: Fred. I've got to talk to you in private.

GUEST: I have been a nuisance in your house. Things I have said about you have enraged your wife.

FRED: (*Sitting down.*) She did say that you'd insulted her. Why did you do that?

GUEST: It comes down to terms of reference, Fred.

FRED: I'll talk business with you. Do you want to buy the house or not?

GUEST: Ah, you forgive the insults?

FRED: I'm indifferent to what most people say about me, or my family. We know ourselves well enough, Mr Guest.

GUEST: I do want to buy the house.

BESS: Don't sell it to him, Fred. It will only mean trouble. I don't trust him at all.

GUEST: I have brought the money, in cash.

FRED: You knew that you'd want the house before you'd seen it? Very adventurous, even for a chancer like you, Mr Guest. What's the game?

GUEST: I need the house.

FRED: That's a good enough reason. Are you going to live in it?

GUEST: No.

(*MARION picks up the briefcase and puts it in front of FRED. She opens it and puts FRED's hand on the money.*)

Money breeds, Fred. When I started out on this mission there ware only two piles of banknotes in this case. They got together during my journey, colliding with each other, bombarding each other, shaking loose molecules, dividing

them so they proliferated. A chain reaction, Fred. How I
held all that energy in my hand is
a mystery.

FRED: (*Starting the count the bundles.*) So, you've done your
homework, that's wasn't difficult. How many in each?

MARION: Ten thousand pounds.

FRED: A lot is at stake in the selling of a house. (*Continues
counting.*) Mr Guest has done some checking.

BESS: Research, not checking. They've dug up all kinds of
things.

FRED: Buyers' tactics. A lot of money is at stake.

GUEST: In the earth's atmosphere there are millions of
statistics masquerading as charged particles. Each of them
is a book, an autobiography of the creator. Or, as you
would prefer it, Fred, an epitaph.

FRED: Even my opinions. That's taking curiosity a bit far,
isn't it?

GUEST: You don't bother to keep your truth to yourself.
You broadcast it very loudly. Everyone must know Fred's
position. You love publicity. Nothing attracts you more
than the limelight.

BESS: Mr Guest, thank you for your interest but we don't
want to sell the house to you. You wouldn't be happy here
– besides, I don't like your behaviour. We're going to have
dinner now and I'm sure you wouldn't want to watch us
eating. That would be a terrible experience for someone
who already finds us so disgusting.

FRED: (*Taking the last bundle.*) Don't be hasty, Bess. Thirty-six.

GUEST: Correct.

FRED: Ten thousand in each. That's twice the price we asked.

GUEST: Half of that will be for your wife. The other half is
for your stepdaughter. There's no need for them to suffer.
Your stepson already has his inheritance.

FRED: Take the dog into the kitchen somebody. He gets upset
if I raise my voice at anyone.

(*JOANNA takes the dog out.*)

GUEST: Who are you going to raise your voice to, Fred?

FRED: All I want for the house is the advertised price.

GUEST: How noble for a nihilist. You've dropped the price
three times since you put it on the market.

FRED: All I want is what I've asked for.

GUEST: All I want is what I've asked for. When I gave you
free will it was not foreseen that you would use it to destroy
the world. Before you chip in, Fred. I accept that it was my
fault. I should have imagined a man as evil as you.

FRED: May we get back to the house?

GUEST: Your house? What of my house? My world is being
threatened, yes, you have undermined its very foundations.

FRED: It strikes me as bad practice for you to try and sell
me religion while I'm trying to sell you my house. Can't it
wait?

GUEST: No longer.

FRED: That's a pity. We were hopeful about making a sale.
The house has to go.

GUEST: If you have your way, Fred, it will only take a thumb
on a button. No. I must be precise: two thumbs on two
buttons. A suicide pact between statesmen on behalf of the
whole world. Why should one soiled thumb in Moscow
and one soiled thumb in Washington act for all the nations
of the earth? (*Pause.*) It will not stop war, Fred. Fear does
not stop war. It makes it.

FRED: So you say. I am not impressed, either with your
argument or your knowledge of my affairs.

GUEST: Hardly hidden your light under a bushel, Fred. Not
your style at all. If anyone can bring international politics
to its senses it is a man who has never seen the inside of a
bushel. Where did your darkness come from?

FRED: I'm flattered that you've taken such pains over me, Mr
Guest. Is the theory that if you buy my house you buy me?

BESS: Fred, you've got to stop taking him seriously.

GUEST: Only himself can be taken seriously. His will, his
existence, because he is without grace or faith, all offers are
considered. There are no rules, you see, no morals, only
his own revelations.

FRED: Frankly, all I'm nervous about is whether he's sane. If
you enter into a contract with a man whom you know is
mad, it's not valid. What d'you say to that?

GUEST: Are you suggesting that I'm taking advantage of you, Fred?

FRED: Do you have any ID? We don't know you from Adam.

MARION: God does not carry ID. Everyone should know him.

FRED: Bess, I want you to call a number.

MARION: No more telephone calls.

BESS: Ian! Joanna! Come here, quickly!

MARION: They are both asleep. And the dog.

BESS: Fred, we must get the police, now!

GUEST: Due north of Sicily, between Stromboli and Vulcano, is a drilling platform. The diamond drillers are now at sixteen thousand feet. They've no idea why. From the rock samples they pull up they are completely aware that there is no possibility of finding oil or gas. It has never occurred to them that they are just boring a hole for Fred.

FRED: Bess leave us, will you?

BESS: Like hell I will! They make no sense to me. How can I leave you with them?

FRED: If I knew who they were, I'd tell you. However, I can guess at their profession.

GUEST: You know we're not agents, Fred. And I realise that you are not corruptible as far as money is concerned. We want to take care of your family, that's all. There are no secrets that you can tell us or sell us. Your wife will need to understand why you have to go. Have you never heard my voice before? Lying on your pillow?

FRED: Bess, go with the woman and see if the kids are all right. Is that acceptable?

GUEST: They are asleep. But Marion will take your wife to see for herself.

(*MARION leads BESS off to the spiral stairs.*)

BESS: You're not going to do anything to him.

GUEST: Check on your children, Mrs Turner. Fred will still be here when you get back, I promise.

BESS: I'm not sure I should go and leave you.

FRED: I want to know they're safe, Bess.

(*BESS and MARION go upstairs.*)

Has she gone?

GUEST: Yes.

FRED: I have heard your voice.

GUEST: I know you have, and you didn't listen.

FRED: How did you do it?

GUEST: To crawl into your corrupt ear was an effort. It is not a place I favour.

FRED: To buy my house you actually bug my bedroom? This is financial acumen of the highest order.

GUEST: For someone who has pushed science to the edge you are still very skeptical, Fred. Why shouldn't my voice find its way into your thoughts when your thoughts are everywhere? They rule the future of this planet. Everyone is affected by them. You have great power.

FRED: I have a house you want. Let's leave it at that.

GUEST: The room where you sleep overlooks the city. From the place where you work one can see over fields and woods to a town full of children. Because you are blind, Fred, it doesn't mean that London is not there, or Cambridge, or the children. They are as real as your calculations. So am I. I am part of your calculations but you obstinately refuse to find me in your answers.

(*Enter BESS and MARION down the stairs.*)

BESS: Ian's flat out on his bed. He's been playing football so he's tired. And he had a few drinks.

FRED: Did he seem okay?

BESS: As far as I could tell.

FRED: Have a look at Joanna. Don't worry Bess – I know who Mr Guest thinks he is now. Panic's over.

BESS: It may be for you. I'm supposed to feel safe in my own home.

GUEST: You're perfectly safe, I have no argument with you.

FRED: Don't forget the dog.

(*BESS exits right with MARION.*)

GUEST: She will mourn you. There is ignorance in Babylon.

FRED: This is the deal then? I agree. I accept the money. We can tie up the paperwork later, Bess is the co-owner so she can give you a written receipt.

GUEST: You'll sell it to me? After all I've said?

FRED: Water off a duck's back. Cash is cash.

GUEST: What powers of self-restraint you have, Fred. You
must follow a discipline of some kind. I must guess at it.

FRED: Thank you for all the trouble you've taken. Good
night.

GUEST: You held back from disliking me.

FRED: I didn't say that.

GUEST: At least from frustrating me. I find that odd in you.
You're a man who has never bothered to control himself
for the benefit of others. Look at the man whose house this
was. Look at his widow. Look at their children. So why
restrain yourself for me? Let rip, Fred. Unleash your worst
side.

FRED: As politely as possible, Mr Guest, I am asking you to
leave us in peace now.

GUEST: In your darkness I cannot be avoided. In the
emptiness behind you eyes I exist. In my existence you are
absorbed, my boy. I am God.
(*Pause. FRED laughs takes off his dark glasses, raises
his face.*)
There are some men who will never look me in the face.
You're one of those, Fred. Miracles are done for the poor
and ignorant, not for the proud.

FRED: You're talking to me from out of a pit of darkness like
anyone else.

GUEST: Only one miracle would convince you, Fred. To
wake up one morning and find that you were in truth the
lord of light, Lucifer himself, sin supreme. Your first act of
state would be – abolish matter, your second – find a way
of multiplying nothing. Your third, and worst – to refuse
to admit that by then you had gone too far. And you have.
You have.

FRED: Oh, excess comes easily to me unlike your good self.

GUEST: Since Einstein and Rutherford opened the gate
I knew that certain sheep would – follow. Some genius
would come up with the idea of splitting the world. It
follows from splitting the atom which is a small world

within itself. Concepts are everything, as you know. But I confess that I had hoped for voluntary restraint. Fred, you puzzle me. How is it that you can show such restraint for a pile of paper money but not for the whole world.

FRED: There is always an onward motion to some minds. I need not be talking about yours.

GUEST: I am what I am!

FRED: That goes for me as well.

GUEST: Deny me now and your death will have no reason to it. Don't resist the knowledge of me. Fear would come in useful. Give it a try.

FRED: If I had resisted the knowledge for which you condemn me it would also have meant resisting the knowledge of you. You are my world-splitter. You are my bomb. All I have done is bring you out into the open where men can see you for what you are.

GUEST: I'll take you with me, Fred. Your fine old house I'll raze to the ground. Every mark you have made on every piece of paper, every sound you have made, will go with you.

FRED: God can't manage that. There's nothing you can do, to fix the past. You have no hold over it at all. It's stronger than God. If there is anything truly all-powerful it is the past itself. And the past is dead.

GUEST: That you should worship death doesn't surprise me, Fred.

FRED: My sad contraption, that little bomb, pathetic machine that it is, goes down the shaft today. It'll lie deep in the earth's crust forever as your headstone. I have buried God. Shake hands with your gravedigger. And have the grace to admit you've lost.

GUEST: I have lost?

FRED: You have.

GUEST: (*Taking his hand and pulling him to his feet.*) You like to dance, don't you? Many an evening when you're alone with your harlot, you dance with her to the record-player. But you will not dance with my world, superman, except to my steps.

(*MARION hits FRED very hard with the pillow, knock-*

ing him flat.
The dog barks angrily off, wakened.)

Fast blackout.

End of Act One.

ACT TWO

*FRED stands by himself near the spiral stairs. GUEST and
MARION are sitting down with BESS, IAN and JOANNA at
a table with a tray of tea cups on it. BESS has a teapot in each
hand and is about to pour.*

BESS: India or China?

GUEST: I don't mind.

BESS: You have to in this house.

GUEST: Then I'll have China. Marion can have India.

JOANNA: Hasn't she got a mind of her own?

MARION: No, I haven't.

JOANNA: It's about time you woke up then.

BESS: Milk or lemon, Mr Guest? Another choice. I'm afraid.

GUEST: Let it stand.

BESS: I beg your pardon?

GUEST: (*Angrily.*) I hate ceremonies.

(BESS puts down the teapots.)

BESS: I'm not sure that I like being shouted at in my own
house.

GUEST: And what have I suffered but that? Crying, begging,
praying, whimpering as well – but mostly shouting. Big
mouthed...obstreperous stupid... Fred, the only advantage
to your cataclysm is that it would stop all ceremonies.

FRED: God is pleading for a little more informality. Can you
manage that?

IAN: Of course we can. Anything he likes. Relax, Ma. Just
because God's come to tea it doesn't mean you've got to
tense up. Are the cups clean by the way?

GUEST: There is a twinkle in your eye, son.

IAN: Ah-hah!

GUEST: That twinkle I would keep. As long as it doesn't
become fixed.

IAN: I'll try to avoid that.

GUEST: Ceremonies, son, ceremonies. I hate them even
on the smallest scale. Anything that stops moving. That's
what worries me about you. A state of suspended belief

180

has stopped moving. Within my universe that is unnatural.
Wake up!

FRED: Don't shout. You'll start the dog off again.

GUEST: For God to be patronised. If I'm not frozen into
some monotonous incantation I'm warmed into the
wandering vagrant of space in need of a hand-out. You
tolerate me no matter what I do. Have me in your house.
Think of me in cemeteries. No one but Fred in this family
knows who I am. And the man is not even nervous.

JOANNA: Lots of people think they're God.

GUEST: Many more think they're divine. (*At BESS.*)
Pain-maker! (*Pause.*) Embracer of axe-heads!

IAN: If you shout at my Ma again, I'll heave you out on your
ear.

JOANNA: Don't antagonise him, Ian.

GUEST: Best keep out of my way, son. This is between Fred
and me.

IAN: You're in our house. Don't boss me around.

GUEST: You're *in* my house. I'll boss you around when I feel
like it!

BESS: Mr Guest has probably come here straight from Hyde
Park Corner.

GUEST: People who are persuaded *en masse* are not
persuaded. They are herded, Mrs Turner. An instinct of
long-standing for killing the mind together. (*Pause.*) Do I
sound foolish?

BESS: Not foolish enough. Have you been to see a doctor?

GUEST: No.

BESS: Fred has told us that you think you're God. That means
you should see a doctor.

GUEST. That's not accurate, Mrs Turner. Fred actually told
you that I am God.

IAN: Fred's tongue never leaves his cheek.

MARION: He meant it. Don't you know when someone is
telling the truth?

IAN: So God is knocking on doors in north London. What are
you collecting for? A sponsored Second Coming?

BESS: If Mr Guest really thinks he's God then I think we
should respect his opinion and talk about something else.

IAN: What? And miss out on an opportunity like this? If he is God then he might be able to answer a few questions that even the newspapers can't manage.

BESS: You shouldn't torment him, Ian. (*To GUEST.*) He does tend to get a kick out of provoking people who appear on the doorstep trying to convert us.

IAN: The best solution to the problem of violence in the world would be if all the violent people could be eliminated. What do you think of that for an idea? Good, isn't it?

GUEST: It is sad to note the influence that you have had on these children, Fred.

IAN: Not on us. We take no notice of Fred at all. TV has corrupted us.

GUEST: You must, be very disappointed in them both, Mrs Turner. They have no respect for their elders. In the old days people were valued for their wisdom and experience. Now it appears to cause nothing but resentment.

IAN: You're going to have some success in this street. The last lot we had were hopeless. All they did was smile and say we'd have to face up to the truth in the end. It was hardly worth arguing with them. But you're not like that, are you? You're a real scrapper.

MARION: Don't be insolent. He is being very patient with you.

IAN: You mean – don't take him on. No one asks you to come round forcing your way into people's homes. You're a nuisance. And you don't do it for us. You do it for yourselves. How many points do you get for tonight?

BESS: You see how offensive he can be? I've seen him reduce Jehovah's Witnesses to tears.

MARION: Fred, why don't you tell your family who this is and why he is here? Make them understand.

IAN: We never believe a word he says anyway. God, how did the milk get in the coconut? That's one you can answer, I'm sure.

BESS: It's just that we get so many of you round here, Mr Guest. It never seems to stop. I'm answering the door all day, all evening, but your deception in pretending to come here to view the house in order to get your foot in the door...well, I think that's going too far.

IAN: Want me to finger his collar Ma?

GUEST: As a physicist Fred, does annihilating all life on the planet fulfil any proven law of matter? Does it make any kind of sense within the detectable patterns? Can you see a gap to slot it into?

(*Pause.*)

IAN: Of course it does. Fred always covers everything.

GUEST: You have great faith in him.

IAN: He's got an OBE.

GUEST: Your husband is the designer of a weapon of total world destruction, Mrs Turner. He is a devil.

BESS: Then I expect he'll get a knighthood.

GUEST: He has to go...I must take him out. Nothing of Fred must remain if I am to save the world.

BESS: Well, we've had plenty come to save the world, Mr Guest, but not enough to buy our house. You've disappointed me tonight. In fact I think you've wasted my time one way and another.

MARION: He is God.

IAN: Good to see you, God. Thanks for dropping in. Now hop it.

MARION: Be serious, please! Fred, can't you see the harm that is being done here?

GUEST: Marion, Marion, don't bother. Pinpricks.

MARION: I can't stand listening to them mock you. Their stupidity, their shallow...sickening smugness... He loves the world! He loves it! And what do you give him in return? You haven't even got the sense to love your own lives. What can be done with such an animal? All you have appetite for is pain, destruction. What are we going to do with them? (*Weeps.*)

(*Pause.*)

BESS: See, you've done it again, Ian. I do apologise, Mr Guest. He doesn't mean any harm. If he had more to occupy his mind it might be better.

MARION: He feels it like I do. Your son knows...he knows... his cruelty is only a way of holding himself together...I

183

forgive him because I know he is suffering.

IAN: Won't work, sweetheart.

MARION: Inside you are different…I know.

BESS: Fred, I think we've done all we can. We've been very polite.

FRED: I can only hear him…imagine him…

JOANNA: But you know who he is.

FRED: He's a phoney…nothing he says can be trusted… he never comes out into the open, makes it clear what he wants. Always it's riddles and contradictions. But I hear him…I even smell him.

JOANNA: But you don't believe?

FRED: He's a liar. He's a hypocrite. He's incompetent. He's mad.

JOANNA: (*Pause.*) Who is?

(*Pause. FRED feels his way over and, sits down.*)

FRED: When did you last talk about anything that mattered?

IAN: To you? Never. What would be the point?

FRED: Think about God. Talk about him, like I do.

IAN: Yes, on television. Give you a microphone and you come to life. But not here, in what you laughingly call a home. Mr Guest, I don't mind at all that you're demented – I truly don't. I admire your style. You should seize this bastard and bang his head against the wall if you want to convert him. Don't try the soft-pedal with Fred. All he understands is force.

GUEST: He will be punished. But the suffering he has caused you is nothing to what he has stored up for all mankind.

IAN: That sounds like my Fred.

GUEST: A billion megaton bomb sunk sixteen thousand feet in the earth's crust in a volcanic fault zone where the continents barely touch. The blast will sunder the world right down the middle. Fred's device is under dual control once connected – the Kremlin and the White House. It is called the No Remedy. Of all its hideous features the name is the one that shrieks most of despair.

(*Pause. The dog whimpers loudly off.*)

FRED: Feed the dog for me.

(*Pause. The dog whimpers on.*)

Come on, someone. You know how he gets if he's not fed
in time.

JOANNA: Deny it, Fred. Say that it's not true.

IAN: Could Fred think on that scale? He hasn't got the
gumption. The blind scientist, the blind piano-player, all
image, all tinkle.

(*The dog whimpers loudly again.*)

All right, all right, hound. I'll come and calm your drooling
fantasies. No Remedy, my arse.

(*IAN exits to the kitchen.*)

MARION: Not to have told your family was grossly dishonest,
Fred.

GUEST: It was ever so. Men go out of the house in the
mornings. They perform evil. They come back in the
evening and it is assumed that because they have worked
nothing but good has been achieved. The labour is secret.
No one asks – what did you do all day?

MARION: Aren't you offended by what he's done,
Mrs Turner?

BESS: No.

MARION: Why is that?

BESS: Because he's done it.

MARION: Does that make it right?

BESS: Mr Guest is the only person who makes things right, if
I understand him correctly.

MARION: What would make you reject what Fred has
created?

BESS: If he has made this thing...I don't mind. If it gets used
I won't mind. We've lived with this since the last war,
haven't we? What's new?

MARION: But the children...

BESS: The first thing children are interested in is destruction.

MARION: This generation of young people are desperate for
security. There is nothing for them...any moments...their
pain is terrible.

BESS: Is it any more of a chance than we had during the blitz
in London? A doodlebug could land anywhere, any time.
The A-bomb was part of my childhood. Then the H-bomb.
I've lived with them all for a long time now.

(*Pause.*)

MARION: We must cherish the young, not break their hearts.

BESS: My first husband was a physicist. Fred is a physicist.
For all I know they could have been working on an atomic
kettle. But Fred's bomb doesn't shock me. It's a world of
bombs. Bombs in the shops. Bombs in hotels. Bombs in
planes, cars... Your briefcase could have been a bomb. All
it could do is kill me. If I die the world dies anyway.

JOANNA: Ma! How could you?

BESS: Tired of hysteria. And the things I love are bombproof
while I'm here. And when you're dead, pet, you're dead.

(*Enter IAN.*)

IAN: That dog of yours won't even let me get the food on
the plate. It'll take my hand off one day. Oh...I see...an
embarrassed silence...someone's said something.

MARION: We must get Fred out of here. She's his strength.

BESS: Hold on, Mrs God, I haven't seen him all day.

MARION: You will be able to make a fresh start, Mrs Turner.
A change of environment would be best. There is no need
for you to be alone.

BESS: Never been anything else at heart. Why should you
criticise Fred so much? He's only brought the whole thing
to a head.

FRED: Bess has no religion, or religious feelings. She's
earthbound.

GUEST: That is a quirk of the mind. No fault of ours.

FRED: But that means she can live with horror. Even my
horror.

JOANNA: Fred, you sound proud of this thing you've made.
You came here every night, ate with us, talked to us,
knowing...

FRED: This is my home, Jo. Why shouldn't I lead a normal
life? How else would I live with the work I have to do?

JOANNA: They should keep you in a cage somewhere.

FRED: Jo, the bomb is mundane. It is almost boring.

JOANNA: I've asked you plenty of times what you do up
in Cambridge. You never gave me a straight answer. I
suspected but nothing as bad as this. At first I thought

it might have something to do with live, animals…live animals! Christ, this is all animals! All of us!

GUEST: You should hate him for it. The boy does so already.

IAN: Not because of some old bomb, but because he's such a dickhead.

GUEST: You were wrong to hate him for trivial things, Ian, my son. Stole your mother. Broke your father's heart. Took over this house. If you had known the full dimensions of his crime you would have been forced to love him for those minor sins. Then hate him for something worthwhile. He would take away the earth from under your unborn children's feet. A colossal, irredeemable crime again Nature. Hate him for that, not peccadilloes.

IAN: All right, God. Anything you say. Peccadilloes are out. Huge, fucking great crimes are in. Let's gnash our teeth, eh?

MARION: You are not the first to mock.

IAN: Oh, let's not get too pious here. All that's happening is I'm losing my home, my mind. But I'm glad you got on to Fred. He needs sorting out.

GUEST: Pour the tea.

BESS: Yes, sir. Right away. Zieg Heil. (*Pours tea from both teapots. What comes out is red.*)

GUEST: India or China it is all the same. For you. Fred, a miracle you cannot see like No Remedy cannot be tested.

JOANNA: He's made the tea go red. If you have to resort to that kind of trick I don't believe in you any more. They could do that just as easy in a disco.

BESS: There's no pleasing them these days, Mr Guest. I do hope you haven't corroded my tea-pots. They belonged to my grandmother.

GUEST: Fred, I changed the water into wine and I changed the wine into blood. Two processes. Both the wine and the blood are red, a colour you have never seen. How can I describe it to you? But you can taste red, can't you? The anger in your mouth, the exhausted hatred of the man in the dark. (*Pause.*) Taste it and tell – what makes you shed the blood of the world?

FRED: If you weren't able to exchange a few molecules…

well…that would be sad. (*Puts the cup down.*) It has always been my view that all the miracles are possible. My disbelief has never been crude. What I don't believe is that you – whatever you are – care a damn. We must do that for ourselves.

JOANNA: By making bigger and bigger bombs?

FRED: Ask him if there's ever been any other logical end to human aggression? I've merely fulfilled his desire. Now any violence…anything at all, could escalate into world: destruction – No Remedy – at a single leap. No one will dare to start it. The reaction is so quick. I have created the ultimate political anxiety.

IAN: Come on, God. Down on your knees. You should thank our Fred. He's given you the best vote – winners since famine and pestilence.

MARION: Oh, don't, don't. His rage can be terrible!

GUEST: No, no, the boy is upset. Comfort him, don't shout at him. Authority is a test, son. Regard your stepfather. He has never balanced his need for me against his need for himself. You could fall into the same trap.

JOANNA: Has Fred done just what you wanted? Have you been waiting for the bomb all this time?

MARION: Before his creation he dreamed of it.

GUEST: He thinks his mind is free of everything but forces, gravity particles rushing here and there. My voice is a cloud in his mind. (*Shouting.*) It's broken! I come rushing out in hail and thunder! Fred, I damn your bomb! I damn it! Total destruction is my province!

FRED: What do you do with such a man as you have made me?

GUEST: Subtract him from his own sum. You have faith. That's because you are blind. That should have been the upper limit of the mind's evolution that I allowed – darkness. But I became fascinated, fascinated by how it was developing. Simplicity was forgotten. I became intoxicated with your elaborations, your strange flowerings of self-destruction, your…accursed ornamentation!

JOANNA: Go on! Go on!

GUEST: Don't you feel it, child? The questions have swarmed

out of this terror he has invented like bees out of a lion's carcase. Life is sweeter because it is imperilled. The danger has made you mad...greedy!

JOANNA: Tell me. I love it when you talk like that.

GUEST: It is not your submission I desire. It's a long time since I heard praises sung. Holy is a word that even I cannot remember understanding. All that is left is...the creation. My greatest work. The love of my life.

JOANNA: That's how he would feel. That's how we feel. I believe in you again. You are God.

IAN: Make your mind up, Jo.

JOANNA: It's not such a big thing – believing. What's all the fuss about? If you've got the ability, use it.

GUEST: Exactly.

JOANNA: Mind if I kiss you?

MARION: No...

GUEST: How many other gods have you kissed?

JOANNA: (*Kissing him on the cheek.*) If you think you're God then I hope you'll be happy. You do it very well.

GUEST: Jo, it was always my hope that the prospect of life would make the young want to live. At the beginning all I had was a sense of adventure. From that I created promise. Promise that must never be fulfilled or the great movement forward would become a known quantity, a cycle only capable of repeating itself. The prospect of life has to be mystery.

BESS: Fred, don't you think God could have been clearer about what he wanted?

FRED: He always was. Inside the universe he put a time-bomb. Ask him why. I don't know. All I've done is to anticipate it so we can face up to the moment and create some peace. But he doesn't want that. Peace is something that God here never intended us to have.

BESS: Well. I've never met a man as interesting as you are, Mr Guest. Fred obviously thinks a lot of you, my children seem to be full of admiration. That seems to leave me. Why don't you come into the kitchen and help me scrape a few carrots for dinner? Let Fred get his breath.

GUESS: We have to go now. Fred, prepare yourself.

BESS: Won't you stay to dinner? It's a long time since we had anyone as entertaining as you...or we could entertain you! That's more like it, perhaps. You have been laughing at us, haven't you, Mr Guest?

MARION: Take the money. The house will be destroyed tomorrow, at seven o'clock. Salvage all you can before then.

IAN: Well, we'd better get packed up, hadn't we, Ma. Got any old newspapers handy? Tea-chests? What a job this will be. All the junk in the attic...and Fred, this must be goodbye, I'm heartbroken.

(*GUEST and MARION stand up. Pause.*)

BESS: Show Mr Guest out, Jo. And see he takes his briefcase.

(*FRED stands up.*)

FRED: Bess, I'll be going with him. I have to.

BESS: Two very ordinary people, Fred, I assure you. I wish you could see them. In the street you wouldn't give them a second glance. Worse than ordinary, love, drab.

FRED: I've expected something, there had to be a reaction. How could he just ignore it? (*Screaming.*) I welcome it!

BESS: You can't leave home, Fred. There's far too much for us to do. Now, sit quietly and forget all this.

IAN: Oh, let him go. They're only nipping round the corner for a pint. Mr Guest, they know Fred at the local. He has a chair that people get out of when he comes in. The barmaid serves him at the table and she is very solicitous. When Fred has finished she rings my mother up to say Fred is on his way home. Will you see that this is done tonight? We wouldn't like him to miss the house and fall into the canal.

FRED: How do you say goodbye to people like this?

BESS: I think it's about time the laboratories accepted that your weekends are sacrosanct, Fred. You've been working under a lot of strain and they still make you go in on a Saturday. That's unforgivable as far as I'm concerned.

FRED: Goodbye, Bess.

BESS: Goodbye.

IAN: I'm off up to my room.

FRED: Goodbye, Ian.

BESS: I'll give you a shout when dinner's ready.

IAN: I'm not really hungry! I had one of those pies at the club and it's sitting on my stomach. Goodbye, Mr Guest. Mrs Guest...good luck with Fred. I've been disputing with the miserable bastard for years and got nowhere. Try and talk him round. (*Goes up the spiral stairs.*)

BESS: Ian's very tired these days. It's doing nothing all the time.

JOANNA: Ian, I know he's God. I can feel it.

IAN: Another of your Bagwans. They're ten a penny. Join his gang if you want to. I'm going to listen to some genuinely crappy music by genuinely bad musicians who think the world is a load of shit and cheer myself up. Night everyone. (*Exits.*)

JOANNA: Don't be hurt.

MARION: In better days he would have been a priest.

BESS.: Oh, a monk at the least. He stays in that room of his for days. Well, if you're going out for a drink don't be too long getting back all of you. It's lamb and it'll only take an hour at the most and you know what lamb's like if it goes cold.

FRED: Goodbye, Jo.

JOANNA: Bye, Fred. God is good. He'll do you no harm. He might even understand you which is more than we've ever done. Bye, God.

GUEST: God be with you is a strange farewell even said so quickly. (*JOANNA kisses him.*) A light heart is something I'm loathe to leave.

JOANNA: I'll do anything for you. Drop me a postcard.

BESS: Don't give him ten per cent of your salary whatever you do.

MARION: You believe that this is the creator, the lord of all?

JOANNA: I do. I think he's terrific.

MARION: You stand in the presence of Almighty God. If you know it, show it.

GUEST: No ceremony. The girl delights me. Let her be.

BESS: I'll have to get going. (*Moves to the door.*) If you're not going out there's some gin in the cabinet and a little bit of dry sherry, I think. I must remember to get some Pernod sometime, that's a drink I like... (*She exits talking.*) ...though you have to watch it.

JOANNA: Now Ma's gone I can tell you. I love him.

MARION: Fred, your stepdaughter believes.

FRED: She has believed before, quite a few times.

JOANNA: Not like this. He's here. I can touch him...can't I?

GUEST: Here I am. Touch me.

JOANNA: I'm touching him.

MARION: She's believed in all sorts. You heard what Ian said... She has followed false prophets.

GUEST: They only prove her need of me. Youth makes it difficult to see clearly. What were you looking for, child?

JOANNA: To be always giving.

GUEST: No heaviness. No melancholy. Such faith! Such eyes. You should see this girl's eyes. Fred. I have taken her from you. What does your mother mean to you now?

JOANNA: Nothing.

GUEST: This house, your childhood?

JOANNA: Nothing.

GUEST: Think before you answer this: the hospital? Ronnie? The old people?

JOANNA: All of them mean nothing now.

GUEST: Unless I tell you to care.

JOANNA: Then I must and will.

GUEST: (*To FRED.*) What can you offer this young woman to compare with what I have given her?

(*Pause.*)

FRED: Goodbye everybody, I've forgotten where the door is.

GUEST: Answer the question! At a stroke I have given her happiness a reason to live, security, a defence against the terror of death.

FRED: It's good to be going. The formula and technical details are in...where did I leave them? Goodbye office. Goodbye memory.

MARION: Poor man. Have mercy on him. He meant no harm.

GUEST: Go away!

(*GUEST sits holding JOANNA's hand and looking into her eyes.*)

MARION drifts off up the spiral stairs.)
Love the world, love the world. Go to your mother.
*(JOANNA kisses GUEST's hand, smiling. She leaves by
the door right.)*
Does she really believe in me? I have my doubts. In fact I
have my doubts about all of them who say they do. Except
you, Fred. I know that you are absolutely certain of my
existence. You always have been.

FRED: I'm going through my goodbyes, in my mind. Now
I know what a lot there is to get through. Always loved a
good cigar.
*(FRED offers guest a cigar. He accepts it and FRED snaps
a lighter in the air, he feels for the flame with his cigar
and GUEST leans forward to light his own, they touch
the cigar ends together.)*

GUEST: Goodbye cigar.

FRED: Dimensions are difficult. I have to think of a world. I
have to think of a cigar. That's space travel for you. And
I'm supposed to be one or the intelligent ones. They can't
cope with the size of it, Guest. You didn't equip them with
a world-sense at all. My bomb would though. It would
crystallise what they had to lose. That's the only way they'll
ever get existence into a true perspective. Threaten it,
totally. Then watch their minds grow.

GUEST. World government, Fred, can only be administered
by me. And I'm not ready for it.
(Pause. GUEST puffs at his cigar.)
My original plan...

FRED: Yes?

GUEST: It doesn't matter.

FRED: What are you trying to do to me? Drive me mad? Tell
me.

GUEST: I'm not sure you'd understand.

FRED: Try me.

GUEST: The earth I saw as a pilot scheme. From this
first experiment I proposed to breed and populate the
uninhabited universe. Things were going well in some
sections. You'd reached the moon, got apparatus onto
Mars, circumnavigated Saturn, virtually hung on the tail

of Haley's Comet: but at the same time as this outward, colonising urge – so vital, so dynamic! – you developed this inward motion towards world suicide. Why?

FRED: Newton.

GUEST: Who?

FRED: To each action there is an equal and opposite reaction. One of your laws.

GUEST: Did I say that?

FRED: You created a totally ambiguous bloody universe! It's full of flaming paradoxes. Oh, get us a drink will you? It's by the door. Whisky and water. Now, that is one of the first things you set up – everything has its opposite, and they confound each other. Nothing is ever straightforward with you. Why the hell did you do that?

GUEST: (*Getting the drinks.*) Thrust has to be countered by thrust. Ask anyone who builds cathedrals.

FRED: That's hardly an adequate answer.

GUEST: (*Bringing FRED his drink.*) If I'd let everything go straight to the point, funnelled all the energy into fast results, the whole thing would have been over in a week. There had to be checks and balances, a braking system… it all comes down to how you deal with energy, doesn't it? Now. I created a finite amount of that.

FRED: Oh, it is finite then?

GUEST: Oh, yes. It has to be.

FRED: But is the source of the energy finite?

GUEST: Ah, that would be telling.

FRED: If the source of the energy is infinite then all energy is infinite.

GUEST: Not so. That would make energy unexpendable in principle.

FRED: But it can be replaced from the source. It is therefore infinite in concept. If not in actuality per particle of energy.

GUEST: Go over that again.

FRED: Are you really God?

GUEST: Of course I am.

FRED: Then what am I doing explaining this to you?

GUEST: This is a good cigar.

FRED: Why did you make it so that there *isn't* always an equal and opposite reaction to any action?

GUEST: Did I?

FRED: You made these exceptions to hide something. What?

GUEST: Well, beneath one set of laws of the universe there is, of course, another.

FRED: We'd guessed that. Hence the anomalies.

GUEST: And beneath that other set of laws there is another set and so on, *ad infinitum.*

FRED: So the laws...! You mean...

GUEST: Never end. Isn't that crafty?

FRED: You impossible...

GUEST: But, ultimately, within all those laws, to each set there is another set that is exactly in equal opposite reaction but...

FRED: But?

GUEST: They're all mixed up.

FRED: In an infinite system there can't always be an exact opposite because that implies a finite relationship.

GUEST: These are very good cigars.

FRED: You don't know what you're talking about.

GUEST: When do I have chance to talk about it? Who is there who'll sit down with me like this and chat? Fred, you're the first person who's had the gall.

FRED: But there is a system.

GUEST: Absolutely. Once you've cracked it the whole thing falls into place. Embedded in the mix-up is the key system.

FRED: How near are we to grasping this?

GUEST: That depends where you're standing.

FRED: Are we close?

GUEST: Not even warm. Split the earth you may, Fred, old friend, but it's hardly scratching the surface. It's a particle made up of a finite number of particles. I can count them. These things go bang every day.

FRED: Then what's all the fuss about?

GUEST: Lonely.

FRED: Lonely?

GUEST: The only reason I came to get you, Fred, is so that

when your device does go off as Washington and Moscow suffer an equal and opposite bout of raving paranoia I won't lose you along with the rest. I'm fond of you. Fred. You've been knocking on my door. I'm letting you in.

FRED: That makes you want to destroy my house...and me?

GUEST: Come off it. Man loves me, loves me, but he is going to destroy my world, isn't he? (*Pause.*) Equal. Opposite. Quite a law. (*Drains his glass.*)

FRED: Now I am disappointed.

GUEST: No. It all makes sense. Was that water as you like it?

FRED: Bess was right. You're just a loony.

GUEST: A well-informed loony. One of the earlier definitions of God. Saint Augustine, wasn't it? What did you expect? No. I'm not God.

FRED: You shouldn't admit it. Now I'm doubly disappointed.

GUEST: I'm a member of God. God is a committee.

FRED: Don't bother with the water.

GUEST: God is a committee of particles. I'm one of the particles. Know how many particles on the committee?

FRED: Give me the bottle.

GUEST: An infinite number. But I'm close to the chairparticle.

(*GUEST hands FRED the whisky bottle. Pause.*)
And on the agenda is change.
(*FRED starts to pour himself a whisky.*)
Let me do that for you.

FRED: I can manage. I stick my finger down the side of the glass to measure it. Ingenious, don't you think?

GUEST: That's about the level of finesse that you've achieved in interpreting my universe, Fred. The committee has passed a vote of no confidence in mankind's future.

FRED: Cheers.

GUEST: This is the most radical decision that the committee has ever taken with regard to mankind because it follows that if there is no confidence in its future there is no confidence in its past. Time, in human terms, has a huge question mark over its head.

(*The telephone starts ringing.*)

FRED: Bloody Ian on to his girlfriend again. She has to live in

Dusseldorf, of course. You should see my phone bills.

GUEST: No, that's your wife ringing for a Chinese takeaway.
Want to know what the order is? I'd prefer Indian myself.
It's the heat I favour... Time, Fred. (*Pause.*) The moment
anyone attempts to set off your device the committee will
abolish history and with it will go knowledge. Nothing will
have happened.

FRED: (*Calling.*) Bess!

GUEST: No evolution, no science, no past. Man will be left
in a present time surrounded by machines and material
he has no knowledge of. Bombs? He will stare at them,
scratch his head and say – whatever was this for?

FRED: Bess! Come here, quickly!

GUEST: You were wrong, Fred. God, that great democracy
of particles, does have power over all Time because it is
Time that holds it together. It is the joint handclasp of the
committee.

FRED: Bess!

(*Enter BESS.*)

BESS: You called?

FRED: Did you order me any egg foo yong?

BESS: No, I didn't order you any egg foo yong.

FRED: Why not?

BESS: Because it doesn't go too well with roast lamb.

(*BESS exits. Pause.*)

FRED: As you were saying?

GUEST: The call to Dusseldorf has cost four pounds
fifty-seven pence so far. This may not be a finite sum by the
time he has finished.

FRED: God, what are we going to do with you?

GUEST: Pity me. Pity me.

(*JOANNA enters with a plate.*)

JOANNA: Ma says you can have these to pick at while you're
waiting. She wants to watch a programme that's on in
about ten minutes, if that's all right.

GUEST: Thank your mother, for me. Tell her that I have been
exposed as a fraud by the genius of her husband Fred here.
There is no need for her to be pleasant to me now. I will
take my angel out of the bedroom where she is listening,

open-mouthed, to the protestations of your brother – in fifth-form German – about the eternal nature of love. Love dies, as angels know, unless it is caught in Time.

JOANNA: Yes. I'll tell her all that.

(*JOANNA exits.*)

GUEST: Complex creatures, young women. They need to be hurt. And they need to be pleased. (*Eats from the plate.*) That is how life is generated – between poles of feeling. In rhythm between poles of feeling. The flapping of a beaver's tail between the river banks as it builds its dam is all the applause I need. (*Weeps.*)

FRED: Perhaps you had better go home, Mr Guest.

GUEST: There's nothing out there. The past has been removed. Nothing ever happened, Fred. What we are doing now is what we are doing now, that's all. It has no future. It came from nowhere. If I stop eating, it is an impression. In fact I am eating now for ever. Like you have been blind for ever. We have to go.

FRED: We'll get you a taxi to take you home.

GUEST: No! Have you any idea what it is like to live in a permanent state of flux? (*Angrily.*) Madness! Madness!

FRED: Is there anyone we can ring for you? A friend...

GUEST: God has no friends. Do you know who taught me... us...to conquer our old enemy, Time? The Communist Party. Fred, they gave God the go-ahead. The past is a piece or putty. Who created the Communist Party? A conspiracy of uniform atoms dancing like gnats in the mind of a Jew whose ancestors dare not even say the word God. Why not? Fred, a burning bush in a tent is a very dangerous thing.

(*GUEST is very upset and agitated. He rips open one of the bundles of bank-notes and starts to eat them.*)

Manna!

(*Enter BESS wiping her hands on her apron.*)

BESS: You should have come in for some more hors d'oeuvres if you were that hungry, Mr Guest. I'm going to turn on the television now. You don't mind, do you?

(*BESS turns on the television.*

JOANNA follows her in and sits down. A programme

comes on but BESS immediately turns the sound down.)
Not on yet. I'm looking forward to this. Fred looks so dis-
tinguished on camera, Mr Guest.

GUEST: It was not a golden calf it was a golden bull and its
droppings were of gold and its urine was of gold and its
cry in the desert was a golden cry over golden sand. They
worshipped it because they could touch it. Hold it. Bang
their heads against it.

BESS: I think Ian might like to see this. You know how he
likes to sit and mutter when he sees Fred holding forth on
television. I'm going to get him.

FRED: Don't bother. We'll only have a row.

BESS: Well, let's have a row. I enjoy rows on days like this.
(Enter MARION at the top of the stairs. She comes down.)
Tell Ian to come down, will you?

MARION: He doesn't want to talk to anyone. His girlfriend in
Germany has given him the push.

JOANNA: Oh, hell. Here we go again. Did she say why?

MARION: She says she has no respect for him. He's not
serious about things that matter, he doesn't work for his
living...all that kind of thing.
(MARION sits down.)

BESS: Why he doesn't go out and find himself a good,
old-fashioned gold-digger, I don't know. They must be
around somewhere.

GUEST: Fred, I apologise...something comes over me now
and then. Can't control it...terrible rage, you know...

FRED: Don't worry about it.

GUEST: You understand? It engulfs me...all this mess!

FRED: Of course.

GUEST: You can watch your programme. But when it's over
we will really have to go.

FRED: That's fine by me. No need to get upset any more.

GUEST: We haven't got time to stay for dinner, Mrs Turner. I
hope you'll forgive us.

BESS: That's all right. We can have it cold if there's any left
over. Joanna's always hungry, aren't you?

JOANNA: Always. The hospital food is terrible. I can't eat it.
(They are watching the television and its silent images.

GUEST packs up the money and puts it carefully under the coffee table.)

I change over to night-shift next Monday, Ma.

BESS: Oh dear. You won't like that.

JOANNA: Can I borrow your bike? There isn't a bus at that time of night – or in the morning if it comes to that.

BESS: You'll have to get some batteries for the lights.

FRED: It's about time you learnt to drive.

GUEST: Evolution is proof that God is always changing its mind.

JOANNA: What's the point of learning to drive if you haven't got a car?

FRED: Well, we might get you one…a second-hand one, cheap.

BESS: I think she'd be safer on the bike, Fred. Ronnie would start borrowing the car. He'd crash it when he was drunk.

JOANNA: Ma, he's not that bad.

BESS: Worse from what I know of him.

FRED: It's about time you accepted Ronnie as a fact of life.

BESS: Oh, I do. A grim one. Here we are.

JOANNA: Ronnie's all right. He's not as stupid as he makes out.

GUEST: *(Shouting.)* Man loves his life! And how does he repay his creator? God had enough of chaos! Living alone in it for aeons and aeons before the spark… shazam!

BESS: I have nightmares imagining that Ronnie has made me into a grandmother. Ah, here go.

(BESS turns up the sound on the television. Music.)

FRED: *(On the television.)* Good evening. This is the third in our series 'The Oldest Question'…

BESS: Don't you think he looks good on television, Mr Guest? I keep telling him but he won't believe me.

FRED: *(On television.)* Last week we discussed the question of the existence of God with three eminent figures, all experts in their own field – the Archbishop of Canterbury –

BESS: Who was hopeless.

FRED: *(On television.)* …A field-marshall and a famine relief organiser. The postbag after this programme was enormous.

BESS: Everybody wrote in to say how hopeless the Archbishop of Canterbury was.

FRED: (*On television.*) ...Which only goes to show how deeply interested ordinary people are in this question. What seemed to provoke most comment was the fact that so many physicists have returned to religion. Can we take it that they have discovered proofs of God's existence while doing their work? Have they found a universal order and, if so, can they describe it to us? Personally I can't but I am only one scientist among many...

GUEST: Oh, Fred. Fred, why persecutest thou me?
(*The sound on the television fades but BESS, JOANNA and MARION stay watching and listening.*)
You profit out of doubt? You traffic in confusion?

FRED: I'm glad you've turned it off. I don't like the sound of my own voice sometimes.

GUEST: They are seduced. Even my helper, my apprentice angel...so easily sidetracked. They have fallen before, they will fall again. She wants to stay. She would if she could but she can't.

FRED: How long will dinner be, Bess?

GUEST: She can't hear you even though she's listening to you. Like you with me, really.

FRED: Bess!

GUEST: No point in shouting at her. Fred. I'll do you a favour. I don't want to hurt your family. They're fond of this old house. Bess never liked the new place in her heart. So I'll leave this standing. But there has to be one alteration. On the outside I'm having a blue plaque put up which will say Fred Turner, scientist, author of the end of the world, did not live here.

FRED: You can't erase me.

GUEST: I have already. I sent a storm into the Mediterranean. No Remedy fell off the platform as it was being lowered into the bore-hole. A strong submarine current is carrying it out through the Straits of Hercules, out towards that trench, you know the one, the deepest part of the Atlantic

Ocean. No Remedy is lost.

FRED: Another one can be built.

GUEST: No. The committee abolished today under its new powers over the past. What is lost today can never be found because it was lost when there was no time. And today you die, Fred. Your death never happened so your life never happened as all men are born to die. Are you keeping up with me?

FRED: Who wants to dispute in a vacuum? (*Pause.*) You'll take care of Bess. I love her in my nonexistent way.

GUEST: She's strong. A peasant at heart. She'll love another.

(*IAN comes down the spiral stairs.*)

If you want to leave a last message, tell the boy.

FRED: Ian, we've decided to go round to the pub after all.

IAN: Can I come?

FRED: No.

IAN: I didn't want to anyway. Hey...Fred...

(*He picks the football up out of the fender and puts it in FRED's hands.*)

Could you get that signed for me by the whole Liverpool football team? It's for the Christmas raffle at the club.

(*Pause. FRED weighs the ball in his hands.*)

FRED: You'd better ask God if such a thing is possible.

IAN: What do you say, Grandad?

FRED: I know the chairman, vaguely.

GUEST: Bring it along.

IAN: You take good care of it, Fred. They cost a fortune these days.

(*IAN walks over to the group watching the television.*)

FRED: When you say the team, Ian, do you mean the regular first team players? D'you want the reserves...

GUEST: He's not listening.

FRED: It's a terrible thing to ask an Arsenal supporter to do, don't you think? Does he imagine I've got no conscience at all?

(*IAN sits down with BESS and JOANNA to watch the television.*

GUEST goes out and returns with the guide-dog in its

harness.)

GUEST: Have to take your eyes as well, Fred. Can't leave anything of you behind.

(He puts FRED's hand onto the harness than goes to MARION who has moved herself to be closer to IAN, leaning against him. GUEST taps her on the shoulder and crooks his finger. Reluctantly she gets up to leave.

GUEST opens the door and ushers FRED through with the dog.

MARION is still looking at the television, not wanting to leave.

GUEST whistles to her.

She exits with him as the dog barks in the street.

BESS, IAN and JOANNA are left in the silent silver flicker of the television screen as the lights fade.

Then the programme fades from the screen into a last point of light and blackout.)

The End.

DAVID POWNALL

KING JOHN'S JEWEL

Characters

KING JOHN

GWYN

WALTER

MIRABELLE

CLAC

GLADMOUTH

Set in England, 1212

King John's Jewel was first performed at the Birmingham Rep Studio on 2 April 1987, with the following cast:

KING JOHN, Julian Glover

GYWN, Ian Puleston-Davies

WALTER, Roland Curram

MIRABELLE, Judy Walter

CLAC, Christopher Ettridge

GLADMOUTH, Shay Gorman

Director, Bill Pryde

ACT ONE

13 August 1212.

A stone circle fifteen miles south of Nottingham. A fallen stone lies off-centre. GWYN lies asleep, wrapped in a robe. He is nearly indistinguishable from the stone he is sleeping by. He stirs and lies still. Dawn coming up. Birdsong. Enter KING JOHN, half-asleep and yawning. He shuffles over to where GWYN is lying and starts to piss over him. GWYN stirs. JOHN hums and looks around, finishes pissing and shakes himself off. Pause.

GWYN: All right if I move now? (*Sits up.*) Didn't want to unsettle your aim.

JOHN: My poor boy…how did that happen? (*Tries to brush him down.*) Keep still, keep still.

GWYN: Fresh morning, isn't it? (*Stands up.*) Weather's improving.

JOHN: Forgive me…

GWYN: Trying to prove a point?

JOHN: I didn't see you lying there. You should have snored.

GWYN: You did it on purpose! I know you. I've never been so insulted in my life. But we'll forget it, eh, Johno?

JOHN: Thank you. That is very generous.

GWYN: And I was having such a good dream.
   (*Pause.*)

JOHN: A dream? What kind of a dream?

GWYN: I'm off home in the morning.

JOHN: You go back tomorrow? That soon?

GWYN: As if you didn't know.

JOHN: Do you want to go home?

GWYN: It's dryer in Wales this time of year.

JOHN: Isn't it discourteous of you to be so glad you're leaving me? I might miss you.

GWYN: Home is home, Johno. (*Pause.*) Being a hostage takes its toll…even if the company is good…you've been very decent to me, I know…pissing on me and all that.

JOHN: Might have made a man out of you.

GWYN: Yes… I'm sure I've improved.

JOHN: Good. (*Pause.*) Strange, but I have no idea of home.

GWYN: You must have some feeling for the place you were born.

JOHN: Oxford? You don't get born in Oxford. You get contemplated.

GWYN: There won't be anything to stop me coming back some time, will there? I might even take service with you.

JOHN: What a kind boy you are.

GWYN: I'll cry tomorrow when I go, I promise.

JOHN: (*Pause.*) Don't make too light of me.

GWYN: I'd never do that, Johno. You've been as good as a father.

JOHN: Better, if it's your father you're comparing me with. It won't take him long to destroy any success I might have had with your education. He'll turn you against me. Your father will think you've been contaminated here, that I've been making you into an Englishman.

GWYN: Not at all. He respects you enormously.

JOHN: Enormously. Well, I'd best get myself prepared. I had no sleep at all last night. We had to work right through again.

GWYN: You should take more rest. There are bags under your eyes.

JOHN: Too much to do! An abbot is coming to ask for my permission to build a new monastery. He wants to erect it right here.

GWYN: What about the old stone circle? Doesn't that have precedence?

JOHN: He wants to obliterate it,   not incorporate it, you follow? Gladmouth crushes, he does not understand.

GWYN: Fond of this man, are you?

JOHN: Always known him. Been like brothers. You never knew my brothers.

GWYN: A monastery, Johno? This doesn't sound like you.

JOHN: Oh, I love monks. Give me half a chance and I'd be one myself. All that security, monotony, would do me good.

GWYN: Odd that I've never noticed this passion of yours before.

JOHN: Oh, yes, I'd enjoy building a monastery, a great abbey church, a secluded, tranquil cloister…eh, the thought of it soothes me. Did you know that I've left orders I'm to be buried wearing a monk's habit when I die? That's what I am, at heart.

GWYN: Which heart is that?

JOHN: Monks can have vices as well. Many of them are riddled with vice. That's why they need to retreat – not from the world, but from themselves. (*Pause.*) I feel very ambiguous about this request old Gladmouth has made. Asking an excommunicated king for his blessing on a new monastery is tactless on the one hand, but wonderfully audacious on the other. No-one else has dared to ask me, which is a pity.

GWYN: Perhaps he feels he's got influence with you…

JOHN: We've always been aware of each other. As children we were sent to the same old brute for what was called… upbringing. We were rivals in everything. (*Pause.*) I have hurt him many times in the past, many, many times. He always deserved it.

GWYN: And he still comes back for more. I look forward to meeting this abbot. He must be demented. Does he regard you as some kind of mortification?

JOHN: Flagellation, Gwyn. I've had Gladmouth thrashed many times. He must still carry the scars, inside and out.

GWYN: Then he must love you a lot, or love being thrashed. Which is it?

JOHN: Oh, both. I shared quarters with him for three years, side by side. Yes, I've had my jaw-teeth into Gladmouth a few times and he has never shaken free. He's an exceptional man, Gwyn, whom you might spare the time to study. No matter how hard I humble him, he returns to me as proud as they come. The last time I brought him down to a point below the line of most men's capacity for suffering. If he looks me in the eye, shimmers with dignity like he used to – then you are in the presence of pride par excellence. Watch Gladmouth. He's good.

GWYN: Like a hawk, Johno. Being your prisoner has made me put a premium on pride.

(*Enter WALTER from left.*)

WALTER: Sire, may I speak with you?

JOHN: I thought I told you to get some sleep, Walter? I want you to join in this meeting with the abbot. He'll be here shortly.

WALTER: A catnap will suffice, sire. During all the years that I have served your majesty I have survived on less sleep than any man I know. (*Pause.*) It is a secret matter, for the moment.

(*WALTER comes over and whispers in JOHN's ear, then withdraws. Pause.*

JOHN is deeply disturbed. He keeps looking at GWYN as if trying to formulate something to say to him, but failing. GWYN is draping his robe over a stone to dry it out, unaware of JOHN's eyes on him.)

GWYN: Well, let's hope we have another sunny day, Johno. Perhaps I'd better set this washed out. I don't want to arrive home smelling of England, do I? No-one would talk to me.

JOHN: As a child, was your father fond of you?

GWYN: I'm not his only son. Took my place in the queue, I suppose. When he did notice me it was usually with indifference or a strap.

JOHN: Has he any reason to hate you? Have you disobeyed him in an important matter?

GWYN: Why?

JOHN: Your father is up with Maelgwyn and Llewelyn in open rebellion against me.

GWYN: Oh, Christ, no!

JOHN: What is your father thinking about? He knows you're held hostage for his good behaviour. Doesn't he care what happens to you?

GWYN: I was setting off home tomorrow…tomorrow!

JOHN: The Welsh lords have little concern for their children, it seems. There are twenty-nine of you held hostage – all fine young men, the future of Wales, no less.

(*JOHN walks swiftly away left, not looking at GWYN again. GWYN watches him go then sits on a stone with his head in his hands.*)

GWYN: No…no…no…I don't believe it…I don't believe it…
no…
(*Enter WALTER. He pulls scarves out of his mouth like
a magician.*)
WALTER: Where is the king?
GWYN: I don't know.
WALTER: He was here a minute ago. I want to show him this
new trick.
GWYN: I don't know! Be told, will you? …He went off…
(*Pause. WALTER sits down close to GWYN.*)
WALTER: Well, young man, it looks as though it is all over for
you and your companions. (*Pulls coins out of his ears.*) What
about this, eh?
GWYN: Go away, Walter…leave me alone…
WALTER: The terms of the contract your father and the other
Welsh lords made at Marlborough last year are perfectly
straightforward. Any rebellion against the king's authority
and your lives are forfeit. (*He brings a flower out of GWYN'S
nose.*)
GWYN: I know that. I'm the last person to need telling…go
away.
WALTER: Just in case you'd forgotten. (*Pause.*) I spent the
small hours drafting a new tax proposal – one of the king's
ideas, not mine. If it is ever implemented it will cripple
our blacksmiths and farriers, wreck our agriculture, bring
mining to its knees and reduce the effectiveness of English
cavalry on the battlefield to zero. But King John thinks he
has hit upon a brilliant new idea for raising money. He
intends to tax horseshoes.
GWYN: Walter.
WALTER: It is an absurd proposal.
GWYN: I have something else on my mind other than horseshoes.
WALTER: Don't let self-pity get in the way of broadening
your mind. Taxation is a fascinating discipline. It can build
or destroy empires.
GWYN: Wales is only stone, Walter, only stone. Do you
believe that the spirit has greater value than the material

world?

WALTER: I have no time for such thoughts.

GWYN: Some people say all matter is evil. Land itself is evil.

WALTER: Who suggested that to you?

GWYN: I read it somewhere.

WALTER: Beware of such books.

GWYN: Now I've made you frown. It was inconsiderate of me to upset your train of thought. You go on, practice your tricks.

WALTER: I have to have another string to my bow. You know the king. He could throw me onto the rubbish-heap any time. And at three o'clock in the morning I often need something to ameliorate his temper.

GWYN: He'll never get rid of you, Walter. You're safe because he feels nothing for you. The time to beware of this king is when he is your friend.

(*JOHN enters left.*)

JOHN: Walter, I told you to get some sleep.

WALTER: I was on my way, sire.

JOHN: Sleep, you little stoat!

WALTER: (*Hurrying off.*) I am asleep, sire. I am asleep.

JOHN: And no complaints from you, Gwyn. Is it my fault you're in danger. My boy, my dear, dear boy. Do you still love me?

GWYN: It's an odd thing but I haven't thought much about anyone else but myself this last five minutes.

JOHN: Be brave. We'll see what we can do. But your life seen against my problems – nothing, dear boy, nothing at all. So, don't harp on about your hanging, will you? Rise above it.

GWYN: Of course I will! I realise that you have a lot on your plate these days. By the way, I don't think much of the horseshoe tax idea. To put a penalty on a symbol of good luck would make you unpopular.

JOHN: You are right. Well spotted, Gwyn. Walter didn't think of that. I would rather tax farting but who would admit their assets. When you grow up do something useful.

GWYN: When I grow up? You mean you're not going to hang me?

JOHN: Oh, Gwyn, Gwyn, if only I could find the means to hate you.

GWYN: Will you watch them turn me off?

JOHN: Oh, no, that's not expected. I can't officiate over such a small affair. Hit me! Insult me! Help me to loathe you. The council has demanded that I exact the full penalty for the Welsh welshing on their words. They do not want the executions delayed. Dithering offends them. Don't dither, they say. Get it over with.

GWYN: Oh, you were never a ditherer Johno. You know what you want.

JOHN: They say it should be tomorrow.

GWYN: As soon as that? Any idea where?

JOHN: They say Nottingham is closest for a good crowd. And they are very particular that all twenty-nine hostages should hang. In fact they have specified that you should go first, as son of the leading rebel.

GWYN: They, Johno? They? What do you say?

JOHN: Don't talk now. You have beautiful eyes. Full of terror.

GWYN: No wonder!

JOHN: I love you, boy. I will have to make up my mind in the next hour. If I go against the council's advice they will be certain that it is only because of you. Never take me for granted.

GWYN: Would I?

JOHN: You mustn't. I have a job to do.   There are twenty-nine hostages held against the good behaviour of those rebels. For twenty-eight of them I couldn't give a fig. You could destroy me, Gwyn. My councillors are not men of any sensibility. If they see what a hold you have over me they could rise up in rebellion themselves. I would lose my whole kingdom...for you. Still, you do not take me for granted. That is such a comfort.

GWYN: Then do what you have to – hang me who loves you because you gave an undertaking never to be shamed by lesser men.

JOHN: We all gave our words at Marlborough. Mine has to have a greater value than most men's...than all men's if I am king at all...

GWYN: Then go ahead and hang me for your word. There is no fitter death for a poet, surely. And to die appropriately must be bliss.

(*Enter GLADMOUTH with CLAC, both in dirty, ragged Cistercian habits and black overgarments.*
GLADMOUTH carries a rough staff his own height long. It has a bit of wood tied across the top as a cross. The hands of both men are stained red. Both GLADMOUTH and CLAC raise their hands in a gesture of peace and recognition.)

GLADMOUTH: Benedictus.

JOHN: Your hands are red, Gladmouth. Have you been fighting again?

GLADMOUTH: Blackberries. (*Bows.*) Sire. There was no stream to wash in. My apologies.

JOHN: You have got thinner.

GLADMOUTH: Sire, this is Clac, one of my choir-monks. He is my head mason and architect. He has been brought up in our order since boyhood. Bow to your king, Clac.

CLAC: (*Bowing.*) You have been father to all my thoughts lately, sire. There has been little else in my head.

JOHN: What kind of thoughts? I would expect any English monk to spare a prayer for his king.

CLAC: Oh, sire, while I was in the brambles all I thought of was clover is the place to think of kings. (*Pause.*) Pardon me if I'm caught staring. I've never laid eyes on you before.

JOHN: Where have you come from this morning?

GLADMOUTH: We have walked all through the night from Burton-on-Trent.

JOHN: Nobody could walk from Burton-on-Trent to here in a single night!

GLADMOUTH: Then we have walked from some other place that your majesty can nominate himself.
(*Pause.*)

JOHN: Is this the mood you approach me in?

GLADMOUTH: Of what consequence are my comings and goings sire? I am your servant wherever I am.

JOHN: Why didn't that shine in your eyes when you said it?

GLADMOUTH: Age, sire, and hard weather.

JOHN: We are equally old. We have both spent the night on
our feet. What must matter is how honest we are. That is
what keeps a man's eyes shining. Are you as pious as you
ever were?

GLADMOUTH: You would have to ask my brethren.

JOHN: Or God. He would feel the brunt of it. Nevertheless,
you are trying to be pleasant with me, Gladmouth. That is
a start. I am feeling quite friendly towards you...but
I have to keep my mind on it.

GLADMOUTH: Is there a reason for this charity, sire?
I know that it cannot be conscience.

(*Pause. JOHN sits down and leaves CLAC and
GLADMOUTH standing.
CLAC puts a hand on GLADMOUTH's shoulder to
steady himself. They are both plainly exhausted.*)

GWYN: Johno, let them sit down...they're dead on their feet.

GLADMOUTH: Do not presume to ask favours on our behalf
– whoever you are.

GWYN: I'm no-one – but very, very close to God.

JOHN: He is, believe him.

GWYN: I am a sensible choice as intercessor at all high levels.
Sit down and be comfortable. The king won't mind.

(*CLAC looks at GLADMOUTH who turns away. CLAC
lowers himself onto the fallen stone.
GLADMOUTH remains standing, defiantly.*)

JOHN: Do sit down.

GLADMOUTH: I prefer to remain on my feet, if your majesty will allow me. It is a form of discipline I favour.

JOHN: Why should a pious man come to beg off a beggar,
Gwyn, my boy?

GWYN: For his good name if he has one, for his blessing... if
the beggar is in a state of grace.

JOHN: Before any mention is made of money this morning,
Gladmouth, I must tell you that I am poor. There's no
point in asking me for money. But I am so poor that I may
be in a state of grace. Is that what you would like from me?
Grace?

GLADMOUTH: If you have any to spare from your own

needs, sire.

JOHN: I thought we would get that out of the way as soon as possible. I have no money. No money. Don't forget that whatever you do.

GLADMOUTH: Sire, may we talk about first things first; this plot of land, the idea of the monastery itself. As you know, we must have your authority to build.

JOHN: It will all come down to money in the end. (*Pause.*) Why do you want to build it here? There is something on this site already.

CLAC: Because it is a good place…solid bedrock… well-drained…not far from running water…out of the prevailing wind…

GLADMOUTH: The stone circle is a heathen temple. It should be destroyed and built over.

GWYN: Does competition worry you, Abbot? Are all the arguments over?

GLADMOUTH: Not in your country, from what I hear.

GWYN: Do you have no respect for the past? All these old stones are doing is bearing witness to ancient truth. No one had heard of Christ when these were raised.

GLADMOUTH: Who is this person, sire?

JOHN: A close friend, let us say.

GLADMOUTH: Must I listen to blasphemy, even from the king's friend?

JOHN: He has a right to blaspheme today. He can curse God if he wishes and I think God would let him get away with it.

GWYN: Johno has a lot of time for anyone who is close to a great mystery. I have been composing a poem over the last week…a nightmare provoked it. I'm confident the king would like to listen to my poem…now.

GLADMOUTH: Sire, I protest! We have come here on serious business.

JOHN: Today he can do anything he likes, even insult my good taste.

GLADMOUTH: I have not walked all this way to listen to a

fool! A poem? What has a poem to do with our purpose
here?

JOHN: Oh, come on, Gladmouth. You and I have chanted
many a verse together. Indulge the Welsh bard. Amongst
his own people he is highly respected for words. Sit down,
man, and listen!

(*Pause. Then GLADMOUTH sits on the ground.*)

GWYN: I am grief's comrade, pleasure's fallen friend.

I number my book-entries for the day of dread,
I make a list of all my precious goods:
First, the world's enigma, the rosebud
hardly opened in the garden's mist,
my finger fumbling for the thorn.
Second, the ecstasy, the game we won, the victory,
the triumph of the body's flight;
Third, the talk of friends, confessions,
brave comparisons, weaknesses admitted,
power admired.
Fourth, the shaking land, my father breaking
in a harsh green wave against the border.
Fifth... Duw, paid a adael nho llad fi...fifth...sixth
Oh. Johno, it's gone!

(*Pause. GWYN breaks down.*
JOHN takes him in his arms.
GLADMOUTH turns away, disgusted.
CLAC watches it all with great peasant nosiness.)

JOHN: (*Over GWYN's shoulder.*) We are very close in thought,
this boy and I. It is a travail of the spirit. See to it that you
finish that poem, Gwyn.

GWYN: Terrible when you can't remember your own work.
(*Walks away.*) Terrible, terrible...fifth...sixth...seventh...

GLADMOUTH: May we get down to business, sire, if that is
all over now?

JOHN: We can do no business until the Jew comes.

GLADMOUTH: What Jew is this?

JOHN: You are here to talk about money. If you talk about
money in England today you must have a Jew. See, you
don't plan, you don't think. The one I have summoned

here will appal you. He is a supernaturally vile creature whose greed is amazing. He is an arch-Jew, the quintessence of usury.

CLAC: We have walked with the Jews for days, majesty. They roam the roads with us. We stay behind them, shuddering to think what is going on behind their beards. Many Jews share our poverty – from the other side of the hedge. Sometimes we split a smile about the justice of your exactions.

JOHN: I have heard that God has a sense of humour, Clac, but he is like me: he only laughs at his own jokes.

GLADMOUTH: If your majesty is bringing a Jew to this meeting, is it right to assume that you have already decided to grant us permission to build on this site? Are we now talking about the design itself and how to pay for it?

JOHN: You may assume what you like. As you know, I'm not to be trusted. I love the sound of the language, not its meaning. (*Pause.*) Your Pope is trying to depose me, Gladmouth. He urges the king of France to invade my country and steal my crown. Your bishops and cardinals curse me from pulpits all over the nation. In an act of phenomenal good nature I went to see old Hugh of Lincoln when he was dying and asked him if there was anything that he'd like me to forgive him for? He had often used bitter words against me. He was virtually a corpse when I spoke to him but he got the strength together to sit up and spit in my face. Now he's up for a sainthood. That is what your Church thinks of me.

(*Pause.*)

GLADMOUTH: Sire, we have already got good title to this land.

JOHN: I know you think so.

CLAC: I can't wait to get my hands on this place. It is full of possibilities.

GLADMOUTH: Any king will build with blessings on his head. But while the Church chastises you? Sire, that indicates a strength of soul and a depth of humility unparalleled, both of which I know you have… somewhere

(*Enter MIRABELLE wearing a starred cloak with the hood up.*)

MIRABELLE: I was told that the king lies here.

GWYN: Not only here, my lady, but everywhere he goes. A Jew, Johno. (*Pulls down her hood.*) A beautiful Jew!

MIRABELLE: Noah of Grantham sent me to attend a meeting.

JOHN: Where is Noah?

MIRABELLE: He died last night.

JOHN: Strange for a Jew to die on the eve of making some money. Who are you?

MIRABELLE: His daughter. (*Pause. She curtsies.*) My respects.

JOHN: Trust Noah to withdraw from the world just at the point when I needed him. That was very badly managed. I am most displeased.

MIRABELLE: My father ordered me to appear before you on his behalf.

JOHN: With his dying breath, no doubt. Business-like to the end.

MIRABELLE: He said it was the duty of our family to help the king if we could. In the past we have served the Crown well. He said you might remember that.

JOHN: Have you reported his death to the sheriff? It is the law.

MIRABELLE: Yes. It was done immediately.

JOHN: Was there no man who could come in your place?

MIRABELLE: I am my father's only child, and his heir.

JOHN: Well, you have had a wasted journey, and you too, Gladmouth. There is no point in carrying on with this meeting.

MIRABELLE: I am competent. My father has trained me as if I were his son.

JOHN: There is no competence without money. The debts owed to all Jews revert to the Crown upon death. So, the barons who owe your father now owe me. That should make me popular. And you are heir to nothing.

MIRABELLE: We are still able to consider this matter.

(*Pause. JOHN looks at her in astonishment.*)

JOHN: You still want to do business? I take everything he has outstanding and yet you still offer me money? Where do you get it from?

MIRABELLE: I have not offered anything yet, sire. But I am here to negotiate if there is anything worth talking about.

JOHN: I take my hat off to the Jews. Hooray for them! What an education you have had. Stand up, Gladmouth, and you, monk. Bow to this young woman.

GLADMOUTH: Bow to a Jew?

JOHN: Bow or I'll have your back broken!

(*Pause. They all bow.*)

Mine is worth a thousand of theirs. I salute you, for your beauty and (*Bows again.*) for your money. Where does it come from?

MIRABELLE: My father studied the law. He knew what would happen to the monies owed to him in this country when he died so he invested much of his capital abroad. Our family is in business in many countries.

JOHN: (*Shouting.*) Walter! (*Pause.*) Walter! Come here at once! Hurry!

(*Pause. WALTER enters at his own speed.*)

WALTER: Sire?

JOHN: How about a tax on all overseas investments of Jews?

WALTER: Impossible to implement, sire.

JOHN Why?

WALTER: It would need the co-operation of other Christian monarchs, with whom you have nothing but bad relations: not to mention the Mohammedans whom you consider to be heathens as well as a bad risk.

JOHN: But this woman holds a fortune abroad! Can't we get our hands on it somehow?

WALTER: Nothing could be easier. Throw her into prison on some charge or other then give her family the opportunity to redeem her for an extortionate fine. They will have to call on their foreign wealth to pay it.

JOHN: Worth thinking about.

WALTER: Then the other Christian monarchs will do the same to their Jews and the money they have invested here will be withdrawn – to our loss.

JOHN: Oh.

WALTER: What is it you want, sire? To be rough on the Jews? A foreign war? Additional taxes? I am here to serve you.

JOHN: Perhaps we'd better stick to horseshoes for the moment.

WALTER: I would it prefer it sire, though my doubts remain on that score.

JOHN: This is Noah of Grantham's daughter. The old villain himself has gone and died on me.

WALTER: I know, sire. He hanged himself.

(*Pause. MIRABELLE looks steadfastly ahead.*)

JOHN: How did you know that?

WALTER: Information came through last night. It did not seem worth bothering you about it when we were discussing more important matters.

(*Pause. JOHN walks over to MIRABELLE.*)

JOHN: When did your father instruct you to attend this meeting?

MIRABELLE: Before.

JOHN: Before what?

MIRABELLE: Before he went into the orchard with the rope.

WALTER: May I go back to sleep now, sire?

JOHN: Stay here. I'll need you if I'm to deal with someone as hard as she is.

WALTER: As you wish, sire.

JOHN: You are looking at her with different eyes, Gwyn. What do you see now?

GWYN: Only someone who has to do as she's told. Why did your father hang himself, sweetheart? There are plenty of people who would have done it for him.

MIRABELLE: He had had enough, as I have, of your cruel, Christian insolence.

(*JOHN strikes MIRABELLE a tremendous blow and knocks her down. Pause.*)

JOHN: I had to do that, my lady. You are in the presence of a man who has taken the Cross.

MIRABELLE: (*Getting up.*) I should not have spoken in such a way. I ask your forgiveness.

JOHN: It is granted. Tell me about this monastery we might

be going to build.

CLAC: Ooooh, sire! Such a place I'll make it!

JOHN: Let it be big, eh?

CLAC: Huge, sire, huge. Colossal, rearing up, stone aroused from sleep.

JOHN: Let it be glorious, ha?

CLAC: Full of light and splendour! Radiant, in fact, luminous.

JOHN: I like the sound of it. Whatever ideas we come up with let them not be sordid or small like the minds of men. My decision will affect the eternal. It will give the infinite another foothold here on earth, if I agree, that is. Divinity must wait on me a while. Before we start, this being the break of a new day, and we being about God's business, the abbot will say mass for us.

(*MIRABELLE starts to withdraw.*)

Where are you going?

MIRABELLE: To allow you room.

JOHN: No, no. Stay and listen. Learn something.

MIRABELLE: I am forbidden.

JOHN: We're not trying to convert you. Look upon it as an entertainment. The abbot will start now. Gwyn, look after this young woman. See that she doesn't get too affected by this Christian ceremony... (*Pause.*) Gladmouth, begin.

GLADMOUTH: Sire.

JOHN: Jew, your admirer will see to it that you are not persuaded to alter your religion. If he sees you are weakening in the face of Christian truth he will refute it for you – in Welsh. Continue, abbot.

GLADMOUTH: Your majesty knows...

JOHN: Do you understand Latin?

MIRABELLE: I do. If your majesty is willing, I would prefer not to hear it in this manner. My studies were for the law...

JOHN: Oh, don't be so fastidious. Think of the marvellous paradox that we are creating whereby thousands of fools at mass this morning will not understand a word of it – and you, a damned and obdurate Israelite, will have a clear knowledge of what is being said and will remain totally unconvinced. It is something for us all to think about. Well, let's get started.

(*Pause. JOHN gestures to GLADMOUTH to begin.*)

GLADMOUTH: Your majesty is aware that I cannot say mass in his presence.

JOHN: This is the prologue to the ceremony. It is essential that there be some dispute over minor details. When they are resolved then God will be praised as He deserves.

GLADMOUTH: You have been excommunicated, sire. At the moment you are denied all Christian ministrations, aids and comforts.

JOHN: (*Standing behind a stone.*) Then I'm not here. Go on without me. God knows I would not stand in His way.

GLADMOUTH: With or without you, sire, no mass can be said in England until the interdict is lifted.

JOHN: Then sing it!

GLADMOUTH: It is the same, said or sung.

JOHN: But we will disappoint the Jew. What will she think we are? Is this the religion that despises her? The king of England cannot hear a few words in a field in the language of Nero and Tiberias? We will have her laughing at us.

GLADMOUTH: Her opinions do not matter to me.

JOHN: (*Furiously.*) But the Pope's do, and he is as much a foreigner! (*Pause.*) Oh, Hebrew, I am sorry that I built up your appetite to witness a Christian moment of togetherness. No doubt you will feel the lack of it as the day goes on. If I may explain, the mass that you did not see is what the monastery that we have not built would house if it were ever allowed to exist. An historic meeting we have here – its logic teems, teems. To whom shall we dedicate this magnificent conundrum of a monastery? John? Saint John the Divine? Yes, the abbey church should be dedicated to John the best friend that Christ ever had: and what a writer!

CLAC: Until now we were thinking more of Saint Rosambertius, sire.

JOHN: Never heard of him.

CLAC: She is the patron saint of mushroom-pickers. (*Pause.*) Our community has lived off little else for the last five years. Without mushrooms we would have starved.

(*Pause. JOHN gives GLADMOUTH a long, hard look.*)

JOHN: Just so, just so.

CLAC: Also, sire, it is the mushroom that we share with the poor and the oppressed, those in despair...lepers... outcasts...our brothers...

JOHN: Yes, yes. Drag me down, do.

GLADMOUTH: With so many beggars and vagrants on the land...

JOHN: Thousands of them. In fact, Gladmouth, the beggars are begging off the beggars. Walter!

WALTER: Sire?

JOHN: A tax on beggary?

WALTER: It would hard to collect, sire.

JOHN: Buggery?

WALTER At the moment that is against the law. We could repeal the legislation and encourage the practice, I suppose, then creep up on them.

CLAC: Mice, frogs and grass, I have eaten. My own dirt and dung I have dined off. I have loved you, sire, even when I have lain on the grass in the morning dew, staring at the ground, waiting for a mushroom to sprout. As that little white head came peeping out, I thought...here comes the king!

JOHN: Well, there's a friend. You see my Welsh bard, monk? He is a foreign friend as well. But he is leaving me. He has things to do in another place. Work awaits him, pain and sweat, a kind of labour that would make the hair of a lesser man stand on end. But he is young and up to it. That is how his father trained him – to be supple in his leisure but stiff in his purpose. He will serve his father as his father serves me. In high places.

GWYN: What are you saying, Johno?

JOHN: Not now, not now...we have all day.

GWYN: Tell me if you've made your mind up. Don't torment me.

JOHN: Be silent, boy! (*Pause.*) Gladmouth, what size of establishment are we thinking about?

GLADMOUTH: The monastery will house ten thousand.

JOHN: Ten thousand hungry monks? How will you feed them? Where will you get such an income?

GLADMOUTH: The Jew must turn her face away.

JOHN: Why?

GLADMOUTH: We are going to allow you sight of an holy Christian relic.

(*Pause. JOHN looks at MIRABELLE and grimaces. She turns away.*)

Show the king, Clac.

(*CLAC takes a bag from under his habit. Out of it he brings an old, dirty sponge.*

CLAC and GLADMOUTH cross themselves.

CLAC holds it up.)

The sponge with which Our Lord was offered vinegar on the Cross.

JOHN: It looks well for twelve hundred years. Those in my bath-house fall to bits within six months.

GLADMOUTH: It goes without saying that this holy relic has miraculous properties of self-preservation, as all of them do.

JOHN: Oh, that kings could be relics!

GLADMOUTH: It was kept in a secret place in Constantinople. When the city was taken by crusaders under Count Baldwin it was given to an English knight as ransom, for a noble prisoner.

JOHN: Very astute, these English knights.

GLADMOUTH: Upon his return to England, the knight – a poor and ragged wanderer by then – fell sick with tertian fever. We cared for him as best we could. When he lay dying on the roadside he gave our community the Holy Sponge as his act of contrition.

JOHN: The Holy Sponge. May I touch it?

CLAC: If you will let me build my monastery, great lord, I will wash your body with it from top to toe.

JOHN: Are you sure it is genuine?

(*CLAC gives the sponge a squeeze and holds it up to JOHN's nose. He sniffs it.*)

Vinegar. (*Pause.*) Who'd have thought it?

MIRABELLE: (*Keeping her face averted.*) Is this...object...to be offered in any way as security?

JOHN: It's worth a fortune. Do you know what the right hand of Saint James takes at Reading every year? Don't be skeptical, Jew. They have something here.

GWYN: Sponges draw sustenance from what is around them in their natural home, the sea. There are men like that, who suck the goodness out of others. (*Pause. GWYN comes over and looks closely at the sponge.*) Some of our Welsh brothers went on crusade and one of them came back with the cock that crowed when Peter betrayed Christ. It was a very old bird bought in a bazaar.

JOHN: What is your name, lovely?

MIRABELLE: I am called Mirabelle.

JOHN: Well, then, Mirabelle. Are we to have a vast loan made on the strength of a sponge?

MIRABELLE: I would need to have its attractiveness proved.

JOHN: Kiss me.

MIRABELLE: That is a command I am entitled to disobey.

JOHN: Hm! Very proud!

GLADMOUTH: Sire, we have yet to discuss the style of the building.

JOHN: Never mind the style. What about the cost? Always, the cost!

CLAC: To build my masterpiece I will need eight thousand pounds to be repaid over fifty years.

MIRABELLE: The interest on that would be sixty per cent.

JOHN: Sixty per cent!? And you would not kiss me.

MIRABELLE: It is a low rate for the risk.

JOHN: On eight thousand pounds over fifty years you would stand to make a fortune... Gladmouth, the Jew is giving a special rate, I think.

GLADMOUTH: She is as rapacious and bitter as all her people. We cannot consider sixty per cent.

JOHN: It is reasonable. Think of her risks! They're gigantic!

MIRABELLE: In our experience of monastic loans over a long period there are inevitably dilapidators from inside and predators from outside.

GLADMOUTH: The administration of Cistercian houses has always been above reproach...

JOHN: So you say.

MIRABELLE: You managed to shut down and lose one monastery. Who is to guess that you won't do the same with another? You have a poor record in these matters.

(*Pause. GLADMOUTH is so angry that he cannot reply.*
He turns away. Pause.
CLAC creeps forward.)

CLAC: We didn't lose it. It is still there. But it is in the old, heavy style. The river is undercutting the foundations. Peasants are stealing the stone for their cottages. The gardens have gone back to wilderness.

MIRABELLE: Would the Crown consider giving a guarantee of some sort that it will not tax this new monastery out of existence?

JOHN: If the Cistercian order will pay for such a guarantee.

GLADMOUTH: We are destitute!

JOHN: Like the Jew you have friends abroad. Your order has over three hundred monasteries who can help you. And the Pope!

GLADMOUTH: How much would this guarantee cost?

JOHN: A thousand pounds.

GLADMOUTH: No!

JOHN: Without it the Jew will have to ask for an even higher rate of interest. Well, there are problems here. (*Pause.*) I need to consult Walter...there may be a way through but it looks doubtful...very doubtful.

CLAC: Sire, help us. We are your people...

JOHN: No, Clac. You are the Pope's people, God's people. You do not live in England in your minds but in Rome, or Heaven. You are outsiders. During fifty years there will be several kings – not all of them as sympathetic to...outsiders...as I am.

CLAC: (*Crying.*) Sire...I beg of you...for the sake of my brethren...give them a home...

JOHN: And there will be several popes in that fifty years. You know what they're like...some of them will hate monks.

CLAC: We were so happy in our old home. Our river had trout in it. At vespers I used to sit near the window and watch them jumping. Where we washed our clothes there were stones with leaves and fish bones imprinted on them, God's drawing-board itself.

JOHN: Yes, yes. I have changed my mind.

CLAC: Joy! We are saved!

JOHN: I think sixty per cent is not right, Mirabelle.

GLADMOUTH: Not right! It is outrageous.

JOHN: It should be seventy. With ten per cent of that paid to the Crown.

GLADMOUTH: You are outdoing the Jew!

JOHN: There is the sponge. If you believe in its powers set it to work. Earn your money. Make your way in the world. (*Pause.*) Does it perform miracles? That always draws the crowds.

GLADMOUTH: Yes. It speaks in the presence of evil.

JOHN: Is that supposed to be useful?

GLADMOUTH: To the pure in heart.

JOHN: Have you ever heard it say anything?

GLADMOUTH: During the time that it has been in the safe-keeping of our community it has maintained an absolute silence.

JOHN: Oh, it would, wouldn't it? Hardly talkative now though, even with, a Jew close by to provoke its wrath!

MIRABELLE: Perhaps it is speechless with indignation.

GLADMOUTH: The last time it spoke was at the fall of Constantinople: the destruction of a great city and the impoverishment of its people by bad government and cruel policies...

JOHN: Oh, I see...that kind of evil. Will that entice pilgrims to the monastery of Saint...Rosambertius? From my observations I think no pilgrims, having walked such great distances, are more likely to purchase a cure for sore feet or haemorrhoids. Does it cure anything mundane?

CLAC: Water that has been squeezed through the sponge cures scurf.

JOHN: Scurf. The Welsh bard has got bad scurf. He finds snowdrifts of it on his pillow in the morning, don't you, boy? Yes, it's true, you must go. Your father must pay the forfeit. There is no way out of it. I am sorry, Gwyn. Such a lot of business today...very rushed, you understand.

GWYN: Why don't you take a moment to think about it? It's my life.

JOHN: There are no moments. I have to use the day as I find it. Tomorrow, around eleven o'clock, at Nottingham. I am very sorry, honest.

GWYN: Nothing I can say will change your mind?

JOHN: No. I have too much to do. I have been thinking about it all the while I have been talking to these people...I cannot let your father get away with it. It's awful, I know.

GWYN: Johno...I'm young, barely twenty-five...no children...

JOHN: Your father will have thought of that. Obviously he wants rid of you, and your line.

GWYN: Mirabelle, I appeal to your woman's heart...speak to him for me. Have you ever heard such cruelty?

MIRABELLE: It you are in receipt of the king's displeasure you may have deserved it.

GWYN: Father Abbot...in the name of mercy... Why should I suffer for my father's actions? I am not treacherous...the king is my friend.

GLADMOUTH: Is he one of the Marlborough hostages, sire?

JOHN: Gladmouth, be cautious. I do not need your help on this matter.

GLADMOUTH: The Welsh lords have been released from any allegiance to you by the Pope himself. A bull has been issued. It was even translated into Welsh, I understand. If there is no allegiance then there can be no rebellion.

JOHN: I am a man who keeps his promises. I promised this man's father that if he ever resisted my authority again I would hang his son.

GLADMOUTH: But you have no authority...in Wales.

JOHN: Nor England, according to your master, the Pope. But even Innocent himself, in all his arrogance, cannot unwrite history. A treaty was made at Marlborough. It was understood, and signed. Now it comes into force.

MIRABELLE: Then you are condemning him for his father's crime, which is not reasonable even under common law.

JOHN: I am not condemning him. I am just hanging him. (*Pause.*) This is nothing to do with the law, Mirabelle. It is outside it, as you are.

MIRABELLE: I apologise to your majesty for speaking out.

JOHN: A scholar will apply learning. Let these financial questions about Gladmouth's monastery wait a while. Tell me, Clac, what will this...edifice look like? Have you any ideas about the design, the style? Architecture interests me greatly.

GLADMOUTH: Time for you to reveal your complete concept to the king. Choose your words well.

GWYN: Johno! Look at me!

(*JOHN ignorers him.*)

Give me some more time...please...let me write to my father...

CLAC: (*Very excited, moving around the stones caressing them.*) This ancient ring. Has it confounded your mind? Who built it? What were they worshipping? I, cementarium magisterium, have cracked that question. On a previous visit, while searching here for food, I had the answer revealed to me.

GWYN: Johno...I know you're busy but...a letter...

CLAC: These standing stones were the legs of the Round Table.

GWYN: I could get it to him in a day.

JOHN: Stop your whining! Remember who you are! (*Pause. JOHN turns to CLAC.*) Go on, monk, you were saying... these were the legs of the Round Table.

CLAC: I have refined those legs down to one great central leg, the base of which encompasses this venerable circle. King Arthur did not design his table out of the air. It was a copy from Nature. In my plan, inspired by one of the low-lying forms in God's vegetable creation – at the top of a great leg that is a thousand feet high, no less – will be the monastery itself. The massive cloister will be big enough to contain ten thousand monks in their thunderous ambulations and prayer. This upper structure, on its tall white tower, will be a huge, flattened dome. (*Pause.*) I see it gleaming white and round in the glowing green fields.

JOHN: One great leg, you say, with a flattened dome on top? This is very bold thinking, radical! Are you sure they have not built one of these new-fashioned monasteries in France? I must be the first.

CLAC: Sire, I assure you there is only one of its sort in the whole world and that is here in my noddle.

GLADMOUTH: Such invention is beyond the French, sire. They are a dull nation at heart.

JOHN: I am drawn to this idea. Your design excites me. Monk, come to your king! Embrace me! I would honour you with my body.

CLAC: I stink, sire…

JOHN: (*Putting his arms round CLAC and starting to crush him in a bear-hug.*) Oh, stand still. Let me hold English genius in my arms. Ah, I hear the strum of Saxon sinews, the crack of Arthur's bones. The laughter of the Round Table.
(*CLAC is gasping for air.*)
You do stink, in truth. What is that smell? Something picked before we get out of bed (*Swings CLAC off his feet and throws him to the ground with a wrestler's skill.*) Oh, you bad man. You lied to me. I know they have one or these new monasteries in the town of Champignon! (*Kicks CLAC.*)

CLAC: Sire! My ribs are broken, my vaults are bending, my arches falling, blood pours out or my crypt! You have tumbled my tower!

JOHN: (*With a foot on CLAC's neck.*) Fungus, in oil I'll have you fried. With pig-meat and hens' eggs! (*Pause.*) Where do you get the gall to mock me with mushrooms?

CLAC: From God's garden, God's dungheap, God's thundercloud. Oh, you wicked king! In your realm the rain is molten lead! No, don't…
(*JOHN goes to kick CLAC.*
GLADMOUTH stands over CLAC and protects him.)
I have taken his blows, master. They have hurt my sides. No more kicking, sire. The abbot will talk to you now. He promised.

JOHN: Gladmouth – you should have spoken before I stubbed my toe on this innocent. What do you want to tell me? (*Pause.*) Can't you bring yourself to say it?

GLADMOUTH: I taught him to mock you. Take out your anger on me.

JOHN: Why didn't you get the monk to stick a knife in me? He'd do it for you, wouldn't you?

CLAC: Oh, yes, yes. A big knife too!

JOHN: You walked thirty miles through the night for a joke? This is not like you, Gladmouth. What do you want?

GLADMOUTH: (*Passionately.*) Why should the meek not mock a monster? The people will kill you in their own time before the land is totally desolated. And we pray to God for that day to come! But it is not our occupation to murder kings. Our occupation is God's glorification through sacrifice...

JOHN: Pshaw! Idle, pretentious, incompetent bawd! All you sacrifice is other men's money.

GLADMOUTH: Royal excrement. Tormentor of the poor. Enemy of the helpless. I will sit on your shoulder and scream in your ear all the black truths of your reign. You have poisoned England.

CLAC: (*Springing up like a hound.*) King John's dog pisses on King John's leg for no oak trees remaineth, the sap is all draineth!

JOHN: This man is mad. He doesn't know when to keep his mouth shut.

GLADMOUTH: Yes, he is mad: that is why I brought him here, to show you what you've done! Clac is only one of twenty madmen in our community. Five years ago they were sane and content. Deprivation, hunger, misery homelessness, have done their work.

CLAC: Ten thousand brothers on a spiral stair, what legs, what legs to be seen whirling upwards...

GLADMOUTH: Clac's mind will never mend. He is mad, till death. The poor man's lunacy was brought on by his feeding off certain mushrooms that cause inflammation of the brain. He knew what he was eating. We had warned him against them. But he was deaf, starving – hungry, so desperate for food that he ate them anyway. Didn't you, you sad creature? Before that you were one of our best – full

of life and God's goodness, a credit to us all…now, this…
wretchedness.

CLAC: Legs is what we're after. Massive, muscular legs…
I have done wrong! I have mocked the king! But have
I wrecked a kingdom?

GLADMOUTH: Blessed is the man that you hate! (*He takes a
sword from the pile of arms. Holding it up by the tip, he puts it
into JOHN's hand and kneels in front of him, bowing his head.*)
I have taught my monks to acknowledge you as Antichrist,
to fear you as Satan. I have taught the common people to
loathe and despise you. Everyone in my community spits if
your name is mentioned. We call you thief, liar, murderer,
enemy of God and man. (*Pause. He looks up at JOHN.*) You
are beyond hope and damned.

JOHN: You have never grown up, Gladmouth. Hell does not
belong to you.

GLADMOUTH: Drunkard, Fornicator. (*Lifts the sword onto his
neck.*)

JOHN: Priests have one great fault…like entertainers.

GLADMOUTH: Sodomite. Perjurer.

JOHN: Because they spend their lives repeating rituals they
imagine they can work the same trick twice.

GLADMOUTH: Kill me, you sinbag! Strike off my head!

JOHN: (*Throwing away the sword. Pause.*) There will be no
more Thomas à Beckets here.   (*Walks away.*) Your old
hero will not make a reappearance.

GLADMOUTH: (*Following him on his knees.*) Give me my
death! You have taken everything else, take my life!

GWYN: My lord Abbot, you must not tempt the king in this
way. (*Hauls GLADMOUTH to his feet.*) Johno has enough
mortality on his conscience for one morning. And what
will the Jew think of all this? We can't have abbots queuing
up for martyrdom. Is this a game you used to play when
you were children, Johno?

GLADMOUTH: To be slaughtered by him would be Paradise!

JOHN: Do you suppose that I learnt nothing from my father?
Letting Becket provoke him was the biggest mistake he
ever made. It was a cold conspiracy: behind it was the

Pope. He authorised Becket's suicide, that is what it was. A sham martyrdom to get my father helpless with guilt.

WALTER: Sire, you go too far!

JOHN: The Pope won that game. My father paid him out for Becket's death. One full third of all English lands ended up in the hands of the Vatican. What has that got to do with God's glory? And what has this sick animal's lust for death got to do with life?

GLADMOUTH: Kill me, I implore you!…let me go…

JOHN: Walter, have these fools put in prison.

WALTER: What are their crimes sire?

JOHN: Holding up the Crown to ridicule.

WALTER: That is not on the statute-book, sire – yet.

JOHN: And put Gwyn in prison as well. He will be hanged at Nottingham tomorrow for his father's breach of contract. And you might as well take the Jew along. I've no doubt old Noah stole that rope. That leaves you. What have you done lately?

WALTER: Me sire? I am the worst thief of all. I am our chief adviser on taxation.

JOHN: (*Pause.*) I wanted to build that monastery, that place of prayer and learning, that fountainhead of charity. The opportunities for a king to create something pure that will last are few. Out or the ruin of that house of witless sluggards that you ran, Gladmouth, I hoped to make something new.

WALTER: I was waiting for a more opportune time, sire, but I might as well add to your despondency now as later. The barons de Vesci and Filtzwalter have raised a general rebellion against you at Chester. (*Pause. WALTER waits for a reaction.*) Sire, have you grasped the full import of what I have said?

(*JOHN stares into space.*)

Sire…did you hear?

(*Pause. JOHN continues staring into space. He frowns.*)

JOHN: What is a general rebellion?

WALTER: Anyone can join in.

JOHN: Why?

WALTER: Commerce is dying, the farmers cannot make the

land pay, tradespeople are being ruined in droves, ship-
building, mining…all bad.

JOHN: And yet I see so many people making money in England. I see fat farmers everywhere. They moan, and moan,
and prosper. What's going on?

WALTER: The country is collapsing under your taxes sire, be
assured.

JOHN: No, it's not. Things are getting better. This is the work
of de Vesci and Fitzwalter. I know them of old. They think
this will shake me. Oho – I'm not going to satisfy them.
This kind of bullying only makes me more obstinate. This
time, Walter, I will have the heads off de Vesci and Fitzwalter. Call the council!

WALTER: They are the council.

JOHN: (*Angrily.*) Then call a different council!

WALTER: We are in the middle of the country, sire. There is
no one we can summon in time to be of any use.

(*JOHN quietens down. He sits on a stone and ponders for
a moment.*)

JOHN: Who's loyal? Tell me the people I can trust.

WALTER: No-one.

JOHN: I see. (*Pause.*) After all I've given them, it all counts
for nothing. Nothing at all. What do they want this time?
All I've got? I cannot be king without money…money…
(*Pause.*) There are friends who will help me. There must
be. I have done more than enough… I've tried… Chester,
that's miles away. By the time I get there they could have
marched past me in the night and got into London…

WALTER: That might have happened already, sire. The idea
of a rebellion in London and the provinces at the same
time is one you perfected during your brother Richard's
reign.

JOHN: They could already be in the palace?

WALTER: News takes time to get here, sire. You know what
the roads are like. Infested with thieves and outlaws.

JOHN: They could already be in Westminster.

WALTER: Or the French may have invaded. King Philip has
got permission from the Pope to depose you, remember?

The French could be working hand in hand with de Vesci and Fitzwalter. Then there's the Welsh. They're already in revolt.

JOHN: Yes, we know all about them.

WALTER: They could be tied in with de Vesci and Fitzwalter and the French...

JOHN: And the Pope. Don't forget the Pope.

WALTER: We know that as soon as your back is turned and you're in the middle of repelling this French invasion, the attack from Wales and the drive south to London from Chester by de Vesci and Fitzwalter, the Scots will come pouring over the northern border. And, while you're fighting on these four fronts, Ireland will go up in flames.

JOHN: Naturally. Is there anyone you've left out? What about the West Country, Walter?

WALTER: As you know, sire, if they see an opportunity to strike a blow at you, they won't hang back.

JOHN: That's the way I read it. And North, South, East... everywhere. (*Flaring up.*) Why wasn't I kept up to date with these conspiracies? What about all the spies we keep in the retinues of people like de Vesci and Fitzwalter?

WALTER: They are cancelled cut by the spies they keep here, sire. Each gives the other false information, almost by agreement.
(*Pause.*)

JOHN: I am betrayed. It is all over.

WALTER: No sire, all that has happened is that you have become too unpopular with too many people at the same time.

JOHN: I should spread it over longer periods, obviously.
(*JOHN stares at his hands.*
WALTER makes no reply.
JOHN looks at the others who are now standing together as if for protection. They are all watching him.)
Well? What are you gaping at? (*Pause.*) How many of the royal guard have I got with me?

WALTER: You had two hundred, sire.

JOHN: Had?

WALTER: They have fled.

JOHN: Men of principle, the royal guard.

WALTER: They have their futures to think of...

JOHN: What do you advise me to do then?

WALTER: Flight, surrender or suicide seem to be the only choices, sire.

JOHN: Not to a son of Henry the Second. My father always used to say, when your back is to the wall, climb over.

CLAC: I can eat grass, so make me the captain of horse. Boiled grass with mint is not a bad breakfast.

JOHN: Breakfast. How thoughtless of me. Here I am with my kingdom falling about my ears and I haven't spared a thought for breakfast. You're not mad at all, Clac. That is good advice. We'll have breakfast.

CLAC: I was not hinting, majesty, but my stomach speaks for itself.

JOHN: Get them to bring some breakfast, Walter.

WALTER: I would counsel against it, sire.

JOHN: Against breakfast? What has breakfast done?

WALTER: The servants have all run away... But they did leave breakfast out for you.

JOHN: Good of them. Go and get it.

WALTER: Cider and peaches.

JOHN: Cider and peaches?

WALTER: That's all there was left. And the barons' spies will almost certainly have poisoned it all before they went.

(*JOHN howls and holds his head. Pause. He looks up.*)

JOHN: I am deserted.

GLADMOUTH: Praise be to God!

JOHN: Thank you, Gladmouth.

MIRABELLE: May I beg a favour of the king?

JOHN: The what? Are you talking to me? King? Where are my subjects? Where is my country?

MIRABELLE: My people bury their dead within the day of death. My father's funeral is being held up until I return to Grantham. As there appears to be no prospect of business here, may I go home?

JOHN: You are lucky, Mirabelle.

MIRABELLE: How so, sire?

JOHN: You have a home to go to.

MIRABELLE: Let me go to my family.

JOHN: No. I need you.

MIRABELLE: For what?

JOHN: You five are all that is left of my people. This circle is all that is left of my kingdom.

(*JOHN picks up the sword, puts the hilt down on the ground and the tip against his heart.*)

One falls on it, doesn't one? What happens now? I just relax? Do I hear anyone say, 'Don't do it, John!?' Ah, your concern is inarticulate. But I think I see tears in your eyes. Oh, England on a sword's tip! (*Throws the sword away.*) There, that makes you feel happier, doesn't it? I'll just wait and see if things improve.

(*Pause. They all stare at him.*)

(*Angrily.*) Well, say something!

Blackout.

End of Act One.

ACT TWO

A few minutes later. JOHN is kneeling, bowed over, his head in his hands in despair. GWYN, CLAC, GLADMOUTH, WALTER and MIRABELLE stand around him like the stones. A long pause.

GWYN: Come on, Johno. This isn't how to behave. Rise above it, remember!

WALTER: Hush, boy! How dare you admonish his majesty. (*Pause.*) Sire, you should not humble yourself before us to this degree.

(*JOHN gets to his feet.*)

JOHN: Bad form, eh, Walter? Why shouldn't I show you how low I've sunk? God, God, what a mess I've made of things. (*He sits on the sponge, which is still on this fallen stone.*)

CLAC: Oi! Don't sit on my sponge!

JOHN: Would you deny me a little comfort, Clac?

CLAC: The Holy Sponge doesn't like to be sat upon: though I suppose it's built to stand it.

WALTER: What do you intend to do about your situation, sire?

JOHN: I can't move from here without protection. I'm stuck, Walter, marooned. All I can do is wait and see what happens. Anyone got any better ideas?

WALTER: Are you asking us, sire? (*Pause.*) Would you like us to be your council? Who knows, something of value might emerge.

GLADMOUTH: Huh!

JOHN: A response from the Church. Was that help you were giving me, Gladmouth? Huh? (*Pause. He gets to his feet.*) Any advance on huh? That's very baronial, huh. They huh a lot in council but I'd rather that you tried to be a little more articulate.

WALTER: Am I allowed my say, sire?

JOHN: Would I leave you out, my trusted scourge.

WALTER: I have always tried to give you my honest opinions in spite of difficulties.

JOHN: Walter is trying to tell you how hard it is to be on my council. A lot of people cannot stand the pace.

GLADMOUTH: Or the threats and the meanness and the cruelty!

WALTER: Father Abbot, it is your duty to assist his majesty if you can. He is in great need.

JOHN: So, Mirabelle? Anything to offer?

MIRABELLE: (*Pause.*) I do have ideas…views on this country, but I dare not give them to you.

JOHN: There is no risk. Say what you like. All of you have my word. There will be no recriminations.

MIRABELLE: But I must remember that you are not a man to be trusted…

JOHN: Ah, the council has got off to a good start! She is attacking me! Mirabelle, go on, go on. I promise you. There will be no memory of this day. Only these stones will bear witness.

MIRABELLE: Then they will probably hear you alter your principles to suit your cases.

JOHN: Wham! Straight between the eyes!

GWYN: I don't think you understand him at all. It takes time and study and patience. His morality is very complicated.

MIRABELLE: The king will patronise me if he pleases; but I don't have to take it from you.

GWYN: Patronise you? Me? That was never my intention. I was only trying to explain. I know him and the way his mind works.

JOHN: Gwyn, don't get in the way of my council's business. If you want the girl, court her in your own time.

GWYN: What time have I got before eleven o'clock tomorrow and my meeting with your hangman?

JOHN: Twenty-four hours can be a lifetime. Who knows what is in store for us? Trust to fate and stop distracting the Jew while she is lecturing me.

GWYN: I could always run away!

JOHN: Oh, we could all run away: but into what? You're safer here; taking a chance on tomorrow. Mirabelle! More criticism, more, more! Crooocify me!

MIRABELLE: It is against my better judgement but I cannot resist telling you to your face that the officers of

English law are the most corrupt in Europe.

JOHN: They are. They take bribes because I cannot pay them. What else do you expect them to do?

MIRABELLE: So there is no justice in England.

JOHN: I am working on it. It will take time.

MIRABELLE: Justice is fundamental to the good government of any nation. Without it there is no central virtue, nothing for people to look up to.

JOHN: I accept your point. You are right.

WALTER: Sire, all she does is argue her own case. The Jews lack justice so they are always complaining about it.

MIRABELLE: That is not so. I make my case as an English-woman.

GLADMOUTH: A what? Now I've heard everything.

MIRABELLE: I was born in this land. I have never set foot outside it. If I am not an Englishwoman, what am I?

JOHN: You are a Jew. I thought that was supposed to be enough.

MIRABELLE: You are a Gentile. Is that enough for you?

JOHN: No, but I do not hold myself apart. I give myself to all. You belong to your race. I belong to everyone who has expectations of me. If I maltreat the Jews in this country, and I do, they at least have the comfort of knowing that I'm a king who is alleged to maltreat everybody. No wonder that you feel so English.

MIRABELLE: I will say no more.

JOHN: Come on, lovely. A council works both ways. Give and take. From your position as an alien tell me how I can improve myself?

MIRABELLE: Don't ask questions to which you already know the answer!

JOHN: Walter, she has found me out. The Jew has known me for an hour and she has opened me up like a surgeon. But not a word on how I can repossess my kingdom from which she makes so much. Does it matter to you who is king? The profit is the same. You Jews would be loyal to the crown if it were stuck on a pole! Go and blaze your beauty somewhere else, usurer!

(*MIRABELLE goes and stands behind a stone.*)

Now we've got rid of one of my critics and one of my weaknesses. This council is going very well. What have you got to say, Clac? Any good ideas.

CLAC: You've heard all my ideas and you didn't like them.

JOHN: True enough. See, Walter, they're just like the barons. Very disappointing.

WALTER: Oh, no, sire. They are thinking. Now, Father Abbot, there must be something from your store of knowledge and experience that you can offer the king.

JOHN: Yes, Gladmouth. You have envied me long enough. To put yourself in my place should not be difficult.

GLADMOUTH: Our father, Henry, was a *great* king.

JOHN: He's been waiting to tell you that. Yes, Gladmouth has the blood royal in his narrow veins. The red poison. One of my father's brood of bastards. That is why he likes to precipitate things. It's the blood urging him on to extremes. Who was your mother? Rosie someone? Wasn't she a deaf and dumb serf who couldn't run fast enough?

GLADMOUTH: He was a great king. He died in despair, a broken man. Thanks to you.

JOHN: Yes, I betrayed him. I did it to him. And everyone does it to me.

GLADMOUTH: We were talking about justice.

JOHN: Oh, yes. He loved me best and I betrayed him best. Did you ever meet him?

GLADMOUTH: He was proud to own me.

JOHN: You were a mistake. The old goat didn't have the sense to spray his seed on the ground instead of into your conniving, big-arsed mother and the other whores he knocked around with, so he had to herd them all into the Church. All my father's ugly, ridiculous, grasping bastards made into bishops and abbots! Oh, what a pollution of our holy places! You have cured me, Gladmouth. A word from you and I stop doubting myself. I am clean. I am pure, when I look at you!

GLADMOUTH: You people here, look at this man – you see the damned, you hear Hell talking. The son of the best king England ever had.

JOHN: He deserved my treachery.

GLADMOUTH: And you are asking us what is the matter with you?

JOHN: If you cannot rule a family how can you rule an empire?

GLADMOUTH: There you have the full depth of your depravity, John. All the world knows that you were his favourite son, and broke his heart.

JOHN: We are not fit to rule each other. (*Pause.*) No one is.

CLAC: Consider the crow that spends its life hopping from chimney-pot to chimney-pot. It believes Man's highest achievement is smoke. Smile, sire. You are soot-black inside and out, I curse you. (*Spits.*)

JOHN: As you say, madman. Rave on. You will spit more sense than I say.

GLADMOUTH: You must abdicate. There is no other honourable course for you.

WALTER: His majesty is sad. He has suffered overmuch lately.

JOHN: No, my old butt and footstool is right. My son is better fitted to rule. He is five years old and still wets the bed. However, he has innocence. This will enable him to treat everyone badly instead of only those who offend him. All government is error. Don't mention God or the   expulsion from the garden. To live any life but your own is a nonsense. Am I the only one who is opening up his heart?

GLADMOUTH: Only because you never mean what you say. This is no agony, John, this is a game. You are leading us on.

GWYN: Not so. I've heard him talk like this before. So has Walter, I know. Is it wrong to doubt, Gladmouth?

GLADMOUTH: Then let him give away his kingdom.

JOHN: I would but I have my father's mistakes to study. He gave away an empire – a piece for Henry, a piece for Richard, a piece for Geoffrey, a piece for John. The result has been twenty years of disunion. What am I, a fourth son doing in first place? Death has put me here, death keeps me here and only death will have me out of here. (*Weeps.*)

GWYN: Come on, Johno...don't weep in front of us.

JOHN: No, let me cry. What harm does it do me? You should all cry with me, having plenty to cry about. Is there anything else left worth doing? Join in. Weep with me.

CLAC: He can cry! He can cry!

WALTER: Are we to take it, sire, that this council is closed? I hope not. We are starting to respond.

JOHN: Closed? It has barely started! I'm just shedding my old state of mind, man, purging myself, preparing my brain for the battery of new ideas that will come from you all. Everyone here would make a better king than I. Everyone in the street. Everyone who can stand up and mumble 'yea' and 'do what you want'. Give this mad monk the crown, or the festering-souled abbot…and this Jew would look like the Queen of Heaven on coronation day. Let John go to his father's and rot. (*Pause.*) Death is the only pleasure of power.

CLAC: Whose death?

JOHN: Oh, mine, mine.

CLAC: No fun in anyone else's? Were they all wasted, my brothers? Her father's? Don't say that. They're part of the brickwork. I don't like to have the king cry.

JOHN: I wish I was as mad as you. It would be a refuge.

CLAC: Change places? Feel the world tilt as you walk on it? Listen to yourself talk as if it were a stranger by your own side. Not a good life, some days. But I wouldn't swop with you, Plantagenet.

JOHN: You are not as mad as you thought, then. (*To WAL-TER.*) Well, malignant! I am getting nowhere, am I? Even down to five and I fail. Can I even rule myself?

WALTER: This is the point in your moods when you usually…lash out. Where would you like me to stand?

JOHN: Stand where you like. There is a lot of room. This is the whole country. God is the sign-post.

WALTER: The sign-post, sire? How so?

JOHN: Many fingers. Many faces. Lots of directions. It will take you so many miles… Oh dear. I have reduced the sign-post to two fingers, so…and God is two-faced. Why are you blinking so much?

WALTER: Er...my eyes are tired, sire. God has two faces? Is this mentioned in the scriptures?

JOHN: Yes. In the gospel of Saint Luke and See. In the gospel of Saint Mark my words. In the gospel of Saint Matthew be so bloody thtupid? (*He rears up to strike WALTER who doesn't flinch. JOHN lowers his hand onto his shoulder.*) You used to be so good at ducking in the old days.

WALTER: The old days have gone, sire. Your blows have ceased to hurt.

JOHN: Have you never seen anything of value in me?

(*Pause.*)

WALTER: To say that God is two-faced is blasphemy surely?

JOHN: Ah, you can still duck the issue. Do me a few tricks.

WALTER: Not now, sire.

JOHN: If I survive this, Walter...hmm? Remember, I can hit hard.

WALTER: I am upset about what you said concerning God.

JOHN: Oh, look after the old fellow, do. Never mind me!

WALTER: Your majesty should...

JOHN: Should? I thought that word was banned between us. As well as ought. The roads of Europe are full of grey and black and white men muttering 'should' and 'ought'. My subjects should and ought to love me, but they don't.

WALTER: Are those who govern us ever really loved, sire?

JOHN: They loved brother Richard the Lion's Arse, the crazed crusader, didn't they? And beggared themselves to raise sixty thousand marks – sixty thousand! that's two year's income for my Exchequer! – to pay his ransom. Would they cough up that much for me? To have me dead, perhaps.

WALTER: Oh. I doubt that, sire.

JOHN: All Richard ever did was frolic around on foreign battlefields. Butchery amused him. But when John fights abroad? A different matter altogether; even though my wars are cheaper, better managed and more profitable. Mirabelle! Thoughts from your womb on war.

MIRABELLE: War is money poured into a bottomless pit.

JOHN: What? The defence of the realm a waste of time?

MIRABELLE: The defence of the realm is not the same as the defence of the country. One – the realm – belongs to the king the other, the country – by nature, belongs to the people.

JOHN: But I am one of the people. My wars are for everyone!

MIRABELLE: How can they be? They are for your own power. The country can exist without the king but not the king without the country. One is necessary, the other a proposition yet to be proved.

JOHN: I am a proposition yet to be proved? That is certainly how I feel. Well, I'm all for this Hebrew logic. (*Pause.*) What do you truly think of us, Jew? What do you say in the safety of your own house?

MIRABELLE: Of you, sire? It is not the day of that degree of fool. I'm sure.

JOHN: Of we English. We drink too much?

MIRABELLE: Y-e-s.

JOLLY: We are idle?

MIRABELLE: Y-e-s.

JOHN: We are too cruel to strangers?

MIRABELLE/GWYN: (*Together.*) Y-e-s.

JOHN: Then what is the difference between us and the French? The Germans? The Italians? Name it for me. (*Pause.*) I can tell you. England is like you, like this council of mine lost here in a field on a summer morning. England is an outsider.

SPONGE: (*From under JOHN's backside.*) Nolens volems nonsense.

(*JOHN half gets to his feet, looking puzzled.*)

GLADMOUTH: It is part of Christendom…of Europe…

(*JOHN gingerly lowers himself back on top of the sponge.*)

JOHN: Another question to the council is this – does England need to be governed at all? (*Pause.*) The laws are only made to be broken. Agreements are made only to be ignored. People take from government what they want and leave the rest behind. Without the Crown and its use of the laws there would be chaos. What is the matter with that? We are accustomed to chaos. We had chaos in brother Richard's reign, chaos with father Henry, King Stephen…we have had a hundred years of chaos and we are still here. All people want is their land. It is the land that ensures survival, not government. While people worship rocks and stones and soil at the expense of justice, reason and basic rights, government in this country will be impossible. It is my opinion, noble councillors, that what people love in the darkest parts of their natures is what will ultimately define their actions. In England that is the land. And the land is evil.

SPONGE: (*Very loudly, under JOHN's backside.*) Fatuous, frantic fool!

JOHN: (*Leaping up.*) Wah!

CLAC: The king has farted! Close the gates!
(*Pause. JOHN looks around the others who are all on their feet now.*)

JOHN: You heard that? (*He looks closely at the sponge.*) It spoke!

CLAC: If the king pours rubbish out of his arse he is at least speaking his mind.

JOHN: In the presence of evil, you said, Gladmouth. That must mean you…or you…or you…

SPONGE: *Eripe me Domine ab homine malo.*
(*GLADMOUTH sinks to his knees.*)

GLADMOUTH: *Deo gratia, deo gratia.* A holy miracle in our midst.

CLAC: Is that all it can say? Rubbish. Tell my fortune, soldier.

JOHN: Which one of you is it talking to? Own up. You must know.

WALTER: You were the one who was sitting on it, sire.

JOHN: That doesn't mean anything…it's in the presence of evil…the presence…you're…we're all in the presence of evil…

CLAC: Sponge, say some more. The crusader said you were always chattering when he had you overseas. You sang him to sleep in Jaffa.

JOHN: No, leave it, when it wants to speak, it will.

GWYN: It has fallen silent. Maybe we were deceived. It could have been your bowels, Johno.

JOHN: No, it spoke. You all heard it. Jew, didn't you hear it?

MIRABELLE: I did hear something.

GLADMOUTH: The Holy Sponge has spoken. It is accusing someone. Have we any doubt who that is?

GWYN: My money would be on you.

(*Pause. JOHN is looking at the sponge closely.*)

WALTER: This is a very serious matter. When was the last miracle recorded in England?

GLADMOUTH: There have been no miracles at any shrine; from any relic, nor have there been visitations or visions granted to anyone since John came to the throne.

JOHN: Ah, I had never been aware of that before. Then this must herald a change. We must tell everyone. I don't think it's going to say any more. (*Pokes the sponge gingerly.*) Its power is obviously exhausted...

SPONGE: Do not touch me, Lucifer.

JOHN: (*Leaping back.*) Ah!

SPONGE: Prince of Darkness.

CLAC: Now it's talking! More! More!

SPONGE: You are evil, John.

JOHN: No...

SPONGE: You are evil.

JOHN: That's not so...

SPONGE: You are evil.

JOHN: (*Covering up his ears.*) Don't

SPONGE: Look at the land. It is being destroyed.

JOHN: It's not all my fault...it can't be...

SPONGE: There has never been such an evil king in England.

JOHN: There has...there must have been...

SPONGE: Name them.

JOHN: Ethelred, Rufus...

SPONGE: Saints in Heaven compared to you.

JOHN: William the Bastard.

SPONGE: In the book of judgement, John, they are your superiors.

JOHN: Sponge...Sponge, Holy Sponge...if you touched the lips of Christ, and He rejected you...you must know how I feel!

SPONGE: Every action that you have ever taken has been calculated to harm and hurt.

JOHN: Evil cannot come from pure confusion. There are thousands who have their answers pat. They are sure of right. They can be evil, because they are over-confident of good. (*Pause.*) Are you listening, Sponge?

SPONGE: Goodbye to your arguments. Even in dread you find excuses for yourself.

JOHN: (*Kneeling.*)   Holy Sponge, you are wise and powerful, they say – but you were offered to Christ and he rejected you. I was offered likewise to my people and they have rejected me. Is this not a sign of our inherent goodness? Also everyone expects us to do miracles. We are brothers, Sponge, comrades! We suffer the same, the same unreasonable expectations...and I am full of bitterness as you were full of vinegar, once... (*Puts the sponge to his cheek.*)

SPONGE: Put me down!

JOHN: (*Putting it down, very gently.*) See, I have even managed to hurt a sponge. Forgive me. I don't know what I did, or said, but I was clearly in the wrong.

CLAC: All the time we've been together the Holy Sponge has never complained of me and it lives in my sleeve.

JOHN: Oh, Clac, you know how to handle a miracle. I've never had my claws on one till now. Sponge, tell me, did you hear him say, 'Father Father, why has thou forsaken me' and 'It is finished'?

CLAC: Of course it did. It was there!

JOHN: Sponge, I, also, am finished. I know how Christ felt. Give me your blessing.

(*Pause.*)

SPONGE: You are evil, John Plantaganet.

JOHN: I deny that.

GLADMOUTH: You are refuting a holy relic, man! Have you no humility?

JOHN: Not when it lies. I am not evil!

GLADMOUTH: Everyone here believes that you are. And now the spirit of God Himself has spoken to you through the Sponge.

JOHN: I don't care. Holy Sponge, what I will say is this: if I am evil in what I must do to govern men in this creation then God is evil.

SPONGE: Aaaaah! (*Switching immediately to WALTER.*) All
bear witness to what the king has just said.

GLADMOUTH: (*Embracing WALTER.*) Well done, well done!
We have him!

JOHN: (*Still in his own thoughts.*) It is part of the power...

GWYN: (*Gently.*) Ssssh. Don't say any more. You've been had.

JOHN: I have tried hard...always done my best...never run
away...tell the Sponge the truth, Gwyn...you know me...

GWYN: Don't say another word. You've been duped.

(*Pause. JOHN looks around their faces, suddenly alert.*)

JOHN: Duped?

GWYN: Walter. One of his little tricks. He can throw his
voice.

CLAC: No, no, it was my sponge. I saw its lips move!

GLADMOUTH: My son, we had to flush the king into the
open. I'm sorry we had to use you but it was for the best.

CLAC: No, it was the Sponge spoke. Honestly!

JOHN: So it was you. Walter. Oh, great fun. Wonderful!

WALTER: Sire, the Father Abbot and myself have been appointed inquisitors for England by the Holy See...

JOHN: Such a trick! I didn't know you had it in you. Wonderful! Who taught it to you?

WALTER: I was taught ventriloquism while on my mission to
Rome to contest your excommunication...on your behalf.
Pope Innocent instructed me in the art himself.

JOHN: You're a Pope's man? You've betrayed me?

WALTER: For your own good, sire, and for God.

JOHN: Then let us hope it was worth it, for both our sakes.

GLADMOUTH: Now we have proof of your heresy. It has
been suspected for a long time. God is evil, you said.

JOHN: Oh, I was playing with words, throwing ideas around.
Never mind all that. But, Walter, Walter, can this be true?

WALTER: Action had to be taken, sire, before you contaminated the minds of the people.

JOHN: Don't talk to me! I can't bear to hear the sound of
your voice! What are you, nuncios, legates, crypto-cardi-
nals?

GLADMOUTH: We have documents to authorise our mission. You can see them. Pope Innocent himself is in charge of this operation.

JOHN: You, I understand, Gladmouth. You have cause to hate me. But this man…God, I cannot even look at him! …we have been so close that he could see into my inner heart. He knows, me and he has seen my problems first-hand… Tell me they forced you to do it…they have a hold over you!

WALTER: I have had to watch you going down the wrong road for too long. Pope Innocent took me into his confidence while I was in Rome. The months I was there opened my eyes. You have been pushing England deeper and deeper into chaos and isolation.

JOHN: And Innocent has helped all he can. Walter, he wants England for his own!

WALTER: No, sire: for Christ who binds us all together. You should know that I was ordained a priest while I was in Rome. From now on that will be my life.

JOHN: Don't apply to be my confessor, will you? That has to be someone I can trust!

WALTER: I pray that the time will come when you can forgive me this necessary deception. Meanwhile, there is your heresy.

GLADMOUTH: How will you get, out of that, John? We all heard.

JOHN: Oh, I said that for effect…don't you find these old stones make you feel odd?…argumentative, on edge… nervous of the truth…they listen for alternatives, don't you?

CLAC: King John is talking to the stones. Better than trying to eat them, which I've tried. These are my teeth-marks.

JOHN: Oh, they do listen, Clac. Have you ever built a church and finished it?

CLAC: No. But I will when you've gone to your fathers.

JOHN: And I will build an English state…but, I fear, someone else must finish it. Oh, I'm so sad, Walter. All those nights around the fire talking about horseshoes and such… I feel ill…probably a fever. Overwork takes its toll. Could be the drink. Long nights. Walter, you're a treacherous swine! I didn't mean that. Gladmouth, my dear brother, why you are of the blood royal yourself. You know our burdens from within...

GLADMOUTH: Squirm all you like. You are lost. John. It is all over with you.

JOHN: Surely the Vatican could anticipate some resentment. Innocent was only trying to be helpful, I know, when he damned everyone in England to perdition, took away all Christian comfort, deprived the dying of consolation, tried to depose me, encouraged the French king to invade, all because he couldn't get the yes-man he wanted in Canterbury. Oh, I suppose I have become confused between religion and the Pope. They're not necessarily the same thing, are they? Religion is what a man thinks in the privacy of his own mortal state and I, of course, am a devout Christian.

GWYN: Johno!

JOHN: Born and bred to it.

WALTER: You recant?

JOHN: Recant what?

WALTER: Your heresy!

GLADMOUTH: Watch him! He's on the move...he's trying to get out of it!

JOHN: Walter, I was not myself...the shock...such a brilliant piece of tomfoolery...I said the first thing that came into my mind...no, I didn't...it was for the sake of disputation, the university mood... I didn't mean it! Oh, why did you deceive me, old friend?

GWYN: Johno! Stand up for our faith! It was hard enough to find.

JOHN: What are you talking, about? What faith? This condemned prisoner doesn't care what he says...he is beside himself with fear.

WALTER: We heard you. There are five witnesses.

GLADMOUTH: God is evil. That is what you said. There can be no greater heresy than that.

GWYN: That's not everything he meant. We've worked it out together – there are two gods, one is evil and one is good. Both of them are creators...correct me if I'm getting this wrong, Johno…and our lives are governed by the conflict between them. It is all war, you see, and that is reflected in the human situation…isn't that right, Johno?

WALTER: You have discussed this with the king?

GWYN: Every day.

JOHN: Would I? With him? A hostage?

GWYN: Come on now, no more lies! Tell them straight! This is the truth. When the Albigensian refugees started arriving from Toulouse we talked to them and found that they shared our ideas. Thousand and thousands of people think as we do. Christianity just doesn't work! Isn't that so?

JOHN: Don't ask me. I've had no Albigensians near me. The boy is mad.

WALTER: We know that you have had them here. Every communication between yourself and your uncle, Count Raymond of Toulouse, that notorious protector of heretics, has been intercepted.

JOHN: I was only interested…academically. There was no intention of allowing them to preach here, or have any influence.

GLADMOUTH: They are everywhere. You have encouraged them. And you wonder why there is unrest and rebellion. It is your own doing.

GWYN: But Johno and I aren't Albigensians, are we? I mean, they're as ornate and cockeyed in their dogma as Christians. That's not anything like the religion we put together for ourselves. Ours is more practical.

JOHN: Be quiet, Gwyn! The boy is raving, raving…

GWYN: You see, we decided that the ultimate power of a man is in the spirit. All the inanimate does – the matter, the mountains, the land – is to challenge him with not being, to argue for the final nothingness. But the spirit cannot believe in nothingness – it cannot credit its own complete destruction. So it creates, and elaborates a hope that the spirit will live for ever. But death stands in the way. The hope becomes impossible and an oppression. So, we say, do not hope beyond the spirit in this life. When we die we become air.

MIRABELLE: He would have hanged you believing that? You try to protect him when he have sent you into nothingness after such a short life?

GWYN: It was his word. His word is his spirit. It was hard, but I accepted it. We have had such a time together working it all out.

MIRABELLE: How can you respect that coldness of heart?

JOHN: Oh, Jew – how else have you survived? Wonderful people, the Jews. With the Old Testament they have at least got half of Christianity right. They've been limping along with us ever since. Damn you, Gwyn! I have a job to do. I never speculated. Whatever happens, the king remains, boy. Look at me. Trapped...lost...

WALTER: He cannot be hanged now, of course.

JOHN: He must! Twice. I'll do it myself, with my own hands.

WALTER: He is a witness. Do you wish to compound your heresy? Must we report to the Vatican that you remain obdurate? There is time for you to change the colour of our findings. If you repent immediately, throw yourself on the Holy Father's mercy, we can argue for leniency.

GLADMOUTH: Leniency! Walter, be more prudent. Lenient, with him?

JOHN: Would you testify against me?

GWYN: A moment ago I would have said no. But you're willing to betray our beliefs, Johno. We worked them out together. I'd have taken the noose, gladly, if you'd kept your word on something that mattered.

JOHN: If you persist in this accusation of heresy what can Pope Innocent do to me? I'm already excommunicated. My kingdom is under an anathema. And that was all over the appointment of an archbishop, a triviality. What has he got left to hit me with?

GLADMOUTH: You know the punishment of heretics as well as I do.

JOHN: Burn a king? That would be an innovation.

GLADMOUTH: We would argue the case, and win.

JOHN: English law is for the English, king and all. In our courts the Pope is powerless. This Jew has more authority

than he has. At least she's here, she has learnt some of our
ways, our language. What is the Pope? An outsider again
but beyond the inner circle of outsiders, an outsider to
even outsiders! Go and track down my guard, tell them to
arrest me for the Pope. You dare not because they would
cut you to pieces. I concede that some of them may act
against me for the rebels, even for the French they could
be that treacherous – but never for the Pope.

GLADMOUTH: He is the supreme authority in all matters
spiritual and temporal. All monarchs must accept that!

JOHN: He is an Italian lawyer. He wouldn't know Jesus Christ
if he fell over him in the street.

GWYN: That's more like it, Johno. Away with all these old
lies.

JOHN: Keep out of this! (*Pause.*) What can a religion of two
achieve? (*Pause.*) How many converts do you think we
have made today?

GWYN: We worked it out ourselves…it's ours. You can't compromise with that, surely…

JOHN: That was all talk, Gwyn. Passing the time.

GWYN: Don't say that…it was all I had to hold on to… going
home to that old brute, my father. I was going to change
things over there you know…make life worth living. Do
you know what I mean? Make some sense out of it.
(*He slumps down, his head in his hands.*
JOHN goes to him.)

JOHN: Gwyn, in the Midi of France, they are, even this day,
slaughtering people of your persuasion. A crusade – there's
a word! – takes place against them. They are being wiped
off the earth.

WALTER: Before proceeding we must consult the instructions
we were given by the Vatican. Are we to take it that you no
longer deny your heresy?

JOHN: Lack of orthodoxy might be a better way of putting it.

GLADMOUTH: We have more than enough proof. You
could be brought before a Papal court, in Rome. We have
your person. You can be taken there.

WALTER: Leave the king to think. If you accept that you have
erred then there are certain proposals we have authority to

put to you but you must see them. They are written out in
the Pope's own hand. I will go and get them. (*Exits.*)
(*Pause.*)

JOHN: You have triumphed, Gladmouth.

GLADMOUTH: The triumph is not mine.

JOHN: It is difficult for me to think with you here. There is
something wrong with the actual air around you. Go away.

GLADMOUTH: What I have done has been for Mother
Church.

JOHN: Your mother has always had a lot to answer for.

GLADMOUTH: There must be a greater unity, John. England cannot survive outside Europe. Pope Innocent's
dream of a huge state sharing common faith and laws is the
design of the future. It will necessitate good government
because it will be built on good principles, not the whims
of unstable men such as yourself. Come, Clac. (*Exits.*)
(*Pause.*)

CLAC: Have you finished with my sponge?

JOHN: The old crusader didn't charge you for it, did he?

CLAC: Only a shilling.

(*JOHN gives CLAC the sponge.*
He puts it up his sleeve.)

We will need a house for all of us to live in again. I'll bring
my bag of tools. Why don't you lot join our community?
She can wash the dishes; he can keep the fires going and
you can work in the garden.

JOHN: (*Absently.*) Yes, yes...fight on...

CLAC: (*Sings.*) Matthew, Simon Peter, James and Tom,
Bartholomew, frere Andrew, Philip, Tad and John,
Simon Canaan, lesser James,
Judas – all write down their names.

Save no coin or all you've bought,
sell your land, destroy your fort,
if you would have your soul set free,
give all away and follow me.

Leave your father at the gate,
tell your mother not to wait
give brother, sister, parting sign,

who loves his blood cannot drink mine.

Matthew, Simon Peter, James and Tom,
Bartholomew, frere Andrew, Philip, Tad and John,
Simon Canaan, lesser James,
Judas – all write down their names.

JOHN: Monk, are you a priest with full powers?

CLAC: Yes, sire…I think so…

JOHN: Marry these two for me.

MIRABELLE: It would never be allowed…

JOHN: You are my ward now. Are you not one of your Father's debts? Marry him. Get her with child, Gwyn. Believe in children if you must believe in anything.

GWYN: Johno…what about tomorrow?

JOHN: Leave tomorrow to me. Take them. Stand them under a tree and marry them then neither of them can go home and be of further nuisance to me.

MIRABELLE: My family would be desolated!

JOHN: If he stays, he hangs. If you stay I'll have you forcibly converted and married to a very old, stinking baron. I want no witnesses to this trumped-up heresy. Don't worry, Gwyn, I'll get out of it, but go! Asia. Africa, anywhere. And when you've finished, monk, why don't you go and be a hermit somewhere?

CLAC: Make your mind up. One minute it's nuptials, the next it's hermits. No wonder people never know where they are with you. (*Shepherds MIRABELLE and GWYN off.*) Stand together…er…lights! Bells! Oh, God…too close to the graveyard…hold hands…is that right? How does it all start? Oi! Watch out! Nottingham? We don't know nothing about Nottingham. We are trying to do a wedding here, if you don't mind.

GWYN: (*Running on.*) Nottingham is yours. They've come to defend you.

JOHN: Keep that mad monk moving. Get married and be off.

GWYN: (*Kissing him on the cheek.*) Stay in one piece, Johno. Don't let them divide you against yourself. Africa, did you say? Africa…

(*GWYN runs off.*)

Enter WALTER and GLADMOUTH with documents.)

JOHN: Ah, the paperwork! I love the paperwork. Did you hear the news? Nottingham is mine.

GLADMOUTH: Where is Clac?

JOHN: They all went off for a piss together. Now, what have we got here? Let me see what that Italian reptile is trying to squeeze out of me

WALTER: We are under the protection of Pope Innocent. If any harm should come to us…

JOHN: You'll hardly be noticed. I have rebels to deal with. You must take your place in the queue. What are you offering me? (*Snatches the documents off WALTER.*) What a hand this is written in. The Latin is atrocious. Yugh! (*Throws the documents to the ground.*) That was all put together months ago, a thousand miles away. What has it got to do with me?

WALTER: Sire, you must do homage to the Pope and become his vassal.

JOHN: Give me that with its exact meaning.

WALTER: You must give Innocent your crown.

JOHN: Ah. That is very precise. I give my crown to Innocent. He already has three on his head. Mine makes four. His neck will break. Good.

WALTER: When you have convinced him that you are purged of heresy and a complete Christian again, he undertakes to give your crown back to you.

JOHN: Ah, a game! I will accept.

WALTER: God be praised.

JOHN: If Gladmouth will accept my offer. (*Pause.*) I think one of my Welsh hostages has disappeared. I have a vacancy for number twenty-nine on the scaffold tomorrow. I will become a martyr to my doubt if you will accept your martyrdom unheralded, unsung, anonymous.

GLADMOUTH: Is this the way for a king to behave – to twist and turn…

JOHN: Who would have ever doubted your answer? Fame commands your spirit, Gladmouth. Sign, sign, I'll sign. If Innocent wants me to be flogged through the streets like a criminal I'll do it. But the wish of my heart would be to lead this country out of the Church.

WALTER: No equivocating, sire...no threats...

JOHN: The man remains. I will swear, sign, do everything
you ask but the man remains.

WALTER: You must submit, with full sincerity by next
Ascension-tide. There can be no cavilling.

JOHN: Ascension-tide is nice. As Jesus goes up, John comes
down. But the man remains. You will not have my mind. I
will kneel and let Innocent put his cursed foot on my neck,
but he will not have my mind. If I am to endure this daily
destruction of happiness, hope, pleasure by being cast as
king, then I must have a hole to hide in. I have business to
attend to. Make up your minds.

GLADMOUTH: He must go to Rome, be tried, humiliated...

JOHN: I took the cross for the Crusades to please the Pope.
Did that regain Jerusalem? Did I have the time to even set
foot in the Holy Land? These are gestures, Gladmouth. Be
satisfied with gestures!

WALTER: You will submit.

JOHN: In public. But not...

WALTER: (*Sharply interrupting.*) I will pass this on. You will
harry and prosecute the Albigensians in England?

JOHN: Burn them, if I find them. Who knows, they may just
melt away.

GLADMOUTH: It will not be enough, Walter. We are letting
him go. Insist on the conditions...

WALTER: We will leave your majesty. There are urgent things
he must attend to. There is this thought – if you were the
Pope's friend these rebels would be excommunicated...not
you. We will wait for you in London.

(*WALTER bows and exits, taking GLADMOUTH with
him by the arm.*)

GLADMOUTH: (*As he is dragged off.*) He will wriggle out of
it, I know him...don't trust him...John! I made you pay. I
made you pay! The bastards made you pay.

(*Enter GWYN from left.*)

JOHN: Oh, God! Not you. Didn't I tell you to go and get married?

GWYN: She wouldn't do it. Against her religion, she said.

JOHN: Escape then. You could have done that. This embarrasses me.

GWYN: The guards are back at work. They won't let me go. I brought you a present. (*Offers JOHN a knife, handle first.*)

JOHN: Is this to cut my throat with?

GWYN: Mirabelle sent it. She had it with her to avenge her father's suicide – which you caused, she says. Not bad for a day's work, John. Forgiven by a Jew. Why, I can't think. If ever a king deserved to be assassinated it's you.

JOHN: Nottingham is with me.

GWYN: Your credit is high with the troops. I've even heard a 'good old King John' or two. Yours is the side to be on, they say.

JOHN: Do they? Loyal lads, bless them. Why did I ever doubt which way they'd jump? The king's name still counts for something then.

GWYN: Horsemen flying in from all over – Leicester's for the king, Derby's for the king, everywhere's for the king. The lanes are choked with them. Nothing but good news streaming in.

JOHN: I'm coming back, Gwyn. And I haven't I done a thing. I haven't done a thing.

GWYN: Johno...don't make me die tomorrow...find a way...

JOHN: Do you know, I doubt if it's seven o'clock yet. We have the rest of the day. Breakfast is what I need. See you, eat well...Gwyn, long journey to Nottingham.

GWYN: Johno! Let me talk to you! (*Pause.*) I'll show him. I'll finish that poem. (*He picks his robe up off the fallen stone, feels it to see if it is dry, then sniffs it.*) Grief's comrade...first, the world's enigma... second, the ecstasy...third, the talk... fourth, the shaking land... fifth...fifth...come on! What's fifth?

Blackout.

The End.

DAVID POWNALL

BLACK STAR

Characters

IRA ALDRIDGE
a black American Shakespearean actor,
aged fifty-seven

AMANDA
his Swedish-born common-law wife,
aged thirty-two

KARAIL
his Polish host, aged thirty-five

NINA
Karail's wife, aged twenty-eight

GOIDZE
a citizen, aged thirty-eight

Set in Poland, 1865

Black Star was first performed at the Octagon Theatre, Bolton on 10 March 1987, with the following cast:

IRA ALDRIDGE, Joseph Marcell

AMANDA, Ellie Haddington

KARAIL, Stephen McKenna

NINA, Mary Jo Randle

GOIDZE, Ray Jewers

Director, John Adams

ACT ONE

April 1865. Eastern Poland. A town called Mubelski.

*The drawing-room of KARAIL's house. It is furnished with taste
and an eye for dramatic colour. There is a rosewood piano and
table with a samovar and food laid out for a late supper. When the
lights go up the room is empty. Pause. The sound of people arriving. NINA, KARAIL's wife, enters in a hurry taking off her coat.*

NINA: Ah, thank God they remembered.
> (*She checks the table, the samovar and the cleanliness of
> the cups and glasses.*
> *Enter KARAIL. He closes the door behind him.*)

KARAIL: Everything in order.

NINA: The servants are improving.

KARAIL: Good. We don't want to upset this fellow more than
he is already, God knows. Give me your coat.
> (*NINA hands him her coat.*)

NINA: He didn't say a word all the way back from the theatre.
I was going mad wondering what to do – make conversation or just keep quiet.

KARAIL: I think he appreciated our silence. Fifty-two people
isn't much of an audience.

NINA: We did all we could…
> (*Enter AMANDA.*)

AMANDA: Oh, it's so nice to be back. I do like your house.

KARAIL: Excuse me. I must hang up this coat. How is the
Chevalier?

AMANDA: He won't be long. Let's say he's composing himself.
> (*KARAIL exits but leaves the door open.*)

NINA: What would you like?

AMANDA: (*Sitting down.*) I'll wait for my husband and see
what he's having.

NINA: He didn't seem very happy at the party.

AMANDA: We have to attend so many. Wherever we go on
tour people give parties in Ira's honour. It is impossible to

refuse when you are in the middle of a strange place.

NINA: Yes, Mubelski in a strange place. Even to us and we live here.

AMANDA: Fifty-two people. I still can't believe it.

NINA: You counted them. I did as well.

AMANDA: For an actor of Ira's standing, it was nothing but a slap in the face. But he'll get over it.

NINA: I hope so. We'd like him to enjoy his stay with us.
(*Enter KARAIL. He closes the door.*)

NINA: Madame Aldridge counted the audience. She made it the same as we did.

AMANDA: I always count the audience. We're on a box-office split, as you know. Only twenty-three people paid tonight. All the rest were complimentaries. Someone's been giving away our money.

IRA: (*From outside the door.*) Oh, my dear ducats! My daughter and my ducats! My ducats and my daughter! Give me justice!
(*IRA enters wearing a full-length red velvet gown and a silk scarf. He stands by the door.*)
O, my dear ducats! Deprived of my ducats. A sealed bag, two sealed bags of ducats! (*Closes the door.*) Of double ducats! (*Pause.*) Eavesdropping. One of my secret vices.

AMANDA: Ira, that's no way to dress for company.

IRA: (*To NINA and KARAIL.*) You don't mind, do you? I must relax or I'll get into a vile mood.

KARAIL: You must wear what you like in my house, Chevalier. If I may be permitted to comment – it is a magnificent garment.

IRA: An old costume, inevitably. I wore it in a new play about ten years ago. Can't remember what it was called or who wrote it except that it was very earnest.

AMANDA: We shouldn't be up too late tonight.

IRA: Oh, I couldn't sleep. I'd have a nightmare. Those yawning seats. (*He goes over to the table and starts looking at the food and drink.*) Ah, this is much better. Sorry I was a bit dull at the party after the show. All those interesting people! Amateur players have so much to say about the theatre.

One of them passed a remark that it seemed to him that I tended to favour my left side. Would you agree with that? What is this wine?

(*He holds up a bottle.*

NINA takes it from him and looks at it.)

NINA: It is Tokay, from Hungary.

IRA: Sweet?

NINA: Yes, very rich.

IRA: Do you think I'm a lop-sided actor?

NINA: No. Would you like some of this wine?

IRA: A bucketful. What's that perfume you're wearing?

NINA: Sandalwood.

IRA: Lovely.

(*NINA pours IRA a glass of wine. She has it up to the halfway when he tips her elbow until it is full.*)

AMANDA: Ira!

IRA: I'm thirsty. This is the worst date I've played for years. Then they accuse me of bias. Thank you, angel.

KARAIL: Some members of our theatre society affect more knowledge and expertise than they have.

IRA: This wonderful man told me that he came away convinced that one side of me must be deformed, that I was hiding it. He said I was like the coins in his pocket –the head always facing the same way.

NINA: You mustn't take such fools seriously. We know who you're talking about. Because he has played on the stage in Warsaw – twenty years ago! – he thinks he knows everything.

IRA: I take everybody seriously when they're criticising my work. Let's think. Maybe he has a good point. 'Yet his means are in supposition: he hath an argosy bound to Tripolis.' Left hand! 'Another to the Indies.' Left hand again! Gods, you'd think I'd use the right – perhaps I believe Tripolis and the Indies are in the same direction? They are, of course. Well, the East Indies but what about the West Indies? Did Shylock know about the existence of the West Indies? I must do some research. If he did then it has to be the right hand. Geography in Shakespeare needs

looking at. Tell your friend that he's been very useful.
Made me think.

NINA: That would encourage him to be even more stupid
than he must be already. Your gestures were beautifully
balanced.

IRA: Margaret, my first wife, taught me to accept criticism
with grace. She said it was part of the European tradition of
good manners to pick holes in each other.

KARAIL: Well, you're almost in the East now, Chevalier.
We have different standards. A high premium is put on
obeisances.

IRA: That's right. The prophet Mohamet knows how to deal
with actors. He forbids the faithful to go to the theatres. At
least we don't get too much criticism that way. Can you be
a Mohammedan round here without getting into trouble?

KARAIL: Oh, yes. We have a long tradition of religious
toleration.

IRA: That's good.

KARAIL: We get all sorts here. Mubelski is a crossroads.

IRA: Then you want to get somebody on it directing traffic to
your theatre.

(*Laughter.*)

(*IRA drains his glass and pours himself another.*)

AMANDA: Wouldn't you be better off with tea, Ira?

IRA: Tea keeps me awake. Tonight I'll need to sleep, and
forget. Oh, vanity, eh? I tell you, I was very glad that we
had such a pleasant home to come to…here. A hotel would
have been agony after all I've been through. Your hospitality is very much appreciated. Two wonderful people, you
are. And kind to travellers. Your health.

(*IRA drains the glass and pours himself another.*
NINA gives him a plate to help himself to food.
KARAIL serves himself with wine.)

NINA: Would you prefer wine, vodka, Madame Aldridge?

AMANDA: If he's drinking wine I'll drink wine.

(*NINA pours her a glass.*)

NINA: Are you hungry?

AMANDA: No. When was the last time that you had professional theatre company in Mubelski?

NINA: Some people came from Moscow last October.

AMANDA: How did they get on?

NINA: Not very well.

AMANDA: What play were they doing?

NINA: Some Russian thing. I can't remember what it was called.

IRA: I don't mind telling you, I felt like walking off the stage and abandoning the performance tonight. That's not my style at all but I have to confess, I did think about it once or twice.

KARAIL: Is that what you were thinking when you used those very long pauses?

IRA: The very long pauses?

KARAIL: Yes.

IRA: Which pauses were those?

KARAIL: It's difficult to put my finger on them.

NINA: Try, if it will help the Chevalier. I noticed them as well.

IRA: These pauses interest me. Silence speaks on stage. You can fill it with emotion. I wish you could pinpoint those pauses for me. If they seemed very long then they were too long.

NINA: Oh no – we knew something was going on in your performance. They weren't uninteresting pauses. You kept moving.

IRA: Ah. What did I do?

NINA: At one point you put your hand to your forehead like this.

IRA: Like this?

NINA: Exactly.

IRA: It's coming back to me.

NINA: What was going on in your mind then?

IRA: I had turned away from Tubal...yes, Act Three Scene One... in my mind, dear lady, was the betrayal...my daughter and...something else. I was angry...the ducats, yes, the diamonds, yes...the injustice of it all...there I was, alone on the Rialto, abused, spat upon...these Christian hypocrites, I thought, they borrow money like water...oh,

I was so angry. The…tension was terrific! Then came the pause. The long pauses. Ah, got it! I remember why. I'd forgotten my lines.

(*AMANDA laughs out loud.*

NINA and KARAIL are surprised.)

KARAIL: Yes, I seen to remember the prompter's voice coming out from the wings soon afterwards.

IRA: Too late, of course. But I never use the prompt. Usually he's two or three pages behind me. Do you know what I do when I dry up? Wait for Will Shakespeare to come booming through the ether all the way from under the green sods of England. Sometimes he'll give me the line, others he just says – Ira, you dumb bastard, can't you remember what I wrote? If you can't then make it up as you go along.

NINA: Is that what you did tonight?

IRA: That is a state secret. Maybe I did. What of it?

KARAIL: Isn't that disrespectful to the great playwright?

NINA: Shakespeare doesn't know the meaning of respect. Human dignity – pah! What Will is after is passion, heat. In his heart he finds all ambition absurd. On the subject of death he's very penetrating. Come on, these long faces? What are they for? We are shocked. We revere our great Polish poets…

IRA: Leave revering to the priests. My own father was a man of the cloth. He wasted his life bowing down to a vacuum. Shall I tell you something? I get too much respect.

KARAIL: That's impossible.

IRA: Only one person talks to me straight – Amanda over there. My Margaret, my Yorkshire terrier, she was the same… If people put you on a pedestal they're getting ready to pour concrete over you. Anyway that's hardly my problem in this town, is it?

AMANDA: Don't start off on that again.

IRA: I didn't say a word about lousy audiences. I was talking about statues. See how stern she is with me? There aren't many famous men who tolerate such uppity behaviour from their women.

(*He kisses AMANDA.*

She pushes him away.)

AMANDA: Oh, stop performing!

KARAIL: Tomorrow we will drag them off the street into that theatre.

IRA: No. You mustn't do that. People must want to go to the theatre. Playing to resentful spirits is a waste of time. What is astonishing is that this old fool, Ira, expected queues. That's what they told me in Saint Petersburg. Those Poles? They'll go mad for you. No culture down there.

NINA: That is just what they would say. They don't know us.

IRA: How many opportunities would the average citizen of this municipality have for seeing a genuine African prince of the Fulah tribe playing Shylock in *The Merchant of Venice*? Is this a feast that the starving local can sit down to every day of his life?

NINA: We were told that you were an American, originally.

IRA: Oh, no, no. Originally I was an African prince even though I was born in New York. Then I became an Englishmen for years for Shakespeare's sake, then Shakespeare and Ira Aldridge became men of the world, together. We can go anywhere we like and make people understand us. Except…What's this place called again?

KARAIL: Mubelski.

IRA: I must remember that name. Ira – where did you reach the end of the line? Mubelski, I'll have to say.

KARAIL: You will never come here again, I fear.

IRA: Would you want me to with my drawing-power? I'm about as popular here as horse-manure in a hospital. Whew, I feel so drained, Amanda – and confused. (*Sits down.*) I'm laughing but I'm crying.

AMANDA: Let's talk about something else.

IRA: Yes, let's do that. I get sick of the theatre. Tell us about your life here in…Mubelski.

NINA: Oh, that would be very boring. Nothing happens.

IRA: So I noticed. Ah, there I go again! (*Gets up.*) Sorry.

NINA: One day is much like the last. When you wake up in the morning you know nothing will change. Can you imagine living a life like that?

AMANDA: It would have its compensations for me. Oh, sit down Ira!

IRA: I can't. I keep seeing those empty seats, damn it!

AMANDA: I like comfort and my own home. Ten months of the year we're on tour. The longest we stay in one place is a week. Sometimes we have one-night stands, weeks of them. All the theatres and the towns end up feeling like the same place.

NINA: I'd love your life, I think.

AMANDA: For a while. Not for as long as I've had to live it. But it's this terrible man here. He won't settle. I think that in his mind he sees a perfect theatre in a perfect town with a perfect audience and he'll keep us prowling around the world until he finds it.

KARAIL: Well, I'm afraid you're a long way from your Paradise here.

AMANDA: It doesn't exist, but don't try telling him that.

IRA: Doesn't a black man doing Shakespeare have novelty value here?

AMANDA: You're being very rude, Ira.

IRA: Yeh, I'm being rude. But not to these people. They've been very good to us. (*Kisses NINA's hand.*) To myself, really.

(*Pause. IRA pours himself another glass of wine and sits down on a settee, spreading himself.*)

KARAIL: Chevalier, I would like to explain.

IRA: Go on. Tell me I'm dreaming.

KARAIL: The problem for us has been the choice of play.

IRA: They don't like Shakespeare?

KARAIL: It's not that. What we are dealing with here is prejudice.

IRA: You don't say. Well I wouldn't know anything about that, would I?

KARAIL: On the posters for *The Merchant Of Venice* you had a second title – I suppose in explanation – *The Story Of Shylock, The Jew...*

(*Pause.*)

NINA: People see enough of Jews in their daily lives not to

want to see them on the stage – especially to pay to see
them on the stage.

IRA: You have a lot of Jews here?

NINA: Yes.

IRA: Why weren't they at the theatre then?

NINA: They don't come to our theatre.

IRA: That's strange. In New York we have lots of Jews in the
theatre. Perhaps you don't make them welcome?

KARAIL: They keep themselves to themselves.

NINA: But they have a lot of power. More than they should
have.

KARAIL: Nina, don't exaggerate now.

NINA: I'll say it if you won't. The vineyards, the timber yards,
both our banks, the school – all controlled by Jews.

KARAIL: Of course they don't control the school, the Russian
government would never allow that!! Don't be ridiculous!

NINA: They have their ways, you know that. They work with
the Russian colonial government here. The Jews are part
of the oppression we suffer. They'll do anything to keep in
with the authorities.

KARAIL: Many of the Jews in this town are poor, Nina –
much poorer than we are. And they get persecuted regu-
larly by the Russian police.

NINA: They look poor but they're not. They have a network.
They support each other. Every family has investments. No
Jew shows his wealth. He keeps it a secret in case he gets
taxed.

(*Pause. IRA looks at NINA and folds his arms.*)

IRA: I'm looking at someone who didn't have too much of a
good time at the show tonight. Didn't you read in Shylock's daughter for me?

NINA: I did.

IRA: You're beautiful. You have a beautiful wife, sir.

KARAIL: Thank you, Chevalier. I think she is beautiful as
well.

IRA: You know what kept me going tonight? Looking at her.
I don't expect too much from the people who fill in the
other parts – people come to see me, not them. Most of the
time I might just as well be alone. Jessica has to be beauti-

ful though. No one would accept an ugly woman in that part.

NINA: I find them repulsive people.

KARAIL: Nina!

IRA: No, let it come out.

NINA: I didn't realise that I was reading a Jew's part until it was too late... Up until then all I could think of was that I was on the stage with a famous actor.

IRA: A legendary actor, darling. (*Pause.*) Margaret, my first wife, came from a place called Yorkshire. Up there they can't stand people who come from a place called Lancashire. Do you know why, Nina dear? Because of flowers.

NINA: Flowers?

IRA: The English are very odd. They'll argue about politics and they'll fight over religion, but they're pretty half-hearted about it. What they really care about is their gardens. So, if you grow red roses, I grow white roses. If I even pick a red rose you pick a white one. Come the annual flower show we cut each other's throats. Shakespeare wrote about it – four plays in all. *Henry the Sixth Part One, Two, Three* and *Richard the Third.* Richard is a absolute villain...but not a Jew. So I guess you might like him.

NINA: If you lived here you would understand. The Jews are not disliked for nothing! They don't belong. They don't want to belong! But everything has to belong to them! They betray everybody.

IRA: At the end of *The Merchant Of Venice* there's one character my friend Shakespeare wants you to feel sympathy for – it's not that bitch, Portia, or that bullshitter, Bassanio... or that asshole Antonio! It's Shylock! Didn't you get that? Then I failed.

KARAIL: Please...Nina, go and see if the children are asleep.

NINA: Of course they're asleep. It's one o'clock in the morning!

KARAIL: I would like to be sure. You can come back down here after five minutes when you're in command of yourself. Go now.

(*NINA glares at KARAIL, is about to say something but*

she holds back.
IRA stands up as she goes to leave.)
IRA: I'll tell you everything he says about you.
KARAIL: Chevalier! She is my wife. I don't like to see her
    upset.
IRA: That's your business. Why keep hatred upstairs?
    (*NINA leaves.*
    IRA wanders back to the table for another drink.)
AMANDA: I think we understand. If someone had advised us
    then we would have chosen another play.
KARAIL: We were   only told that it would be Shake-
    speare. It was not until your posters arrived for distribution
    that we found out that it would be Shylock.
IRA: Where do these Jews live?
KARAIL: They have their own district.
IRA: I'll go up there tomorrow and see them. Maybe I can
    talk them into coming to the show. We could have reduced
    prices for all Jews. No. They're so rich, according to your
    wife. Let's double the prices for the Children of Israel.
    They'd get the point.
KARAIL: My wife's attitude to the Jews is not peculiar to
    herself.
AMANDA: But you don't share it?
KARAIL: No. I only have so much anger. In my case it is
    reserved for those people who hurt me most. But the Jews
    must look after their own interests. They're used to that, I
    think.
IRA: With you it's the Russians?
KARAIL: Yes.
IRA: It has to be somebody. Do you know who it is with me?
    Work that one out.
KARAIL: I daren't.
IRA: People who don't go to the theatre,
KARAIL: We have always allowed the Jews to live in Poland.
    They did not invade us. The Russians are here as oppres-
    sors and conquerors. Our country was just part of the
    division of spoils after the last war... Austria has this bit,
    Prussia that bit, Russia this bit. We were not consulted. But

it is most impolite of me, to harass you with our problems. The Russian authorities in Saint Petersburg must have acquainted you with recent events.

IRA: Yes, they mentioned some rebellion two years ago. But what are we to do about tomorrow? I'm not playing to another empty house, not me.

KARAIL: Could we have another play? Something different?

AMANDA: We haven't got the costumes or props for another play.

KARAIL: When I heard that you wore coming – the greatest living exponent of Shakespeare, the foremost tragedian of the English classical stage – I had a hope that you might give us *Macbeth.*

IRA: Oho! Don't mention him. Bad luck, that one.

AMANDA: We're forbidden to perform *Macbeth* in any Russian territory.

KARAIL: Oh, are you?

AMANDA: The government censor in Saint Petersburg told us we mustn't perform *Macbeth* or *Hamlet* or *Lear.*

KARAIL: I see.

AMANDA: He was very specific about *Macbeth.*
(*Pause. KARAIL gets up and gets himself a glass of wine.*)
How did they know that you would want *Macbeth* down here in the wilds?

KARAIL: I think you know why. How long has the Chevalier been touring in Europe? He knows what it is like to play the killing of kings and the vulnerability of kings to people who need it.

IRA: That's true. I've had some nights with that play. In Vienna the performance was a revolution in itself. But it started, it stopped. The people went home. As far as know, the emperor is still on his throne. I didn't change much from what I can see.

KARAIL: We are a long way from Saint Petersburg and we are Poles not Austrians.
(*Bell jangling.*
KARAIL jumps up and opens the door.)
(*Calling.*) Nina! Answer the door will you?

NINA: (*Off.*) Coming!

KARAIL: People don't know when to go to bed.

AMANDA: We should be going, Ira. You need your rest.

IRA: No, I'm not tired. You go if you like.

KARAIL: Thirty-two men from this small town were executed by the Russians when the rebellion was put down. Some of them were mere boys. Give us *Macbeth.*

IRA: Do you know that you're talking to a man who has performed in front of all the crowned heads of Europe? I've got awards, honours, medals in all the capital cities. When I wear all my regalia I look like a king myself.

KARAIL: Give us *Macbeth.*

AMANDA: It's wrong of you to ask.

KARAIL: Call it something else. All that matters is that the Poles recognise Macbeth, someone the Russians fear. We know nothing about the play in detail, except that a king is assassinated. The Chevalier performs in English anyway. We can't follow it line by line.

AMANDA: They knew what was going on tonight.

KARAIL: Shylock is a universal figure…his hair, his clothes, his skullcap, the way he rubs his hands – but Macbeth? What is it about him that makes the Russians so afraid?

IRA: He was a Scotsman. When I do him I wear a kilt.

KARAIL: Chevalier, you could do this great thing for us in any way you like – but if the Poles knew that it was Macbeth, that it was a prohibited performance that you were doing it for them, it would be delightful. You, on our stage, with Russians watching – and not knowing! We would know and we would be able to laugh again.

IRA: Don't laugh too much. It's supposed to be a tragedy.

AMANDA: I'm sorry but it's completely out of the question.

IRA: Hold on, hold on…

AMANDA: Ira, we only just got permission to do this tour. We're here on sufferance. If we step outside the limits they've set then we can never come back.

IRA: I don't like people telling me what plays I can perform.

AMANDA: We signed a document.

IRA: You signed it. You don't do the acting in this outfit.

I do.

(*Enter NINA. She closes the door behind her.*)

NINA: It's Goidze.

KARAIL: (*Getting up quickly.*) What does he want?

NINA: He says that he was passing. He saw the light and thought he might meet the Chevalier.

KARAIL: Tell him it's too late.

NINA: He heard the Chevalier's voice and recognised it. He was in the audience tonight.

KARAIL: I know he was. (*To IRA.*) This man is a Russian informer. We all know him.

IRA: And he just happened to be passing. Bring him in. I can duel with secret agents. Played 'em plenty of times.

KARAIL: Well, if you wouldn't mind. It would probably be best.

NINA: Be careful what you say in front of him. He's treacherous.

IRA: So was Brutus, but you could talk to him. Lets have a look at this fellow.

(*NINA exits.*)

KARAIL: He is very intelligent. A local man, one of our best families. But the Russians have got him in their pocket. His father despairs of him.

(*Enter NINA, followed by GOIDZE. He is a handsome, impressive man.*)

NINA: May I present Goidze Kainardski – the Chevalier Aldridge, Madame Aldridge.

GOIDZE: I am charmed and honoured. (*Kisses AMANDA's hand.*) If I was not sure of my welcome in my friend's house I would not have called at such a late hour.

KARAIL: You must have been taking the long way home, Goidze.

GOIDZE: (*Sitting down.*) Chevalier, I live on the other side of the town. My friend Karail is telling you that my arrival here was no accident.

IRA: Now we know that you're a man who goes visiting when he feels like it. (*Pours himself another glass of wine.*) You were in the audience tonight.

GOIDZE: Yes, I was.

AMANDA: Then you were two per cent of it.

GOIDZE: The attendance was unusually poor. Even our own amateur productions get better audiences than that.

AMANDA: That will be because of local ties. Everyone's relatives and friends come along.

GOIDZE: The standard of performance in our theatre society is quite high. We have a good reputation. People will travel from other towns to see us.

IRA: You act yourself?

GOIDZE: In a small way. I enjoy the discipline.

IRA: Yes, you would have an excellent presence. Perhaps your voice has been trained?

GOIDZE: No, this is my natural voice. What I came to say was that I thought the drama you performed was a terrible piece of writing.

IRA: That was William Shakespeare!

GOIDZE: So badly put together. Such unbelievable characters.

IRA: He doesn't like Shakespeare. Do you know what you're saying?

GOIDZE: He's a very old-fashioned writer. In those days they made many elementary mistakes. The characters talk too much and they take far too long to explain themselves.

IRA: That's poetry. Poetry always takes too long and it never knows how to explain itself. You're a man with firm opinions, Mr...

GOIDZE: Goidze, if you please.

IRA: Yes, we were introduced... Well, I reckon they need you back in Oxford or Cambridge to sort them out. Those people are walking around totally deluded about Shakespeare. They think he's all right.

GOIDZE: I am referring in my criticism to this particular play. There are others that are much better.

IRA: Now we're getting somewhere. (*Holds up the wine bottle.*) No one has offered you any refreshment and you've been wandering around in the dark worried about English literature

(*KARAIL is about to protest but GOIDZE heads it off.*)

GOIDZE: It is too far into the night for me to think about my stomach. What concerns me, Chevalier, is the rest of your engagement here. We cannot have that play performed again. Not only does it offend us because it restricts the entertaining aspects of your craft, but it is also repugnant politically and socially.

IRA: You don't say.

GOIDZE: Obviously the Russian government have not studied the play or they would have never allowed something so inflammatory and upsetting to be seen on the public stage. I feel it in my duty to ask you, and the amateur society to cancel tomorrow night's performance.

(*Pause.*)

IRA: Well, that's straight enough.

GOIDZE: The Jews are not to be encouraged to get above themselves. That is my understanding.

IRA: Shylock doesn't get above himself. He gets destroyed. His daughter betrays him. The Venetians cheat him out of his pound of flesh. He's lucky to get away with his life. I tell you what, I'll write a new scene for the end in which he gets crucified. How about that?

GOIDZE: Any play about Jews is a provocation. We don't want then on the stage. They get too much attention anyway, for what they're worth.

IRA: Which is what?

GOIDZE: They are not part of our future. I hear *Othello* is a good play.

IRA Oh, I can do *Othello*. Isn't it true that the real reason you don't want Shylock on again is because the Jews have complained about having a negro impersonate a member of the Chosen People?

GOIDZE: They are certainly capable of that attitude but I haven't heard any of the Jews voicing it. As you tour around doing this Shylock do Jews actually have the gall to say that to you?

IRA: No, I thought it up myself.

GOIDZE: Wouldn't you think *Othello* was a better choice,

Nina?

NINA: I don't know.

GOIDZE: It's about a general who goes mad with jealousy
and slays his wife. He's a black...like the Chevalier himself.

IRA: Should go down well at the army barracks.

AMANDA: Are you here in any official capacity?

GOIDZE: I come as a friend. But I have influence as your
hosts know. You would be well advised to listen to me.

IRA: Your English must be pretty good if you followed *The
Merchant* so closely.

GOIDZE: I have a Russian translation which I read before
coming to the theatre. It gave me an idea of the plot and
the characters.

IRA: Well, you sound a very cultured man to me.

GOIDZE: I am an ordinary citizen but I support the new re-
gime. Russia is our future I believe. You will have noticed
that your hosts have not offered me food or drink. That is
not an oversight.

(*Pause. GOIDZE stands up.*)

I will call at ten tomorrow morning for your answer. It
should be *Othello*, I think. Good night to you all.

(*He leaves the room, followed by KARAIL.*
Pause, the door offstage opens and slams.
KARAIL re-enters in a fury.)

KARAIL: Did you hear all that? The incredible arrogance of
that man! I could strangle him!

IRA: He knows that.

AMANDA: For an informer I found him quite honest, didn't
you?

IRA: He was worth watching. As an actor, I learnt a few
things.

KARAIL: No, no! He is disgusting. Horrible!

IRA: If you don't know what's just happened here I do. I've
been told not to perform *The Merchant* again, and I've been
instructed to do *Othello* instead.

KARAIL: He has no authority!

IRA: He has enough for me.

AMANDA: Would *Othello* be acceptable to the society?

KARAIL: At his dictation! Never! (*Pause.*) I apologise. You have been put in an impossible position. Under the circumstances it would be better if you did not perform at all.

AMANDA: We will have to be compensated. There is a contract.

KARAIL: That will be arranged, I assure you.

IRA: So you want us to leave town?

NINA: We might as well see *Othello*. It will be better than nothing. The Chevalier has come all this way.

KARAIL: That is no longer possible. The committee would condemn me.

NINA: Surely they would understand?

KARAIL: No. Most of them will already know by now that the Russians want *Othello*. *Othello* might just as well be a Russian! Too many layers, Chevalier, too many whispers and listening-posts, too many pairs of ears. It is shameful that this has come about. God knows what you must think of us. Everyone is using you.

IRA: Now I know why I feel at home. Got any serfs?

KARAIL: No. (*Pause.*) My father has.

IRA: So everyone gets well used around here. Will you inherit your father's possessions?

KARAIL: The serfs are in the process of being liberated.

IRA: And who's doing that for you? If the Russians weren't freeing the serfs, would you be? Do you realise how like brothers the Czar and Abraham Lincoln are to me?

KARAIL: It is a sign of my ignorance and insensitivity that I did not think of it that way. I apologise.

IRA: It's a tangle. It's a maze. All you can do is keep hold of who you are and try not to get lost. My grandfather was a slave. My father was a preacher. Between those two was there any better job than acting? Amanda, I want you upstairs in five minutes. Good night.

(*IRA exits. Pause.*)

NINA: We didn't mean to make him bitter.

AMANDA: He's not bitter. Ira is just protecting himself. In England his dilemmas were ten times worse. I've seen him with plantation-owners in his dressing-room offering him congratulations and champagne.

KARAIL: But did he drink it? That's what matters.

AMANDA: He did. You see, they owned the theatre. Good night.

(*AMANDA exits, leaving the door open.*

KARAIL gets up and shuts it.)

KARAIL: We have treated that man abominably. That talented man. He came here to act masterpieces for us and now – squalid, petty politics.

NINA: He loves it. He loves it all. Forty years he's been touring Shakespeare round Europe, he told me. Wars, revolutions, they're scenes in his plays. His problem must be – when are things real?

KARAIL: When he looks at you, I think.

(*They both exit.*

Blackout.

Ten o'clock the following morning. Lights fade up on the drawing-room.

GOIDZE is standing there alone waiting. The door is open. Enter IRA dressed for hunting.)

IRA: Good morning, Goidze.

GOIDZE: Good morning, Chevalier.

IRA: You've come for my answer.

GOIDZE: I have.

IRA: I'm going hunting for bears. Ever been hunting for bears? In New York it's a popular pastime. You have to be up early and quick on your feet. New York bears are man-eaters. Honey they dislike. Show them a salmon river and they'll look at you askance.

GOIDZE: All the posters for *The Merchant Of Venice* have been taken down during the night.

IRA: Did the Poles, the Russians and the Jews all co-operate in doing that? Makes a change. Perhaps I'm creating history here?

GOIDZE: There is a printer who can produce a playbill by two o'clock. Distribution will be arranged by the authorities.

IRA: You're pushing me, Mr Goidze. It's my decision, remember.

GOIDZE: Everyone is anxious not to lose an opportunity of seeing you in the great role of *The Moor of Venice* not *The Merchant.*

IRA: Sounds like you stayed up all night reading the play again.

GOIDZE: Are all Shakespeare's characters so stupid? All that business with the handkerchief, it's so obvious. Tell me, Chevalier, do you think Shakespeare understood men of your colour at all?

IRA: You don't want me to do *Othello* any more?

GOIDZE: Oh, yes. There are stupid people in life, why not on the stage?

IRA: We can talk about the handkerchief afterwards. *Othello* then?

GOIDZE: Wonderful. This will not be forgotten. To help keep the peace is a noble undertaking, especially for a stranger.

IRA: You'll have to be there yourself, I'll be looking for you.

GOIDZE: Nothing would keep me away. I will buy my ticket as soon as possible and bring my family as well.

IRA: Well, I'd better get after these Polish bears. My host has gone over to a neighbour to borrow some dogs.

GOIDZE: You will enjoy our beautiful countryside. We have some sunshine today. But I'm afraid you will find no Polish bears.

IRA: Is it the wrong season?

GOIDZE: Poland has not existed for the last two years. As a country it has disappeared. This is Russia. Until tonight. Farewell.

(*GOIDZE exits.*

As soon as the outside door closes NINA comes into the room.)

NINA: That loathsome man seemed very pleased with himself. Have you satisfied him?

IRA: How long's your husband going to be getting those dogs?

NINA: I don't know. Another half an hour, perhaps.

IRA: Let me come up to your bedroom.

NINA: No.

IRA: Because I made Mr Goidze happy?

NINA: No. Because I respect my husband and you should respect your wife.

IRA: My wife won't mind.

NINA: Well I say she should. What did you tell Goidze?

IRA: That I'd be doing *Othello.*

NINA: Oh.

IRA: You sound disappointed. I feel disappointed. It must be exactly the right day to go out shooting large animals. Change your mind.

NINA: If I change my mind will you change yours?

IRA: If you change your mind. But you're not going to, are you?

NINA: Do you approach women this way in every town you tour through?

IRA: They follow me like they follow the circus. Do you know some towns are emptied of women when I leave? They hang on the outside of the train. 'Take me with you!' they scream through the window but I just carry on smoking my cigar. I want you to read Desdemona tonight.

NINA: Who's she?

IRA: Othello's wife. You'll read the part, in French as you did Jessica. And I'll have to strangle you. Want to rehearse?

NINA: The Russians will be pleased.

IRA: Of course they will. My Margaret used to say – you can't please everybody. I've spent my life trying to prove her wrong. Do you like Amanda? She's a good woman. When I took up with her on tour she fell pregnant. My Margaret was still alive then. She took Amanda into the family. The child was brought up with two mothers. When that little Yorkshire woman was dying she told me that I had to marry Amanda after six months of mourning. Six months was respectable. I said yes to please her. And you said no to please yourself.

(*Enter KARAIL dressed for hunting with dog leashes wrapped round his wrist and two guns. He gives one to IRA.*)

KARAIL: We are ready, Chevalier. Lets get up into the hills.

IRA: One of my remote ancestors on the distaff side was a man called Davy Crocket. He could shoot the eyes out of flying crow at a thousand yards, God bless him. Amanda will give you the scripts you need for tonight.

NINA: You assume that I'll do it for you? (*To KARAIL.*) It's Othello.

IRA: Trust me. (*To KARAIL.*) Would it be possible to get a message to our friend Goidze? He's done some acting, so he tells me. I'd like him to read in a part or two tonight, I've decided.

NINA: You expect me to go on stage with him?

IRA: This is the theatre we're dealing with, Nina, light of my life. We have the hero, we have the villain but what we don't have is barriers. Anyone can go on the boards. I've even played Lucifer himself. All the world's a stage, as Shakespeare muttered somewhere.

KARAIL: Do as the Chevalier asks.

IRA: Amanda has a script for him. Send it round with the message. I don't think he will be able to refuse. Goidze is the kind of man who likes dressing up. (*Shakes his gun.*) Tally-ho! Where's that bear?

KARAIL: Nina, let the committee know that it is the Chevalier's express wish that Goidze be part of the performance. It is not my idea.

IRA: That's right. Don't get into any trouble on my behalf. Ah, the hills! You should see the ones we have round South London. No bears but a lot of foxes. What I'm waiting for is an invitation to join the Norwood Hunt. That would put my Legion d'Honneur into the shade. As paramount chief of the Fulah tribe I am the only man in West Africa who has the right to hunt the black rhinoceros, a species long extinct in those parts.

(*KARAIL crashes his gun butt to the floor.*)

KARAIL: May I ask why it has to be *Othello*!

IRA: I'll explain as we go. Tragic heroine, farewell.

(*IRA claps KARAIL on the back and pushes him out of the door.*

KARAIL is numbed with disappointment. It hardly reg-

isters with him that he is leaving the room.
NINA sits down, miserable.
AMANDA enters with a pile of papers and books in a box.
She puts them down on the table.)
AMANDA: Have the boys gone out to play?
(*NINA nods.*)
(*Going to her.*) What's the matter? You're crying.
NINA: It is nothing.
AMANDA: You don't want to talk about it?
NINA: Do you love your husband?
AMANDA: Ach! Don't worry about that.
NINA: Do you love him?
AMANDA: Just because Ira wants to make love to you –and
     he's said so by now, I imagine – it doesn't mean I hate
     him. Nor does it mean that he doesn't like me, which in
     more to the point. Is that what has made you cry?
NINA: No. He explained about the way his life has been. It's
     my husband I'm crying for.
AMANDA: I shouldn't do too much of that. He seems to be a
     very capable man.
NINA: You should look closer. He wants to die.
AMANDA: Nonsense. No one wants to do that. Ira says that
     you will arrange to send this script to Goidze.
NINA: Haven't you looked in my husband eyes?
AMANDA: I suppose I have when I've been talking to him.
NINA: His elder brother was hanged by the Russians. On that
     day his eyes changed. There is nothing behind them.
AMANDA: Will you be able to get the script to Goidze? It is
     very important.
     (*AMANDA holds out the script to NINA. Pause.*
     She takes it then puts it down on the floor beside her.)
     Shall I call a servant?
NINA: (*Flaring up.*) No! I will do it!
AMANDA: We have a lot of work to do. Ira will have to
     rehearse with you all for at least three hours before
     the performance.
NINA: You must think we're all mad.
AMANDA: No, I'm used to it, that's all. Wherever we go

people expect too much.

NINA: We don't get out of this town enough. I've told Karail – let's go to Paris, or Berlin. He won't. All he wants is his shame.

AMANDA: That's not healthy.

NINA: No.

AMANDA: How long will it take to get the script to Goidze? Does he live far away?

NINA Oh no, not far at all. The chevalier has added to the shame but in all innocence, I suppose.

AMANDA: I wouldn't go that far. Ira usually knows what he's doing.

NINA: He would deliberately insult my husband, here, under his own roof? What kind of man would do that? Only an immoral beast!

AMANDA: One with a discreet and selective conscience.

NINA: Oh, that's hard. I thought the next thing you'd say would be that he couldn't help it, that he was still a primitive.

AMANDA: Oh, no. He's quite civilised really. He stopped filing his teeth years ago.

NINA: Would he ever hit you?

AMANDA: Not to hurt me… Maybe, for amusement, or to let off steam.

NINA: Poor Madame Aldridge! Heaven. (*Pause.*) You must be very brave… How does one cope with a barbarian like that?

AMANDA: Laugh at him.

NINA: God, Karail would go mad if I laughed at him.

AMANDA: Ira's quite good, at comedy. Better than he thinks.

NINA: What's your child like?

AMANDA: Oh, brown.

NINA: It must be strange to have a child by him. You wouldn't know what was going to arrive. Did you find that exciting?

AMANDA: Yes. I enjoy suspense.

NINA: You haven't asked about my children.

AMANDA: I'm sorry. I didn't think you had any.

NINA: I haven't. Karail says it's me, but I don't think so.
When the Chevalier gave you a child was it because you
had asked him to?

AMANDA: I'm not as articulate as Ira. If you've been that
deep in conversation with him, he will have planted
thoughts in your mind.

NINA: You are encouraging me to say yes?

AMANDA: Not if you find him unattractive. However, such a
person as Ira won't be entering your life again.
(*NINA laughs.*)

AMANDA: What is so funny?

NINA: I'm talking about shame to someone who doesn't
know what it means.

AMANDA: I'm just going along with what you are thinking
and not saying. Be more open with yourself.

NINA: No. I'm only playing. (*Pause.*) He should do *Macbeth* for
us.

AMANDA: You still think he's a knight in shining armour?
I thought we'd got beyond that. (*Pause.*) Have you helped
his people in America? What have you done for the Union
side in the Civil War?

NINA: What could we do from here?

AMANDA: Send money. Sympathy. What about a Polish
Women's League for The manumission of Slaves? You
could be the head of it with all your experience. (*Pause.*)
I'm sorry. Sometimes I get bitter about it all.

NINA: He wants to be used. Your husband knows he is a
symbol, he recognises it. To glitter like he does, oh, what
an advantage!

AMANDA: Symbols tinkle too. If you needed to damage Ira it
would be easy enough. Tell him what you've just told me.

NINA: I wouldn't want to.

AMANDA: Don't speak too soon.

NINA: Karail says that your husband has the authority of
the oppressed. He got so excited when he know you were
coming. This black man, Ira Aldridge, will set fire to this
town, he said. Blow them up into the sky! He'll show them.

AMANDA: All very well for the reception committee – but

what's coming is a working actor who takes his profession
very seriously. He believes in his talent. Take that away
from him and he'd just curl up and die.

NINA: No, no, he must be everything. When he arrived we
could feel it. Here was someone extraordinary, someone
who had suffered and risen above it. It's in his eyes, the
way he carries himself...

(*Pause. AMANDA smiles.*)

AMANDA: I must tell Ira that you think he has moral charisma.

NINA: Don't you dare. Oh, God, what have I been saying?
He confuses me. Tell him he's far too exotic for a simple
country girl.

AMANDA: I'll tell you something very dull about Ira. It
might dispel your confusion. For as long as he's been able
to afford it he's put aside a quarter of his income to buy his
own people in the slave markets of America and set them
free. Each month we send the money by bank draft all the
way across the Atlantic from here, from wherever we are.
He's done the work, played the parts, earned that cash by
his talent. That's as far as he can go within his own understanding. Ira is not a political man, God help him. But he
does what he can. (*Pause.*) Don't worry about the script for
Goidze. Send the servant to me and I'll sort it out.

(*Pause. NINA hands over the script and exits.*
AMANDA sorts two scripts out of the pile and some letters.)
Here's two parts for you, Bright Eyes, Desdemona and
Lady M. A letter for the local rabbi, one for the boss of the
serf organisation if we can find one...

(*Fade to blackout. Lights fade up fast. A scream.*
IRA and KARAIL holding up a huge bloody bear skin
with head. They roar and hurl it at the feet of the women.
Both men are covered with blood and drunk.)

IRA: How about that? What a chase we had! This creature
could run!

KARAIL: Have you ever seen such a brute? He towered over
us. Killed two of the dogs.

NINA: Get it out of here! You're ruining the carpets!

IRA: This is the carpet! Throw out that other stuff. If you
don't want it I'll have it. I'd like to have him looking up at
me from the floor when I get home. Graaah! Put up your
dukes an' fight, man!

AMANDA: You'd better sober up. I've called a rehearsal
down at the theatre in an hour's time.

IRA: That's fine. Ever eaten bear meat, Amanda? You ought
to try it. The liver is best.

NINA: Go and have a bath. You smell.

KARAIL: Don't you want to hear the story? The Chevalier
says he will dine out on it for years. For two hours we saw
nothing, nothing…

(*NINA walks out of the room.*)

Go on! Turn your back on me! Ira, I haven't had such a
good time in years. You're a friend, a true friend.

AMANDA: A bath isn't a bad idea. And the blood in getting
all over the furniture. You've had a good time but I think
you ought to tidy up now.

(*Pause. KARAIL laughs and grabs hold of the bearskin by
a leg. He hauls it towards the door.*)

KARAIL: Grrrrr, eh, Chevalier? Grrrrr! What a wrestle?

IRA: Grrrr, old bad-tempered bear! (*Gives the head a kick.*)
Gave me a fright when he came out of the bushes, I can
tell you. I couldn't get the gun up to my shoulder but
Karail here – bam! Straight through the heart. The old
monster looked really surprised. Hey? What you doin'?

KARAIL: A lucky shot! (*Drags the bearskin out.*) Nina! Nina!
Come down! Let me tell you about it.

(*AMANDA closes the door. She takes a handkerchief out
of her sleeve and wipes IRA's face.*)

AMANDA: Was he brave?

IRA: Yeh.

AMANDA: And you?

IRA: Oh, I was brave as well. You know me.

AMANDA: How drunk are you?

IRA: Pretty drunk. Did you get everything organised?

AMANDA: Yes. What are you going to do? Have a bath and
some rest?

IRA: That's not a bad idea. We had a crazy time up in the

hills. Couldn't stop laughing, both of us. As that poor old bear went down we just couldn't stop laughing. And it was dying, Amanda.

(*AMANDA puts his arm over her shoulder and they walk out of the room together. With his free hand IRA wipes his face with the handkerchief. Blackout.*)

End of Act One.

ACT TWO

The first act set has been struck for the most part but there are still sections to be removed. As the stage hands work on this a backdrop of hills, rivers and woods and a great sky of clouds flies in. IRA enters. He is wearing his red robe. Pause. He watches the stage hands work for a moment then looks at the backdrop. All the stage hands exit once the last item of the act one set has been cleared. Pause. Enter AMANDA.

IRA: They've stopped for tea. Good lads, I'd say.

AMANDA: The dressing room is dreadful.

IRA: Cosy though. Once we're all in it there's so no need for a fire.

AMANDA: This time, Ira, I don't have to prophecy. It'll be a disaster.

IRA: You're always right, Amanda. That's what occasionally bores me about you. *(He kisses her.)* Who cares?

AMANDA: And if they put you in prison?

IRA: What d'you mean? I have a British passport. The whole might of the empire would come down on them. A gun-boat would be dispatched. War would not be out of the question. Lord Palmerston himself would be over on the next train. Don't forget the Crimea, my dear. We showed 'em, Russian bullies. Don't worry. We've been far too cute for them. They'll never cotton on.

AMANDA: As you wish. I don't mind if the tour is aborted. It'll mean we get home earlier.

IRA: Yes. You miss your garden. April! Everything is happening in the garden and you're not there to be part of it. One day, Amanda, we'll give it all up and sit in the garden watching the grass grow.

AMANDA: I'll believe that when I see it. Do they fully understand the risks they're taking doing this show?

IRA: Of course they do. Listen, this in how they live. They're always taking chances. One thing they don't want from me is tameness. You wouldn't want me to be a spoilsport, would you?

AMANDA: Thank you for taking my opinion into account.

IRA: I'll have plenty of time to rot. (*Pause.*) Have you noticed anything about this place? The way people walk up the sides of the streets like nuns. No one talks more than they have to in public. Look out in the fields. You can hardly see the people working out there because the earth and their skins are the same colour. Can't you smell it? The cookhouse, the cabin, the man on the corner with a gun and a gleam in his eye? I bet they even live off beans.

AMANDA: Promise me that this is our last tour.

IRA: Yeh, yeh.

AMANDA: I beg you.

IRA: I said yeh, didn't I? You deaf or somethin'?

AMANDA: Don't shout...

IRA: I'll shout if I damn well want to. Don't start naggin', woman! Who keeps you, eh? Who feeds your child? Yeh, I'm a great butter an' eggs man. (*Pause.*) Sorry.

AMANDA: It's pointless talking to you.

IRA: Have those people asked me to do the things I have to elsewhere? Those entr'acte performances you love so much, the old coon songs from the cotton fields, the servile nigger? In England I had to do that in the damn intervals! No rest, even doin' *Lear, Hamlet*! No, get back out there with your goddamned banjo, buck, and sing. What these people want may be dangerous but it's dignified.

AMANDA: Dignified? It's a travesty you're planning, Ira.

IRA: Pullin' the lion's tail is dignified if you're a monkey.

AMANDA: If you start drinking so early in the day I've told you before that you mustn't stop or you'll get into these ridiculous moods by late afternoon. Your system simply can't take it any more.

IRA: Don't tell me how to drink!

AMANDA: Have something now. I'll send out for some brandy.

IRA: I'll drink when I want to, not when you tell me too. Anyway, I've got a bottle in the dressing room. Amanda, Amanda. (*Takes her in his arms.*) All I'm doin' is havin' a little fun.

(*The stage hands enter, they stand and look at the black man with the white woman in his arms. Pause.*)
This is when I bite her in the throat.
(*IRA kisses AMANDA on the neck.*
The stage hands stare then turn to their work. They start building the dressing room stage left.
AMANDA exits.)
(*Standing near the stage hands.*) Now you boys, you can work faster 'n that, surely? What you had for breakfast? Hell, I'd say you wasn't pullin' your weight. Hey, hup! Swing that hammer! Drive that plough. What are we buildin' here? These shinin' walls! These crystal floors! Hell, if it aint the New Jerusalem!
(*The dressing room is recognisable. Two skips and a rack of costumes have been brought on.*
IRA gets in among the stage hands and starts to change into his Othello costume.
A set for 'Othello' is erected stage right consisting on an archway and a few battlements.)
Now a mixture between a Russian and a Pole is a role, so I'm your man. That's the sad island of Cyprus you just knocked together. Home for an American-born African Englishman translatin' Shakespeare into indignation. I'm a travellin' man. I go where I want to. I'm free. Got more clothes than Beau Brummel and Beau Nash put together. Now where's my mirror? And is it clean? Must see my face in that mirror. Sweet Jesus! Is that me? Now I know what's pullin' the crowds.
(*KARAIL and NINA enter and start to change into costume and make-up.*)
Hello, folks. Now is the time to dedicate yourselves to God in all his glory. He don't ask that you come to Him naked or without war-paint. He says, boy, do your best with what you got. Don't be drab. Lift that eyebrow a little. Put something in your eye to make it glitter. Now your nose is a problem. Not aquiline enough. Lord, ain't you ever seen the snub-nosed eagle circling overhead? His sable plumage in highly prized as an adornment for the bonnets of mutes

at state funerals.

(*All stage hands have exited by this point.*)

Put some bags under your eyes.

KARAIL: Ah, yes. Worry!

IRA: You've been out all night trying to track down your daughter. The previous night you were out with the lads. Let's say that old man hasn't had any sleep for a week. And lengthen your nose.

NINA: And me, Chevalier? Will I do?

IRA: Desdemona was a girl. She had no brains, no common-sense. You've seen them, wide-eyed. Spots of colour on their cheeks. (*He puts on some colour for her.*) A beautiful summer swallow. They don't have any brains either. And don't forget your handkerchief. Has it got strawberries on it? If there are no strawberries on the handkerchief we're doomed. Desdemona has strawberries on her old family escutcheon – fruity, fragrant but soft in the middle.

NINA: You don't respect Desdemona as a character?

IRA: I find her kind of innocence irritating. Don't make your mouth too red. You'll look like an old tart. Where's that idiot, Goidze?

AMANDA: I saw him in the foyer earlier.

IRA: He should be here. We go up in fifteen minutes, for God's sake. What was he doing?

AMANDA: Nothing, really. Just hanging around.

KARAIL: He'll be very nervous.

IRA: Does Goidze suffer from stage-fright? It's a terrible affliction. I remember appearing at the Theatre Royal, Glasgow with a young man of my own colour. What was it we were doing? Ah, yes. *The Padlock.*

AMANDA: Awful play. Always hated it. Coon comedy at its worst.

IRA: My young colleague stood in the wings waiting to go on. Suddenly he slid to the ground. His face was grey and he couldn't move at all. Nor could he speak. It was only when the theatre manager picked him up and shook him till his teeth rattled that he could make his entrance. After that he was very good, I thought.

(*Enter GOIDZE. He slams the door.*)

AMANDA: Mr Goidze, in the theatre you never slam doors.

GOIDZE: Something has made me very angry.

AMANDA: Well, don't take it out on the woodwork.

IRA: Where've you been, Goidze? The call was for seven o'clock.

GOIDZE: The audience is full of serfs and Jews! Out in the foyer it is chaos. The gentry are very upset about this, Chevalier.

IRA: Are Jews and serfs forbidden to go to the theatre?

GOIDZE: No, that's not the point. Usually it's not their practice to come. They make their own amusements.

IRA: They won't mind sharing ours for once.

GOIDZE: Not when you've given them all free tickets. The box office is under siege. This was madness on your part.

IRA: Get into costume. Goidze. It's my money. Can't the gentry get seats? I calculated that there'd still be plenty of room if every merchant and every army officer in Mubelski came tonight.

GOIDZE: Well, the crisis has past, but you should have told me. What are they going to make of it? The Jews don't speak English, they don't speak French – the serfs can hardly speak their own language never mind anyone else's! – so what good is this going to do? They'll just make a nuisance of themselves.

IRA: They're my guests. They can watch my gestures, the way I open and close my mouth, Goidze. I've been playing to uncomprehending but admiring masses for donkey's years, man. All I do is stand there, wave my arms around – mustn't forget to use both tonight – and resonate! The timbre of my voice makes the air…luminous
(*GOIDZE is struggling to get into his costume.*
IRA gives him a hand.)
You see, Goidze, language is artificial. Shakespeare knew that better than anybody. What people can feel when I'm out there is conflict, the tension of opposites, war! – well, how can I put it to you – it's a battlefield of the spirits, my son. As long as they can see the armies and recognise the uniforms, they understand.

GOIDZE: I've got a lot of friends and influential people here tonight. If I hadn't invited them they probably wouldn't have come…

IRA: They will be astonished, Goidze. Folks of quality appreciate being put in the way of an unique experience. No doubt you'll shoot up in their estimation. Look dignified. Come on, you're the Duke of Venice, the Doge, a man of immense power in the Mediterranean Sea – is that all you can manage? Do you know what dignity is?

GOIDZE: The evening has already lost much of its style.
Once that's gone you've alienated your discerning patrons.

IRA: Hush! Amanda, off you go, and you two. As rehearsed.
(*AMANDA puts down her sewing and leaves the dressing-room. She goes out onto the stage.*
KARAIL and GOIDZE follow her.
Lights up on stage.)
Take your script, Goidze. You're not coming back in here before we start.
(*AMANDA addresses the audience.*)

AMANDA: Ladies and gentlemen, the Chevalier Aldridge, Knight of the Royal Saxon Ernestinischen House Order, Member of the Prussian Academy of Arts and Sciences…
(*GOIDZE translates into Russian.*
KARAIL translates into Polish.)
Holder of The Grand Cross of the Order of Leopold, and the Imperial Jubilee de Tolstoy Medal of Saint Petersburg…
(*GOIDZE and KARAIL translate.*)
And Honorary Captain in the Republican Army of Haiti…
(*GOIDZE and KARAIL translate. There is a pause before GOIDZE makes his translation.*)

IRA: We begin! *Othello*, in parts!

GOIDZE: Whoe'er he be that in this foul proceeding
Hath thus beguiled your daughter of herself
And you of her, the bloody book of law
You shall yourself read in the bitter letter
After your own sense.

KARAIL: Humbly I thank your grace.
Here is the man!

GOIDZE: What say you to this? Speak, Othello.

IRA: I do confess the vices of my blood,

So justly to your grave ears I'll present
How I did thrive in this fair lady's love
And she in mine.
GOIDZE: Say it, Othello.
IRA: Her father loved me, oft invited me,
    Still questioned me the story of my life
    From year to year, the battles, sieges, fortunes
    That I have passed.
    I ran it through, even from my boyish days
    To the very moment that he bade me tell it:
    Wherein I spake of most disastrous chances,
    Of moving accidents by flood and field.
    Of hair-breadth 'scapes in the imminent deadly breach,
    Of being taken by the insolent foe,
    And sold to slavery, of my redemption thence
    And portance in my travels' history:
    Wherein of antres vast and deserts idle,
    Rough quarries, rocks and hills whose heads touch heaven
    It was my hint to speak, – such was the process;
    And of the Cannibals that each other eat,
    The Anthropopaghi, the men whose heads
    Do grow beneath their shoulders,
    The three weird sisters of the Caledonian heath
    And Burnam forest's march to Dunsinane.
    This to hear
    Would Desdemona seriously incline:
    But still the house affairs would draw her thence:
    Which ever as she could with haste dispatch,
    She'd come again, and with a greedy ear
    Devour up my discourse: which I observing,
    Took once a pliant hour, and found good means
    To draw from her a prayer of earnest heart
    That I would all my pilgrimage dilate,
    Whereof by parcels she had something heard,
    But not intentively: I did consent,
    And often did beguile her of her tears
    When I did speak of some distressful stroke
    That my youth suffered. My story being done,
    She gave me for my pains a world of sighs!

She swore in faiths 'twas strange, 'twas passing strange:
'Twas pitiful, 'twas wondrous pitiful:
She wish'd she had not heard it, yet she wish'd
That heaven had made her such a man: she thanks me,
And bade me, if I had a friend that loved her,
I should but teach him how to tell my story,
And that would woo her. Upon this hint I spake:
She loved me for the dangers I had pass'd
And I loved her that she did pity them
This only in the witchcraft I have used.
Here comes the lady; let her witness it.
(*Enter NINA as Desdemona carrying a script clutched to her breast.*)

KARAIL: Oh, see my daughter, noble lord! A maiden

never bold;
Of spirit so still and quiet that her motion
Blush'd at herself. A spotless virgin of such purity
Clamp'd into the sooty bosom of such a thing as this?
                                                    Oh, no!
Oh, never, never! I'll kill him ere it be so.

IRA: Then, to please you both, divorce proceeds immediately.

NINA: Was the hope drunk
Wherein you dress'd yourself? Hath it slept since?
And wakes it now to look so green and pale
At what it did so freely?

KARAIL: Desdemona! How com'st though so forward and
                                                 so lewd?

NINA: I have given suck and know
How tender 'tis to love the babe that milks me
I would, while it was sailing in my face
Have pluck'd my nipple from his boneless gums,
And dash'd the brains out, had I so sworn as you
Have done to this.

KARAIL: God be with you! I have done.
I had rather to adopt a child than get it.
Come hither Moor.
I here do give thee that with all my heart
Which thou has got already.

(*IRA embraces NINA. All four of them turn and bow to the audience then hurry off. Lights fade on stage.*)

AMANDA: How is it going?

KARAIL: The audience is listening very carefully. The Chevalier conveys so much by subtle changes in his tone of voice.

GOIDZE: Smells like a farmyard out there. All those ruffians are completely lost. (*Pause.*) There're lines I can't find in the script...

IRA: God, man, the original is four hours long. I have to edit it down to a reasonable length. Move Goidze, you've got a costume change while we're doing the next scene.

GOIDZE: We should at least have the same script...

IRA: Oh don't fuss, man, for God's sake! We're doing very well. Look, I haven't had *Othello* out of storage for three months. It's very difficult to remember which play is which when you've got thirty or forty milling round in your memory.

GOIDZE: I realise that but we have to be true to the play...

IRA: Incidentally, Goidze – you're very good. Don't you think so, Amanda? Come on, you two.

(*IRA exits with NINA and KARAIL.*

AMANDA helps GOIDZE to undress for his costume change. She does this very expertly.)

AMANDA: Yes, you are good. My what a firm body you have.

GOIDZE: I like to keep in trim. The Chevalier is impatient with me.

(*AMANDA pulls his shirt open and down over his am and makes the movement into an embrace. She kisses him full on the mouth.*)

AMANDA: Oh, dear. What am I doing? With you? And me? Can you imagine what it's like being tied to such a man? He's a brute.

GOIDZE: Madame Aldridge...if there is any way I can help you...

AMANDA: There is, Goidze. There is. Make me into a woman again.

(*They embrace and kiss then go down behind the rack of costumes.*

Enter KARAIL with script.)

KARAIL: (*To audience.*) In which Othello is sent to the island
of Cyprus to defend it against a Turkish invasion. Desdemona, his bride accompanies him. Upon arrival at Cyprus
it is discovered that the Scottish king Duncan has got there
first and has invested the fortress with his own troops.
Othello is forced to accept Duncan's hospitality. After a
banquet Desdemona and the Scottish king take the air. (*He
puts on a crown, he points to himself.*) Duncan, the Scottish
king.
(*Enter NINA in a nightgown, with lighted candle.*)
This castle bath a pleasant seat; the air
Nimbly and sweetly recommends itself
Unto our gentle senses.
You will like it here.

NINA: From Venice, my lord, is a long way, I faint
with tiredness and would retire to my chamber.

KARAIL: The temple-haunting martlet, does approve
By his loved masonry that the heaven's breath
Smells wooingly here: no jutty, frieze,
Buttress, nor coign of vantage, but this bird
Hath made his pendant bed and procreant cradle:
Where they most breed and haunt, I have observed
The air is delicate. Birds in nature
Are my passion.

NINA: The raven himself is hoarse; and the crow
Makes wing to the rooky wood, my lord.

KARAIL: Except I be by beauty in the night,
There is no music in the nightingale. Come to my
chamber.

NINA: My lord, I will not! Respect a new bride's
virtue!

KARAIL: I command it or thy life is forfeit. (*Exits.*)
(*NINA weeps.*
Enter IRA.)

IRA: My dearest love, what ails thee?

NINA: Come to my woman's breasts
And take my milk for gall you murdering ministers! Unsex
me here,

And fill me from the crown to the toe, top-full
Of direst cruelty.
IRA: What's ado? From whence comes this unnatural rage?
NINA: Lechery, by this hand! The Scottish king
Would leap into your seat,
IRA: O, that the slave had forty thousand lives!
One is too poor, too weak for my revenge!
Like to the Pontic sea,
Whose icy current and compulsive course
Ne'er feels retiring ebb, but keeps due on
To the Propontic and the Hellespont;
Even so my bloody thoughts, with violent pace,
Shall ne'er look back, ne'er ebb to humble love,
Till that a capable and wide revenge
Swallow then up.
If it were done when 'tis done, then 'twere well
It were done quickly: it the assassination.
NINA: Assassination? Vengeance, surely, for great wrongs
Performed upon our state and honour.
Such an act would claim applause from angels.
IRA: Ah, that but this blow
Might be the be-all and the end – all here,
But here, upon this bank and shoal of time,
We'll jump the life to come. But in these cases
We still have judgement here; that we but teach
Bloody instructions, which being taught return
To plague the inventor: this even-handed justice
Commands the ingredients of our poisn'd chalice
To our own lips.
NINA: When you durst do it, then you were a man.
IRA: Oh, what a rogue and peasant slave am I?
If we should fail?
NINA: But screw your courage to the sticking-place,
And we'll not fail.
IRA: Am I a coward?
Who calls me villain? Breaks my pate across?
Plucks off my beard, and blows it in my face?
Tweaks me by the nose? Gives me the lie i' the throat,

As deep as to the lungs? Who does me this?
Ha?

NINA: Glamis thou art, and Cawdor, and shalt be
King of Cyprus: yet do I fear thy nature;
It is too full o' the milk of human kindness
To catch the nearest way.

IRA: It cannot be
But I am pigeon-liver'd and lack gall
To make oppression bitter.

NINA: Art thou afeard
To be the same in thine own act and valour
As thou art in desire?
(*Enter KARAIL to upstage in a nightshirt carrying a
candle. He lies down upon some pillows, then puts the
crown over the candle.*)

KARAIL: My lust is kindled. Ho, there! Mistress!

NINA: He calls!

IRA: I'll do it. Oh, adulterous thief, thine end is near.

NINA: Take thou this handkerchief to wipe thine hands withal.
The maker sewed in strawberries upon a field of

inno-
cence.
Make thou those fruit into real stains of blood.
Upon black vengeance rampant!
(*NINA gives IRA the handkerchief and exits.*)

IRA: Is this a dagger which I see before me,
The handle toward my hand? Come, let me clutch thee.
I have thee not, and yet I see thee still.
Are thou not, fatal vision sensible
To feeling as to sight? Or art thou but
A dagger of the mind, a false creation,
Proceeding from the heat-oppressed brain?
I see thee yet, in form as palpable
As this which now I draw. I see thee still;
And on thy blade and dudgeon gouts of blood,
Which was not so before. There's no such thing:
It is the bloody business which informs
Thus to mine eyes.

(IRA starts to advance on KARAIL who has his rolled-up script under his nightshirt.)

KARAIL: Ah, I hear her tread! She comes! Oh, ecstasy! *(He raises the script under the nightshirt.)*

IRA: Now oe'er the one half world
Nature seems dead and wicked dreams abuse
The curtain'd sleep; witchcraft celebrates
Pale Hecate's offerings; and wither'd murder
Alarum'd by his sentinel the wolf,
Whose howl's his watch thus with stealthy pace,
With Tarquin's ravishing strides, towards his design
Moves like a ghost.

KARAIL: *(Smiling, his eyes still shut.)* Is that you, Desdemona?

IRA: Thou sure and firm-set earth
Hear not my steps, which way they walk, for fear
The very stones prate of my whereabouts
And take the present horror from the time,
Which now suits with it.

KARAIL: Why, who would not make a husband a cuckold to make him a monarch? I should venture purgatory for it. He may have this island so I have his. For love's the world and worth all in 't.
(A bell rings.)
That's one o' th' clock.
You've kept me waiting, chuck.

IRA: *(Raising the scimitar over his head.)*
Hear it not, Duncan, for it is a knell
That summons thee to heaven, or to hell.
(As he starts to bring the scimitar down a bear rushes on roaring.
IRA rushes off right pursued by the bear. Pause.
The rolled-up script goes down under KARAIL's nightshirt.
Blackout. Lights up on the dressing-room.
IRA bursts in.
GOIDZE and AMANDA jump up from behind the rack clutching costumes to cover themselves.)
Good God! Damn it to hell, Amanda!

AMANDA: Ira! I thought the scene would last longer.

IRA: No, it's not true. It mustn't be! Can't I leave you alone for five minutes? God almighty, Amanda. What have you done?

(*Enter the bear.*)

See what I've found waiting for me, Nina? Goidze and Amanda making the beast with two backs.

AMANDA: Ira, I can explain...

IRA: Yes, by God, you'll explain when I get you in private with a riding crop, you randy bitch! You'll do some talking.

(*Enter KARAIL.*)

Hey, you know this character Goidze here. Is he in the habit of going round forcing himself on defenceless women?

KARAIL: What has happened?

IRA: In flagrante! Right under my nose. Only one thing makes me able to bear this. It was his youth, wasn't it? Don't say it was because he's not black or I'll tear the skin off my face!

AMANDA: It will never happen again, I promise.

IRA: I appeal to you, Karail. What would you do if your wife was unfaithful to you?

KARAIL: Break my heart.

IRA: There you are. Goidze. That will tell you what it feels like for me, you ram! My heart is broken.

(*IRA starts changing his costume tearing one off and throwing another on.*)

There's nothing disgusted Shakespeare more than adultery. Marry, here's grace and a codpiece; that's a wise man. Oh, don't just stand there with your mouth open, Goidze. Never been caught before? I bet this is a sweaty little town. Nothing to do. Nowhere to go. You get the itch, Goidze. Know what that is? A warning to get yourself a pair of sheep-shears and geld yourself, you bastard!

(*IRA throws his costume on the floor and slumps down at the table.*

AMANDA goes to him.

She touches his shoulder.

He reacts violently.)

Get off, you whore!

AMANDA: Forgive me.

IRA: Strumpet! The soiled horse goes to it and the gilded fly. Prostitute! Asshole!

NINA: Your wife is crying.

IRA: Let her! Anyone can cry. What matters is does she mean it?

GOIDZE: Chevalier, I don't know what made me behave in this way.

IRA: Don't speak! Whatever you do, keep quiet. I have an absolutely ungovernable temper, Goidze. First things first. The show must go on. We only have a few minutes to get ready. Oh, Amanda, my love! (*Sobs.*) After all these years.

AMANDA: I'm sorry, Ira. He was very insistent.

IRA: Would you have done it otherwise? Goidze, get into costume! Well done, Nina, darling. You made a first-class wild animal. Goidze, I can't begin to tell you how seriously I view your betrayal.

GOIDZE: (*Getting dressed.*) Somehow I will make amends.

IRA: Too damn right you will! I come from a proud people.

(*NINA takes off the bear-skin and changes into another costume.*

KARAIL changes.

IRA starts altering his make-up.)

GOIDZE: How is the play being received, Chevalier?

IRA: You wouldn't know, would you? A very appreciative, intelligent audience. One might be in Paris, they're so sophisticated. Pick everything up. Now, this act coming up is crucial to the action, Goidze, so concentrate. Othello has to kill Iago.

GOIDZE: Who's Iago? Me?

IRA: No Karail is Iago. Now Iago had a special privilege at the court of Cyprus. He was allowed to wear a crown.

GOIDZE: Why?

IRA: Because he'd been on a pilgrimage to Jerusalem.

GOIDZE: The crown was a symbol of religion?

IRA: Exactly.

GOIDZE: Ah.

IRA: A simulacrum of the crown of thorns.

GOIDZE: A simulacrum. I don't remember a bear in *Othello.*

IRA: Part of the entertainment in the banquet-scene.

GOIDZE: I don't remember a banquet-scene either.

IRA: Well, there is one. You know what Russian translators are like – drunk, most of the time. Trying to translate Shakespeare is like trying to unpick the hair shirt of Mohamet. God, you've shattered me, Goidze.

GOIDZE: Will you be demanding satisfaction?

IRA: I have to. It's a matter of honour. Not only that, Goidze, but I'll have choice of weapons. How d'you fancy assegais?

GOIDZE: Aha! I see a twinkle in your eyes Chevalier. You've forgiven me, already.

IRA: Not so loud. You'll upset Amanda. God, man. I could draw this out for a fortnight. We actors have to have our dramas within our dramas.

GOIDZE: So, you have no sense of honour. I am surprised. Even an actor should have some self-respect.
(*Pause. The others stop moving around as they change.*)
Because you do plays does that mean you can have no commitment to anything real? Isn't there a moment when the game stops? Without honour and self-respect life is hardly worth living.

IRA: You been talking behind my back again, Amanda?

GOIDZE: Oh, that was a casual moment. Your wife takes it in her stride. When you were coming here there was a lot of interest at a high level. We thought that you must be a man to be reckoned with. But that was a mistake. Saint Petersburg got it wrong.
(*Pause. IRA keeps working on his make-up.*
KARAIL, NINA and AMANDA resume their dressing.)
Shakespeare is a great disappointment.

IRA: Ha-ha.

GOIDZE: I regret that I allowed myself to be involved with such a shabby business.

IRA: Goin' to walk out on us, Goidze? There's desertion in the face of the enemy. There's drunk and refusing to fight. The worst crime in the soldier's calendar is abandoning a battle because it aint good enough. You're not capable of that, are you?

GOIDZE: If I felt that you were genuinely committed to

something it would be different. You have no feeling for
fundamental issues.

IRA: Commitment? Last time I heard that word was when
my old Uncle Sam was being put in an asylum. C'mon,
you know my type, Goidze. I'm a lotus-eater. (*Puts the
crown on his head.*) In fact I'm the king of the lotus-eaters.
All that matters to me is eating. If you get between me and
the lotus beds I put my palace guards onto you and call it
philosophy. (*Pause.*) Iago's crown. I'm not a rich man. The
expenses of touring are vast, Goidze, vast. So this isn't only
Iago's crown. It's Claudius's – the adulterous poisoner in
Hamlet – it's Lear's, the mad incompetent old sentimen-
talist – it's Richard the Third's the demon king. It has to
make do for all the kings.

GOIDZE: Has it been worn on this stage tonight?

IRA: The Scottish king had to have his crown. Poor old chap
is bald.

GOIDZE: What Scottish king? There's no such character in
Othello.

IRA: Oh, you didn't read it carefully enough. The Scottish
king is a colonialist. He's got his foot on the neck of the
Cypriots. Now you never see any of those in *Othello*. Does
that mean they don't exist?

GOIDZE: God what have you done? (*Snatches at the crown.*)
Give me that!

IRA: What? Strike the crown? It's a bauble, Goidze. A piece
of tat. The buttons for my braces have more function and
significance. Lets awa'!

GOIDZE: (*To AMANDA as he exits.*) I know you now for what
you are.

IRA: Oh, stop whining, man! What does it matter? It's only
tawdry, shabby old make-believe, signifying nothing.
(*IRA finishes his make-up. He gets up keeping his left pro-
file in view. He shoos the others out of the dressing-room.
AMANDA stands near the door. As he goes out IRA smiles
at her. She closes the door then goes out onto the stage. The
others remain in the wings.*)

AMANDA: (*To the audience.*) Ladies and gentlemen, the
Chevalier Aldridge has commanded me to make an an-

313

nouncement. As paramount chief of the Fulah tribe of
Senegal it is his duty to put on certain princely decorations
of his person to coincide with precise gyrations in the pas-
sage of the planets on this day. No matter where he is or
whatever the circumstances of the moment he must put on
particular signs and signals. He asks that you do not let this
affect your enjoyment of the   play. It is merely an act of
respect for his god. (*Pause.*) Also it is William Shakespeare's
birthday.

(*IRA steps into the light. The right hand side of his face is
painted completely white.*

AMANDA exits, to the dressing-room.

IRA slips the crown over the end of his scimitar.)

IRA: A composition of my own in honour of my friend and
patron, gentleman of Warwickshire, chief of the Fulah
people of Senegal. William Shagsper, blood brother,
totem-pole and ancestor.

In a country to your taste: better than Illyria,
Or oven Prospero's isle! Bohemia! Troy or Athens!
Who else 'ud do your work in Nowhere? Now y'see it!
Now you don't. By process that you'd understand
This country disappeared – stroke of a pen. Playwright
Mightier than the sword? I hear you mutter from the sod.
But they left a board to play on. It exists. (*Stamps.*) There.
Shagger, between your name and mine I'll brook
No false division, no empire, no Jews or Christians,
Moors and maniacs, officers and censors! All away!

(*He slings the crown off the end of the scimitar across the
stage.*)

An empty gesture that no one here misunderstands
Even wi'out my language. But empty gestures
Have the power of what they mean.
An actor's life sparkles in the heaving void
To demonstrate that even emptiness is cramm'd
With possibilities. Ask no more of us,
We're not your servants apes, or appetites,
We're not your passions or your acolytes!
We're Daniel cast into the fiery furnace of your minds,

Waiting for rescue.

(*IRA sheaths his scimitar. He nods to KARAIL.*)

KARAIL: Chevalier, farewell. God guard you.

IRA: Proceed! Announce the scene!

KARAIL: I have to go. Long live Poland! Destruction to her
enemies! Down with the Czar!

(*KARAIL runs off. Pause.*)

IRA: Strange war-cries these Scots and Cypriots have. Ladies
and gentlemen, my acting company has been summarily
reduced by one…

(*NINA whispers into IRA'S ear.*)

Sorry. Change that. By two. The script will have to be
reshuffled somewhat but we'll get something together, we
always do. On the road we often have to cope with sick-
ness and desertion. But the show goes on! The show has to
go on! Welcome to all the ploughboys here, all the soldiers
and moneylenders, all the free men. In which Othello kills
his wife and himself and the king goes scot-free. Which
cuntree is this? Make up your minds. To be or not to be
that is the question as MacHamlet says…

GOIDZE: (*Running through the audience to the stage.*) I denounce
this! You are performing a prohibited work upon the public
stage. I call upon you all to witness that once I knew what
was going on I drew the attention of the authorities to it.
The Chevalier is not to blame. He has been misled by
Karail Rusinkski who I denounce as a traitor.

IRA: Whether 'tis nobler in the mind to suffer
The slings and arrows of outrageous fortune,
Or to take arms against a sea of troubles
And by opposing end them.

GOIDZE: Stop no more, please! (*He climbs onto the stage.*) It is
all over. You must abandon the performance. (*Pushes him
off.*)

IRA: To die; to sleep;
No more; and by a sleep to say we end
The heart-ache, and the thousand natural shocks
That flesh in heir to…

GOIDZE: Please go to your dressing-room and wait there
until the police come. They will want to take a statement

from you.

IRA: 'Tis a consummation

Devoutly to be wish'd.

GOIDZE: (*He pushes IRA into the dressing-room and leaves.*)

Wait there. Don't try to leave the theatre.

IRA: To die, to sleep;

To sleep: perchance to dream; ay, there's the rub.

AMANDA: Well, I thought we had him fooled.

IRA: I went too far as usual. I think it was the crown that worried him. You were brilliant, of course. What was he like?

AMANDA: Unimaginative. D'you think we'll get into a lot of trouble?

IRA: Nah. (*Starts to clean his face.*) We wuz misled.

(*Enter NINA into the dressing-room.*)

Did he get away all right?

NINA: I think so.

IRA: Has he got somewhere to hide?

NINA: Yes. It was a stupid thing to do. You shouldn't have gone along with it.

IRA: Why not? I thought it was fun. Shakespeare would have bust a gut laughing.

AMANDA: When will you see Karail again?

NINA: They're always watching us. Karail will talk his way out of it once things have calmed down. He's been in trouble before.

IRA: Loves trouble, your old man. Thrives on it.

NINA: Yes, I'm afraid so.

IRA: Why didn't they get rid of him before? Perhaps he has a charmed life. I know what it's like to have a licence to unknowingly agitate – but the conscious ones I've met have all ended up in jug, or dead.

AMANDA: Ira, for God's sake!

IRA: What's up with you? She knows what he's like. The man's a Polish patriot and he wants to be treated like one. The Russians know how to give him the respect he needs.

AMANDA: There's no need to be so cruel. Would you run his risks?

IRA: Don't have to, do I? All I have to do is stand there an' be my little ol' black self.

(*Pause. IRA has wiped off most of the white. He rubs at it with a cloth.*)

Oooooh, shit! I shouldn't have let him talk me into it. Nina, I'm a fool. But I didn't mean any harm.

NINA: I know that.

IRA: It was the fresh air, the hills, too much excitement in a strange place. You see, I've met hundreds of men like your husband all over. They come to me and ask for help. Sometimes they say carry a gun, join the demonstration, make a stand. Get off the stage! But I don't because I'm safe on the stage. You're looking at a coward.

NINA: No, I'm not.

IRA: Karail doesn't care any more. That's something you know anyway.

NINA: All he wants to do is goad them, provoke them. One day they will oblige him with a bullet.

IRA: Well, I regret that we didn't get into the second act of our collage. There was some good stuff in there. And I didn't get to sing *Possum Up A Gum Tree* or play the banjo. Mubelski will be the poorer for it.

(*Shots off. Pause.*)

No, he'll have got well away. Your husband can run. I've seen him when we were up in the hills. Runs like a goat.

(*NINA starts to weep.*

IRA indicates to AMANDA that she should comfort her.)

AMANDA: You don't know what's going on out there. Ira's probably right.

IRA: Damn guns always going off. That's one of the things I like about Will's stuff – there're no damn guns. It's not a natural sound at all. Nothing else sounds like that.

NINA: It was him. I know.

IRA: Runs like a goat, that man. We had a marvellous day up there. A picnic, few bottles of wine, plum brandy…oh, and the scenery! It's a long time since I've felt so good. It's what he wanted, Nina. If he's got it don't pity him too much.

NINA: Those bastards! I hate them! Lumps of lard!

(*Enter GOIDZE. He has a coat thrown over his shoulders.*)

GOIDZE: Nina, I have to bring you some grave news…

IRA: She knows, she knows. Where are these policeman who want to see me?

GOIDZE: Out of respect for your position as a visiting artist the authorities have asked that I take the statement as I am acquainted.

IRA: That's very delicate of you, Goidze. Do a lot of police work around here?

NINA: Did he die well?

GOIDZE: He was shot at the corner by the water-pump.

NINA: (*Screaming.*) I said did he die well?

GOIDZE: I don't know what you mean.

IRA: Had he his wounds before? Was he running away?

GOIDZE: No. He had turned.

(*Pause.*)

NINA: Thank you, Goidze. I hope you go to Hell one day.

GOIDZE: Chevalier, I must take this statement. Ladies, would you leave us alone for a while?

(*AMANDA looks at IRA.*
He nods.
AMANDA takes NINA out of the dressing-room onto the stage. They sit down. AMANDA has an arm around NINA.)

IRA: So, what is it you want from me?

GOIDZE: The police want to know how this…charade came about.

IRA: It was his idea.

(*GOIDZE takes out a book and a pencil.*)

GOIDZE: That's what I thought. Why did you go along with it?

IRA: Boredom.

GOIDZE: A common enough artistic malaise.

IRA: Well, see it my way, Goidze, old man. Forty years I've been in this business. I've seen them all come and go. I'm not that boy with stars in his eyes any more. I need excitement.

GOIDZE: That incident of mine with your wife…

IRA: Nothing to do with it, Goidze. She fancied you, that's all.

We theatre people tend to be very bohemian and freethinking about these things. Amanda just responded to you, physically.

GOIDZE: Oh.

IRA: You got her going. That's your credit. She's no actress.

GOIDZE: Well, that's a comfort.

IRA: She likes you. And you were very co-operative as far as I was concerned as well, you know, agreeing to be in the play, at such short notice, coming on stage, doing your bit. We couldn't have got it on without you.

(*Pause. GOIDZE looks at his note-book.*)

GOIDZE: Are you prepared to leave Mubelski this evening if I can arrange it?

IRA: Well, tomorrow morning would be more humane. It's getting pretty late. We're not packed up or anything.

GOIDZE: I would advise you to go tonight. If the provincial headquarters send someone over here to investigate this you would be stuck here for days.

IRA: If that's your opinion, Goidze, I'd better move.

GOIDZE: Will you describe to me step by step, in detail, how Karail persuaded you to undertake this...

IRA: Collage, dear Goidze. Here, give me your book. I'll write it and save time. Would you be so good as to start packing that skip with those costumes: fold them carefully or I'll end up with a huge bill for ironing.

(*IRA takes the notebook and pencil and starts writing. GOIDZE watches over his shoulder for a moment then starts to pack a skip.*)

NINA: I don't want to stay here, not without him.

AMANDA: Have you got any family you can go to?

NINA: No. I'll have to get away somehow.

AMANDA: Won't they leave you alone? It wasn't your idea, after all. Say Karail forced you to take part.

NINA: Goidze will become a nuisance.

AMANDA: Became?

NINA: I would have to kill him. Goidze has known me since I was a child. At one time our parents were arranging a marriage until I met Karail. I wasn't indifferent to Goidze at all.

I quite liked him. But I know that he has no soul. He would come round, even now, and ask me to like him again. If I don't he'll make my life a misery.

AMANDA: You're not a bad actress.

NINA: No, I'm not.

AMANDA: There's a lot you can learn. Not an easy life.

NINA: I would think not.

AMANDA: Some things would be inescapable, I promise you. One of then is talking fast in the dressing-room right now.

(*NINA laughs then checks herself.*)

NINA: God, he's not dead an hour and I'm laughing.

AMANDA: That could mean that you're already one of us.

NINA: Karail would agree with this; I'm sure he would. Oh God, not to even stay to bury the man? Can I do that?

AMANDA: Meat. Think nothing of it. The man will stay with you.

(*IRA hands the notebook over to GOIDZE.*)

IRA: That's the story. No embellishments.

GOIDZE: I'll got you a carriage. Wait here until it arrives.

(*GOIDZE exits. He goes across the stage.*

AMANDA and NINA see him go and return to the dressing-room where IRA is packing things up.)

AMANDA: Did you get out of it?

IRA: No time to talk. I've done a deal with Goidze. He wants us out of town now, tonight. Tell everyone to get ready to follow on by train. Goidze is calling us a carriage.

AMANDA: Nina's coming with us.

IRA: I knew she'd say yes one day.

AMANDA: She thinks Goidze will try to stop her.

IRA: Get in the skip.

(*NINA climbs into the skip. They put costumes and props on top of her.*)

AMANDA: (*As they pack the skip.*) I'll tell Goidze that you've gone home.

IRA: He won't be thinking about her, he'll be wondering about how safe his hide is. All for Will Shakespeare, hell that man is good at causing mayhem. No wonder he died when he was only fifty-six. I reckon they had him assassi-

nated. First time I did Shakespeare I was eighteen, in New
York. Now here I am, still doin' Shakespeare in Poland
all these years after and I still don't know which way the
bastard would vote. Is that power or is it chicken?
*(They have finished packing as GOIDZE hurries back
across the stage and enters the dressing-room.)*
GOIDZE: The carriage is waiting! Hurry up!
IRA: Will you give me a hand with this, Goidze. It's too heavy
for me to handle by myself.
*(AMANDA takes a smaller skip and pulls it off.
GOIDZE takes the other end of the skip containing NINA
and they lift it.)*
GOIDZE: What a day, Chevalier. I hope to find quieter times.
(They start to carry it out and across the stage.)
IRA: You're right. I hope you'll be able to explain to the
authorities so I can contemplate continuing my Polish tour.
(Pause.) Sorry, my Russian tour.
GOIDZE: Oh, I think so. This will be a nine-day wonder.
IRA: Quite right. When it comes to agitation we actors don't
achieve much, even in innocence. Phew! Do you mind if
we put it down for a minute?
GOIDZE: We have to hurry…
IRA: All right, Goidze. I'm not as strong as I was. So I can
leave that to you? Tell them I was only playin' around.
GOIDZE: I'll do what I can. If Nina will assist me in denounc-
ing her husband that will help. She's a good woman at
heart.
IRA: Oh, I think you can take that for granted.
GOIDZE: I had to go to the station to find the carriage. News
has come in that Abraham Lincoln has been assassinated.
*(Pause. IRA sits down on the skip. He hangs his head then
wipes at his eyes with the handkerchief.)*
IRA: I'm a very tired pigeon.
GOIDZE: The assassin was an actor, Chevalier. And the kill-
ing took place in a theatre. Can you imagine?
*(IRA stands up. Pause. He lifts the skip with GOIDZE.
As IRA carries the load off he lets out a soft, African cry
of mourning that builds into a high, pain-filled lamenta-*

tion. Blackout.)

The End.